The Cost of Not Educating the World's Poor

T0300350

In *The Cost of Not Educating the World's Poor*, Lynn Ilon observes from her 30 years of travel and work in some 20 developing countries how global instability, problems of environmental degradation, spread of global disease, migration and political instability are a cost of viewing the uneducated poor as separated from a network of fast-growing global knowledge. This book shows how powerful global learning systems are rapidly forming and linking the rich world with the world of the poor and developing nations. Using a narrative voice interleaved with concise introductions to the underlying theories (economics, development, learning, technology and networks) it shows us how changing our ways of thinking can lead to new possibilities. *The Cost of Not Educating the World's Poor* is based on an emerging theory of development economics and the author's own vast experiences and stories. It also discusses, among other issues:

- international development and how it has evolved toward an emphasis on knowledge;
- how networked human capital creates new potential for poorly resourced countries;
- the formation of a global system of learning networks;
- the digitization of knowledge;
- how nations improve their well-being through knowledge and equity.

This inter-disciplinary assessment of international learning inequality and the methods to overcome it will appeal to researchers concerned with emerging concepts of global learning networks and their effects on development. It will also be of interest to students and policymakers studying national inequality, economics and global development.

Lynn Ilon is Professor at the College of Education, Seoul National University.

The Cost of Not Educating the World's Poor

The new economics of learning

Lynn Ilon

Routledge
Taylor & Francis Group

LONDON AND NEW YORK

First published 2015 by Routledge

2 Park Square, Milton Park, Abingdon, Oxfordshire OX14 4RN
711 Third Avenue, New York, NY 10017

Routledge is an imprint of the Taylor & Francis Group, an informa business

First issued in paperback 2017

British Library Cataloguing in Publication Data
A catalogue record for this book is available from the British Library

Library of Congress Cataloging in Publication Data
Ilon, Lynn.
    The cost of not educating the world's poor: the new economics
    of learning/Lynn Ilon.
    pages cm
    Includes bibliographical references and index.
    1. Education—Economic aspects. 2. Education—Social aspects.
    3. Education—Aims and objectives. 4. Educational planning.
    5. Education and globalization. 6. Human capital. I. Title.
    LC65.L64 2015
    338.4'337—dc23
    2014044533

ISBN: 978-1-138-88749-7 (hbk)
ISBN: 978-1-138-57585-1 (pbk)

Typeset in Galliard
by Florence Production Ltd, Stoodleigh, Devon, UK

Contents

Acknowledgements

Many thanks to Rayton Kwembe for his extensive help on an early draft of this book. Thanks also to M'zizi Kantini and Bethel Ghebru.

Preface

As I write this, the Ebola virus is in rapid expansion in West Africa. There is a growing fear among the public that the disease could spread to the West. Yet, reportedly, the disease is not easily contagious and, given proper conditions, can be contained and managed. The spread of this disease is a perfect example of the *cost of not educating the world's poor* and why I wrote this book.

In August 2014, two US health-care workers were flown in to Emory University from West Africa for treatment of the disease. Both eventually recovered. When they were received at Emory Hospital, there was virtually no fear that their arrival posed any threat to bringing the spread of the disease to the United States because the disease, properly handled, is rarely contagious. One has to be exposed to the bodily fluids of the person with *active* Ebola in order to catch the disease. Avoiding contact with the bodily fluids is a matter of clothing oneself with protective suits and of isolating the patient and handling their bodily wastes properly. This protocol was being followed in Emory University and in West Africa. Except for the occasional mistake (such as the mistakes where the two US health-care workers were exposed), the disease can be contained (Kaplan, 2014). So, why is it spreading in West Africa—seemingly out of control?

People need to get their relatives to a containment area as soon as they appear to be sick. But they are not doing so. Throughout the region, people distrust the government and distrust the outside medical workers. Many believe that the disease has been brought on by the presence of the Western doctors and clinics or can be cured through local means such as eating onions (Botelho *et al.*, 2014; Eldred, 2014). Not only does this show a lack of basic disease knowledge, but it shows a distrust of outsider people. It is reasonable to ask, and rightly so, why would these outsiders suddenly appear with what must be expensive clinics, equipment and health-care facilities if people have needed the most basic of health care and schooling in the region for generations. Surely, this new effort must have something to do with the self-interest of the outsiders (Nossiter, 2014).

Of course, the communities are not wrong. Without containment of the disease within Africa, a disease that otherwise should be manageable can become a global problem (Reuters News, 2014). So, one of the containment strategies has been to build trust and education within the villages (Public Broadcasting Service, 2014). But, as Harvard Medical School points out, we live in an interconnected world and such a view is the *central core* of not only solving the Ebola outbreak (Pickett, 2014) but, I maintain, preventing such spread in the future. If the right type and quality of education had been laid down in West Africa ten years ago, the vast cost (of managing the disease, loss of life, cost to commerce and future political, social and commercial costs) could have been avoided. Nor would there have to be trust built first, because the West Africans would be familiar with the global ties that link them to the rest of the world.

But this is not the only education that needs to occur. The Western world and the educated world need also to be re-educated to understand that the rich world/poor world concepts that have underlain foreign aid since the Second World War are now problematic. Simply sending in foreign aid when there is a crisis not only does not solve the problem, it can breed distrust. Many foreign aid programs are isolated—geographically, sectorally and programmatically. The obvious linkages to the rest of the world, other sectors and local social systems are not transparent. These linkages and the ability to use these linkages are needed by the people who should be involved in solving the complex problems. Ebola is a complex problem—medically, educationally, culturally, politically and socially—and it requires skilled medical experts, community workers, politicians, social workers and transportation and communication analysts.

Our old way of approaching the problems of the poor are outmoded. They assume that we can go in and handle isolated crises when they occur. But "hotspots" throughout the world—whether they be disease, climate, political, social, terrorist, financial or virtual—now spread across the world; isolated containment does not work. We need to approach the world as a linked, interconnected world where the resources of everyone are put into play. And . . . it begins with the most profound, the most fundamental and the fastest-growing resource of all—learning. Learning, put on the world's networks of knowledge, is quickly becoming a vast resource that links everyone and can be utilized to solve and mitigate these globally linked problems.

Without this understanding, the whole world pays a high price—not just the cost of containing Ebola or other global diseases, but of containing the cost of terrorism, ecological and environmental disasters, spreading political and social instability, refugees, disruption to communication and transportation channels and financial instability. We also lose the potential human gains of building new possibilities and ideas. The cost of not understanding these global linkages and how they affect our world is decreasing our quality of life and ability to generate new potential at a time when such potentials are just over the horizon. Equally, the cost of neglecting the world's poor means that global disaster is brought to our door, thus draining the world's resources, reducing quality of life and shortening the time span we have in this world. The cost of not educating the world's poor can only be solved by understanding, in a humane way, our global linkages. This book lays them out through my eyes and supplements this narrative with the underlying theories that are rapidly in development.

References

Botelho, G., Wilson, J. and Brumfield, B. (2014, July 31). In Ebola fight, security forces to make villagers comply with medical plan. Retrieved from www.cnn.com/2014/07/30/health/ebola-american-aid-workers/index.html

Eldred, S. (2014, July 2). How can ebola be stopped? *Mashable.* Retrieved from http://news.discovery.com/human/health/how-can-ebola-be-stopped-140701.htm#mkcpgn=rssnws1

Kaplan, R. (2014, August 3). CDC director: "We can stop" ebola from spreading. *Face the Nation.* Retrieved from www.cbsnews.com/news/cdc-director-we-can-stop-ebola-from-spreading/

Nossiter, A. (2014, July 27). Fear of ebola breeds a terror of physicians. *The New York Times.* Retrieved from www.nytimes.com/2014/07/28/world/africa/ebola-epidemic-west-africa-guinea.html

Pickett, M. (2014, August 1). Global cooperation needed to stop the spread of ebola virus disease. Retrieved from www.health.harvard.edu/blog/global-cooperation-needed-stop-spread-ebola-virus-disease-201408017314

Public Broadcasting Service (2014, July 28). Medical workers use education to combat ebola outbreak. Retrieved from www.pbs.org/newshour/bb/faced-challenging-ebola-outbreak-medical-workers-use-education-combat-fear/

Reuters News (2014, July 31). Fears of global spread of ebola virus as death toll hits 729. Retrieved from http://rt.com/news/177048-ebola-virus-sierra-leone/

1a Introduction

My memory, now, turns to a hot, sticky day in rural Nepal—near the border with India. I sat in the simplest of grass huts and spoke with a young mother, a small baby in her lap. Her five-year-old daughter was attending the village school; her husband was off tending crops. Her dwelling was sparse and mainly one small room. Outside stood a round structure on stilts, intended to protect the rice crop from rats and other vermin. I had seen the village men as my driver wended his way to the remote location; they carried huge bundles of green foliage on their backs—seemingly much too large a load for their slender bodies. I asked the woman a simple question: "Why did you decide to send your daughter to school?"

The question and her response required the best of my thinking, the best of my knowledge and the best of my experience. For it wasn't clear to me that, were I in her position, I would send my daughter to school. As she answered in her hesitant manner, I asked myself again—as I had in so many parts of the world I'd visited—whether I could ever have the strength of this woman—the determination, the will and the sheer force of conviction—to give my child up to a school for hours each day. Her daughter was the water carrier, the fuel gatherer (for cooking meals), the babysitter and the house cleaner. The mother worked hard, long hours in the rice paddies—small baby strapped to her back. Every moment spent doing something else meant less food for the family already living on the edge—already at risk of slow death from lack of food. And yet this young mother, completely illiterate, with no literate neighbors, no examples of success from education, gave up a precious labor source each day: her daughter. She did so out of some conviction that there had to be a better life somewhere and her daughter would have a chance at that life if she had an education. The family lived even closer to the edge of existence for nothing more than a hope—a hope that life could be better for their daughter.

It is all too easy to see this as a singular decision—as it is treated in the literature and in much of the press. They are viewed as individual families who now have access to a local school and choose, for various reasons, to educate the very first generation. But, in fact, what I knew and the mother did not, was that she did not face many choices. The outer world was encroaching; education would be the new norm and not to have it would put little Pima (we'll give her this name) at the future margins of even this—seemingly remote—society. For the village would see many changes. The latest crop technology would be introduced and feed more people—a change that marked the turnaround for Korean society some 50 years earlier. This would bring with it the need to participate in a monied economy. The pollution and variations in weather that result from a world already well into industrialization would change the environment for growing a family's daily food. The chance to access basic health care would arrive with vaccines, birth control, dentistry and antibiotics, but its access would be severely limited for those not in a cash economy. In fact, by educating Pima, they were merely ensuring that she would have a regular, normal life in a much-transformed society. Normality in that village would change from subsistence farming to crop farming for small markets and only the educated could be assured of a relatively secure life in that evolving local economy.

The more difficult question to address is how the world of the educated and privileged is affected by the life of this mother and her daughter in Nepal. Little influence, seemingly, moves the other way—up the chain of influence from poor, rural, uneducated, to wealthy, industrialized, urban, educated populations. Yet the apparent distance is an illusion. The ties are strong. The days when the world might appear to be comfortably divided between rich and poor or even educated and uneducated are long past—comfortable as those days might have been for the educated. The clock cannot be turned back to those days of apparent comfort, control and power for the privileged any more than the Nepalese woman can prevent crop development, formal-sector markets and educated neighbors from encroaching upon the life of her daughter.

The notion that the ties are simple is also an illusion. Foreign aid is sent to poor countries to support the education of the daughter and this appears to be a simple bond between the two worlds—a transfer of funds from the rich to the poor. But this link is anything but simple. The linkages of trade, formalization of economies and integration of labor markets ultimately benefit consumers in wealthy countries more than those in poor countries. When was the last time you went to a large discount store and bought the running shoes on sale, the microwave with new features or the sheets for your bed? For that matter, when did you last buy a computer at a price much less than your last one, or try on that cute embroidered silk jacket at your favorite boutique? Without foreign aid, your purchases would be more expensive, less varied and less plentiful. It is the cash that went to the poorest countries, that provided the education, that allowed manufacturers to move production, that linked the consumer markets, that lowered the trade barriers, that dictated the rules of exchange rates, that put that computer in your lap (and mine now).

But what else links us with our Nepalese woman? Modern infrastructure such as roads, ports, electricity and water provide the means for international production and trade and also provides a road near where she lives. Small markets grow around her and district buses become available to her. She can visit her relatives more easily, but increased exposure to other people increases her risk of contracting tuberculosis (TB)—joining 90,000 of her countrymen who also have the disease. Her formerly isolated community is now susceptible and becomes part of the widening footprint of TB throughout the world. Not to provide the village with the medicine that cures TB will make it harder and more expensive to prevent TB in its growing global circle—in Paris or Kansas City. Epidemiologists will tell you that uncontained spread in one part of the world means lack of control of the disease worldwide. The cost of your medical insurance just went up. Your grandson who decides to teach English in Thailand is now at a higher risk of contracting a deadly disease.

As Pima grows up, she may well find a way to achieve a higher income for the cash crops the family grows. She'll have heard something on the radio that made sense; have listened to an agricultural worker or talked over changes with a neighbor who grew a new strain of rice. The family will generate a very small income that allows them to buy more cooking oil, to install a water pump in the back yard or buy new shoes. She'll learn to access health care, and when she becomes a mother she'll go to the local clinic to give birth. Her children will have a better chance of living to adulthood. Life expectancy will increase and the village will grow. (Later, more education will cause families to choose fewer children.) The surrounding ecosystem will be challenged to support the growing population at the same time that factories upstream need some of the water and have deforested the land. The acid rain, degraded water flows and additional carbons entering the atmosphere will pollute the skies and oceans and drift into other lands. The temperature in your back yard will ascend and the price of your shrimp dinner will rise. The cost of global cleanup goes up exponentially.

But what of the child who doesn't get an education? The world around her changes: the village gets more crowded; the health clinic is a reminder that, if she could access health care, she could recover from the infection on her leg; the water supply in the village is dwindling; the fortunate children in the next hut have gone off to get factory jobs; her best friend now has AIDS and so does her friend's child; and the means by which her family traditionally fed itself is deteriorating. Life can no longer be sustained in the old ways and her own prospects are bleaker by the day. Although uneducated, she can see that these changes are a result of a larger world encroaching upon hers. She is angry. She has neither the means of understanding the changes, adjusting to them nor being advantaged by them. Her quality of life and life chances are narrowing despite any effort she might put into them. She is susceptible to the inspiring words of a group forming at the edges of her social life—a group that is organizing in protest against the perceived global enemies. Political and religious fanaticism doesn't look fanatical to her—it is the only way she has of protesting against changes that she doesn't control, can't understand and can't adjust to. This is how terrorist organizations grow their base. Your safety to fly, travel and live your life just receded.

But what if things could remain as they are for established, industrial nations? Or, better yet, return to a time that seemed more secure, less global and more prosperous? Leaving aside that Pima's world was never very secure or prosperous and that her opportunities expand with an education, health care and good protection of the environment, the life of the wealthy may seem to have been better off when foreign aid and foreign trade were not major concerns of Western governments. If you are from such an older industrial economy, you'd have to give up your cheap microwave, running shoes and computers. Speaking of computers, your nation can't really secure its borders because the global computer networks that track illegal money for terrorists can't work without global electronic networks and strong diplomatic relations. National companies would have to close down all those factories abroad so, if you own stock in IBM, Citibank, Nike—almost any large corporation—their value would now recede. Your retirement portfolio would shrink. Your job in BMW or Microsoft or R. J. Reynolds might vanish since exports would disappear. Your bank fees would increase because your financial transactions couldn't be handled in Ireland or India any longer. The internet might work within the country, but the ability of Nokia or Amazon or Bayer to compete globally would recede as they couldn't access the latest findings or participate in research with their counterparts in other countries. Your country's competitiveness would fade.

The value of the nation's currency would contract because their markets were no longer far reaching and powerful. The ability to discover and exploit new forms of energy would shrink as exploration and high-quality research cannot be conducted without global engineering and research networks. The cost of computers and all technology would escalate because Western labor is far more expensive than that of Thailand or China, who now make most of the world's computers. The cost of clothes, medical supplies, farm implements, backpacks, radios and jet engines would increase for the same reason. The financial industry would be at high risk of collapse as would the IT sector, communications sector, much of the tourism sector and many universities.

As the rest of the world moves forward, the country could not maintain its economic, political or military power—even the power it had before computers and global communications. Other countries would move forward and your country's ability to compete would recede. The voice in world politics, economics and military affairs would get less powerful. The clout on the world stage to determine markets, trade, politics and economic contexts would shrivel. Not only would the country fail to maintain today's world, it would not be able to maintain yesterday's world, and its role in forming that global framework would be small. The country would become an ever smaller player in a world that is moving rapidly forward. The authority of passports, travel, communications, innovations, educational systems, financial reach and global clout would shrink. No country can turn away from the global world any more than Pima can.

Part of the disconnect here—the simplistic, naïve and misguided notion that a former world of control, dominance and plenty is disappearing because of international connections—stems from the lack of understanding of how the world has changed, how it continues to change and how change looks, feels and requires adaptation. Many in older industrial economies long for a world that was—but is no more. They believe the "world before" was better because they lack the education to understand an increasingly linked world. They don't understand that it is not the country's foreign policies, diplomatic links or military might that underlie these linkages: it is, rather, the human spirit.

And so, this book is written to educate. It is not a book for Pima or for her mother. Rather, it is a book for "the educated" about the "uneducated" and about the world that is increasingly part of a networked world of learning. As these linkages grow, the power and importance of the connections of learning and knowledge are beginning to dominate the importance of financial or market linkages—in fact, they are beginning to define and control the financial and market linkages. So, understanding Pima's education is central to understanding the future of the world's prospects; her education is no longer a cost, it is a resource for a better world. Our understanding of this is also a vital resource for this better world.

1b Introduction to the theories

I originally wrote this book as a narrative, to invite the non-academic reader into the world I see, having worked in or with more than 20 countries for over 40 years of my life. But, even as a narrative, I planned the chapters around the various emerging theories that either demonstrated how the world was linked or helped readers understand what actions could be taken in such an interlinked world; the actual "theory" chapters were written later. The theories are still developing, but now have enough shape and specificity to write about. Even more interesting, they are converging.

While each theory might reference the economics of knowledge, many do not use this theory as a launching point. Some, like *new learning theories*, used the growth of knowledge as a reason for building the theories, but the theories themselves emerge from a body of work in the field of educational psychology. Other work, like that of *network theory*, began largely independently of knowledge economics but is merging with it—particularly in the areas of complexity and crowdsourcing.

Two themes seem to pervade all the theories: the first theme is linkages. Although not all the theories began with the point of linkages, all have reached the stage where the examination of linkages (whether global, community or personal) are central to understanding how the theory works. The second is technology. In all cases, the theory evolves differently because technology is increasingly pervasive or *ubiquitous* throughout the world. This is not just a convenience or a tool, but has changed the environment and ecosystem of the linkages in which the theory works.

As an economist, I tend to approach the theories through that particular lens, but the theories are converging. And, since the book is about how the world's poor must now be viewed within the context of a linked global world, it made sense to begin with the older worldview: that the world was divided between "them and us," rich and poor or North and South or West and everyone else. Chapters 2 and 3 talk about the older views of development and the role of education. Where did these views come from and how are they now being challenged? The theoretical underpinnings are neoclassical development economics and human capital theory.

Chapter 4 shows how the world began to change with the fall of the "second world"—the Soviet economic bloc. How the convergence of world markets created an environment where raw materials, manufacturing and labor began to link across the globe into a single world market setting the stage for competition on a different realm: knowledge. Chapter 5 introduces the theory that can help explain how these global linkages work: network theory. Yet this theory, seemingly simple, emerged out of the study of biological systems and had sophisticated assumptions about sustainable systems that, over time, set the stage for a much larger, more powerful analysis.

This analysis is introduced in Chapter 6, where the growth of networks spawned a huge growth in the spread, storage and building of new knowledge. Because knowledge was easy and cheap to spread and store, it began to take a different form and meaning than it had in its physical form (books, teachers, professors, film) so knowledge migrated from a static, to a process, to a dynamic. Chapter 7 describes the properties of knowledge that allowed it to make this migration once freed of a physical form. Such properties gave it resource characteristics unlike any resource contained in neoclassical economics. Further, it had process properties that allowed it to spread within networks: social networks.

Chapter 8 is an introduction to the economic theory that is evolving to explain knowledge as a resource. It is known under several names but is most popularly known as "new growth theory." But viewing knowledge purely through economic eyes is a mistake. Knowledge makes a contribution through many sectors and parts of society and operates unlike industrial products or services. So, Chapter 9 talks about how knowledge works as a social contribution including new resilience theories that incorporate equity and diversity. This part of knowledge theory shows that a more equitable spread of knowledge benefits society, and shows how the theory of networks and knowledge economics views the importance of diversity.

Although the book focuses on the new learning environment, what goes on in a formal learning environment—such as schools—is clearly impacted, so Chapter 10 introduces new learning theories and collaborative learning to show how learning environments inside and outside schools are being rethought in light of the advances in networks, knowledge, technology and the changing learning ecosystem. Finally, Chapter 11 wraps up the theory chapters by explaining how all these theories are now contributing to rethinking how society improves itself. The old notion that society's welfare can be measure in industrial production is substantially challenged in this new environment; alternative measures and concepts of societal welfare are emerging.

Chapters 12 to 14 do not have theory chapters as they contain my thinking, as a result of theories. My thinking is extended because of my observations and because of trends in the theories. Perhaps, in a few years, there will be extensions of these theories that might explain these last few chapters.

2a Development

The sense of global connectedness has not always been with us. As recently as 1994, when the genocide occurred in Rwanda, the global community felt powerless to take action even though some of its most powerful members were being informed as it happened. When the general public found out later that thousands of people were slaughtered by their own neighbors using machetes we were horrified. We just could not imagine how this could have happened. How could people who had lived together for generations turn against each other one day and kill each other with knives, and rape their own cousins? And, as horrifying as all this was, how could we feel so distant, as if this human tragedy belonged on a different planet—almost to a different species?

For those hearing about it in the living rooms of Asia, Europe and the Americas, the distance to Rwanda seemed great but, nonetheless, there was compassion, but the sense of frustration at not being able to do anything is not such a mystery. It was only a few years ago that this sort of information became available to us in full color, with little time lag. These days we might actually know someone who has traveled to one of these distant countries or even comes from one. Now, with today's technology, there might be a reporter who can report immediately via satellite phone, even if the usual communication lines are cut and electrical lines are down. Even if reporters are banned from the site, local citizens can use their cell phones to record the events and get the word out—not one or two reports, but dozens, or hundreds or thousands.

Today's media bring home the stories in ways that make our worlds seem more joined. But more is going on than media. Today's world is joined by education. Rwandans are teaching in universities in the United Kingdom, Dubai, China and Germany and the citizens of Europe and the United States are teaching in Rwanda. People in all these countries are writing about other people's countries and marrying across nationalities and ethnicities. Children are being born and growing up who have dual nationalities and dual race and language. People are watching videos and television programs in real time about other people's countries. Twitter, YouTube, Wikipedia and numerous websites are educating millions of people about each other. The physical distance is being eclipsed by the cultural, psychological and—more importantly—the learning distance, which is narrowing.

But to understand why Rwanda seemed so distant, to understand why the West apparently "did not know" the event that was eminently knowable and how a powerful Western world was apparently powerless to intervene, one must go back to a time when the world appeared to be fundamentally split between rich and poor, educated and uneducated, East and West. The concept of comparing countries on a scale of "development" began just after the Second World War.

The Three Sisters

Three sisters were born in 1944 in a small town in New Hampshire called Bretton Woods. Still known as "the Three Sisters," these were the powerful world organizations that continue to control the interplay of global financial flows to this day. The International Bank for Reconstruction and Development (IBRD)—later more commonly known as the "World Bank"—was born on the heels of that war; its twin, the International Monetary Fund (IMF), was born at the same time; a third institution, the World Trade Organization (WTO) also started at that time under the title of the General Agreement on Tariffs and Trade (GATT).

An economist from the United Kingdom, John Maynard Keynes, first proposed the establishment of the institutions as a means of stabilizing the world's economies. The war had shown leaders that national welfares were linked—what one country did affected another. So, in the small, sleepy New Hampshire town of Bretton Woods, the world leaders met to hammer out the institutions that would monitor and attend to the economic links that bound countries together. The three sister organizations would be known as the "Bretton Woods Institutions." The IMF would look after the economic health and viability of countries: if a country veered far off course in managing its finances, the IMF could step in and correct it. Later IMF policies were blamed for many of the problems of international development, but at its beginning the IMF was viewed as a "father" that would acknowledge his children's independence but be ready to step in with advice and a loan if they reached a financial crisis point.

The International Bank for Reconstruction and Development would serve to loan money for economic reconstruction and growth, as its official name implied. Initially, it loaned money to much of Europe to rebuild its industry and get those economies back on firm ground. The loans were generally for infrastructure—rebuilding roads, bridges, airports and shipping ports, along with electricity and other utilities. The loans were highly successful and much of Europe recovered, returned to financial health and repaid the loans.

The GATT was, at this point, not an institution so much as an agreement between countries on principles for world trade. There were general principles of fairness governing world trade, but the specifics got messy. Few countries wanted a world organization to dictate their tariffs, trade policies and levies on imports. GATT meetings took place on a regular basis to continue to define fair rules of the game. The fall of the Soviet economy and globalization of world markets moved, many decades later, to suggest rewarding nations that could link their production. GATT then became the WTO.

There was no doubt in anyone's mind that the world was split between "them" and "us." There were the industrial powers and then there was "everyone else." The World Bank, IMF and GATT were designed to regulate industrial economies. If there had been a slaughter in Rwanda in 1945, no one would have thought this was relevant or even mattered, except perhaps the colonial magistrate who needed to get transport out of the country. There was no thought that the peoples were joined or that "humanity" was affected across such borders as these. If there were financial flows at all, they didn't involve banking, stock markets or commodity markets as we know them today. If commodities were affected, it was only those that were exported back to colonial powers. The Three Sisters were established to stabilize the industrial powers and grow industrial markets. The member countries were exclusively European and North American, except for South Africa which was, of course, British dominated at that time.

These economies had been devastated by the war and needed to get industrial production up and running again. Further, the war had convinced them that their economies were connected as war production was linked—the production of one economy clearly linked to the welfare of another economy. So international production and trade needed to be promoted and managed.

The goal was reconstruction; trade and growth were unhesitatingly self-promoting, largely with the thought that promotion of markets benefited both donor and recipient. The United States had substantially geared up production and now had thousands of young men returning and looking for work. It needed a new placement for its productive capacity. By helping to create the IBRD (World Bank) and loaning money to Europe, it created markets for its production and, later, had good trading partners who, in turn, grew the United States through imports of US goods. The Marshall Plan and the rebuilding of Korea would, later, have similar results. Meanwhile, the economies of much of Europe had been disrupted by the war and now faced a common problem—underproduction and poor infrastructures.

The results of this investment were rewarding. National economies in Europe, which had been devastated by the First World War, grew 20 percent in the five years after Bretton Woods; world trade increased by 25 percent. In this same five-year time span, the World Bank loaned out over $300 million US, which was nearly all returned with interest. US markets grew apace. In the ten years after the Second World War, the US economy grew by 4 percent per annum—some years reaching growth rates as high as 9 percent. Its role in both the World Bank and in the Marshall Plan proved a boon to its own economy. The Western (first world) and even the Soviet (second world) economies entered a period of rapid growth.

The goals of Third World development emerge

Although the World Bank of today is largely associated with helping poor countries, their roots are firmly planted in the reconstruction of Europe after the Second World War. Their stated purposes remain the promotion of global markets and world trade—not the reduction of world poverty as is often thought. Although membership has later expanded to include even non-industrialized countries, its official stated purposes remained the same—promotion of global trade and markets rather than poverty reduction.

The World Bank began to incorporate poorer countries, not through a broader notion of world linkages, expanding notions of humanity, stronger communication ties or extended relationships with foreigners. Rather, it was through the extension of the notion of their original (and still continuing) purpose—building world trade and markets.

Can world markets expand to include poor countries and, ultimately, benefit the poor? Irrespective of whether humanity is linked through some broader notion of social benefits, communication, interlinked lives, environment and health, does market expansion benefit the poorest members of the world? This is a very real question and it is difficult to answer empirically. Market-oriented economists at the World Bank would tend to answer it this way.

When people join markets, their opportunities expand. As their opportunities expand, they become more productive, especially if they can also expand through additional education. This expanded education increases their resource base and allows them not only to produce more, but, in turn, to consume more. This improves their lives. Thus, market expansion is both a cause and a consequence of improved lives. Market expansion is a good thing.

But others would argue that the world has a limited amount of resources and not all of the world can continually expand both consumption and production—someone has to give up something. Thus, as parts of the world expand their consumption or production, someone else's life will, inevitably, deteriorate. The earth can only produce so much lumber, oil, gas, clear water, cotton, corn, fish and rice at any given time. So, constantly expanding markets means that societies must live ever poorer quality lives. Therefore societies must learn to recycle, conserve and sustain.

There are other views as well, but the point is that the World Bank is a "pro-growth" organization, both by design and by stated purpose. Its stated purpose is to grow global markets and encourage global trade of goods and services. Their view has been and continues to be that the poor can "grow" (i.e. see their incomes grow) by making the right investments.

The initial strategy of the World Bank was to simply build the infrastructure as they had in post-war Europe. Build the dams, bridges, roads and airports, it was assumed, and industry would flourish. But industry did not flourish. Later, the World Bank realized that the poor countries were lacking the human infrastructure necessary for industry, so investments in education and health were ramped up. But even this did not seem to make a difference. Attention was turned to institutional infrastructure such as finance, courts, government and policies. Eventually, parts of Asia began to take off and growth was rapid although it is not clear it was the World Bank's investment strategy that was working. In fact, as East Asia began to grow, it rejected World Bank investments in favor of internal or regional investments, which did not require stringent financial conditions. Strict adherence to educational growth and industrial growth policies seem to have been behind the tandem growth of industry and education.

A linear path for development has been a guiding principle. As a bank, the notion is that money can be invested, then that money can pay returns and the returns pay off in the form of increased growth. All loans are made on this basis— all must be justified on the grounds that the initial loan will result in a return to the country that can be measured. As with Europe before it, investments should grow economies and economies should grow markets and trade.

Soon after the Three Sisters were designed, the world split into three "worlds"—the first world (the Western trading partners), the second world (the Soviet trading partners) and the Third World (the non-aligned countries—largely poorer countries); foreign aid was used as much to buy political influence and attract countries into the first or second trading worlds as much as it was to built markets. Ownership of and growth of markets dominated by the super-powers was a means of gaining global power. Although the second world appears to have diminished (perhaps now being replaced by the rise of China), the notion that markets could and would be dominated by particular partners in the world of trade had not necessarily been anticipated when the World Bank constructed its terms of agreement, which focused on building such markets.

Small, start-up markets or markets that grow out of local initiatives, or grow from neighborhoods to regions to nations to cross-borders, are difficult to foster when the initial development monies are explicitly meant to build the ties to existing (mainly large, first-world dominated) world markets. Emphases on building gross national product (GNP) when a huge percentage of production within an economy is rural in nature (largely consumed before it ever gets registered in the national accounts) means that the welfare of rural farmers is not taken into consideration when the World Bank, IMF and—following their lead—bilateral partners assess the strength and viability of a country's economic prospects.

An integrated world

But the world is really not so simple nor always built on markets as Rwanda reminds us. The tragedy in Rwanda occurred not because markets grew or failed, not because the World Bank made investments or failed to do so. It was a human tragedy and the failure was one of human awareness—or a weakness in human awareness. It is not that no one knew what was happening—some were making phone calls to Washington DC and the UN and getting the word out quite early; it was because the people at the other end of the phone were caught in an old view of the world. The old view maintained that countries need to or should intervene when the links between them are substantive—a divided view of the world. Links are relative and when markets, trade and personal relationship links are weak but political and economic costs of intervention appear high, then action may not be warranted. The high-level political players in the UN, the US and the UK had powerful positions, but the systems in which they operated appeared to lack viable ways of responding to such an unfolding event.

There are international laws that forbid wholesale slaughter of one's citizens—especially where such slaughter is waged against a particular ethnic group. To label the Rwandan situation as genocide would require immediate UN action, but there was not enough evidence or political will to take that argument forward. It would take much more time, evidence and persuasion. To ask for action by one country would require that country to act unilaterally against another without time to define an enemy or a course of action. Who is the enemy? What course of action?

And so, for days, the insiders were paralyzed into inaction and thousands were slaughtered. The world heard a few reports but couldn't confirm the reports. Yesterday's technology couldn't get enough reports out to confirm that such a horrific event was truly occurring in a widespread fashion. Weeks later, when outsiders were able to get into the country and take photos and do interviews, the world wondered how it all could have happened without the world intervening.

This view of the world is not so easy to justify today even though the global view (paradigm) of development still operates primarily on a them/us point of view. The reality of a media that is linked in real time has meant that the world's population has moved far beyond this thinking, even if the global institutions have not fully made the shift. Today, with the internet, cell phones and satellite phones, we cannot imagine how such an event could not have resulted in some international response—let alone go unnoticed. None of us can envisage a similar situation where we are not engaged in some attempt to stop the bloodshed if it were to happen today.

And yet, the world of development is still conducted, in large part, as if the world is separated between rich and poor, North and South, educated and uneducated, as if solutions can be implemented for specific populations without taking into account the integrated nature of the entire world. We can put a school in Pima's neighborhood, hand her a textbook and pay a local teacher and not think about the project in the next village, which has corrupt local officials who are taking some of the teacher's pay. We don't have to think about the political instability, medical issues, environmental problems or technology possibilities that will impact her education or create possibilities for her. We can be naïve about her education because it is easier than thinking about an integrated world. Let's take an ecological system and follow its layers upon layers of integration throughout the world.

Global warming affects us all—or if you do not agree, let me state this fact for the sake of argument. Further, let us agree that greenhouse emissions are heavily contributing to global warming. Then, we could also agree that the global climate system passes such gases around the world and causes changes in climates throughout the world—some get warmer, some get rainier, perhaps some are less affected. So, by itself, global warming is a global system.

Now, let's look at one of the systems at work that might help reduce greenhouse emissions—alternative energy innovations. These new industries require employment of educated people because such industries are, in fact, largely knowledge-dependent. That is, they grow through innovation. When such industries grow, they increase the demand for more educated labor. This changes the nature of labor throughout the world by demanding more educated labor globally. Where such people are employed is also where these new technologies can be afforded and where there might be some pressure to adopt such technologies. So, now, the solutions to greenhouse emissions are tied to labor markets, socio-economic status and political pressure.

On the other hand, the dependence on older forms of energy is in poorer countries, which are experiencing rapid growth in their economies. Suddenly, they are developing middle classes who want electric heaters, television sets and hair dryers. Energy demand is growing rapidly as it once was in wealthier countries. To meet this rapidly growing demand, the governments can hardly afford to build modern power plants, much less new technologies. Rather, it is cheap to burn coal and worry about pollution consequences later. Political stability is often tied to economic growth: a citizen who sees her life improving year by year, is less likely to be dissatisfied with an undemocratic system of government and more likely to tolerate some corruption and curbing of freedoms. Thus, there is little incentive in poorer countries to raise the cost of development. If the cost of electricity can be kept cheap, even at the cost of greenhouse emissions, so be it. Here, global warming is tied to political stability and economic growth.

China is a good example. China's economy continues to grow between 8 and 10 percent year after year (since about 2000). This requires a lot of energy. People's incomes are growing and industries are expanding. Yet the average person has only a little more than $4,000 to spend. Clearly, China cannot be in the high-priced nuclear or solar energy investment arena in any big way. Rather, they are largely investing in coal-powered energy plants. Coal consumption has more than doubled since the year 2000 and, along with it, China's carbon footprint. Pulmonary disease is on the rise and there is a movement to shift the worst of the plants outside the Beijing area to lower pollution rates. But one can easily see why the government is caught in a difficult bind.

Early in the century, China's economic growth rate was the envy of the world and my trip to Shanghai in 2010 showed me the impact of such rapid growth. China has a growing middle class that is only too happy with its new-found stability and ability to buy modern housing and the latest gadgets, and feed a family high-quality food. Faced with a huge population and tremendous regional disparities of wealth (from Hong Kong and Shanghai at one end to huge expanses of poverty in rural China at the other), growth is spreading hope to much of China's population. Keeping the cost of growth down is a high domestic priority.

Even if the salaries and lifestyles of those in the richer countries are benefiting by developing alternative energy sources, these countries depend heavily upon growth through increased consumption in the rest of the world. Microsoft can export more software, Ford can manufacture more cars, Princeton can bring in more top international students, Pfizer can sell more drugs and Boeing can build more planes if these countries continue to increase demand. The economic links of the world are such that their survival depends upon growth of consumption throughout the world. Further, all of them face new competition from rival companies, not down the street, but across the world. Cars, planes, drugs and software are emerging industries in high-growth countries such as Brazil, China and India. So, the wealthier world does not really have a lot of incentive to push their new greenhouse gas-reducing technologies on these poorer countries. After all, they do want those economies to grow and they don't want to alienate the governments by insisting that the governments "go green" when the governments feel that political stability partly depends upon keeping electricity rates low. Finally, the large oil companies, who have influence over the policies of their often wealthy home country, are not anxious for alternative energy sources to become big players in the energy market, so everyone has at least some interest in maintaining the status quo.

So, we can include the following systems that are all part of the global warming picture: international politics, labor markets, economics, political stability, job markets, trade and oil markets. A development approach that assumes one simple investment—whether it is in markets, governance, trade, industry or labor markets—will not tackle this problem. And it really is a development problem. Countries are growing and demand energy. Their linkage with world supplies of sources of energy and world markets of commodities and world markets of consumers is key to the entire development issue. Actual development within a given country cannot be tackled effectively without consideration of the political and economic global linkages involved in global warming, energy and greenhouse emissions.

Learning in an integrated world

We may all have learned that global warming involves a global system—a system of global climates—or one climate with many facets. But what we did not learn was that it was integrated with global systems of politics, economics, labor markets, world institutions and trade. We did not understand that it involved an old way of viewing development as a single, isolated country that could, unremarkably, grow at its own pace, increase its markets, build labor, increase consumption and, without consideration of its world integration, not affect the politics, economics, labor markets, consumption and production patterns of its neighbors or the globe. And yet, as we know from systems theory, a small change in one place can, potentially, have major effects on a system elsewhere. So, the old view of development is not only completely outdated, it can potentially do the world great harm. It can lead us to the false conclusion that development is always a good thing when, in fact, it has consequences far beyond its apparent borders and we do not examine these consequences. Let us examine the educational implications, now, of global warming.

Somewhere in Nepal, a curriculum specialist, no doubt supported by a grant from the Asian Development Bank, the World Bank or some bilateral agency (US AID, the British or some other government) is deciding on a curriculum for Pima's education. She will be taught about global warming as part of her science curriculum. She will be taught that destroying the trees around her village is a bad thing. The fuel needed to cook her meals should come from another source—perhaps a solar oven. She should join a club to plant trees or learn to conserve water. Of course, the means to conserve is limited because the ecological options within her poor community are quite limited, but she will understand these basics.

What she might not understand is that the decisions of her government to alter trade agreements, shift government expenditure and delay environment protections in order to attract industry are part of a larger geo-political picture that involves local, regional and global politics, economics and trade. In part, they may benefit her in the short term while jeopardizing her health in the future or keep existing politicians in power or, possibly, put her country on the path to growth, but none of this will be part of the science curriculum. Global systems are not part of her curriculum.

But neither will that be taught in the classrooms of the schools in Birmingham or the elite schools of Seoul or Mumbai. Some of the world's most educated people understand this or it might be taught in the graduate classrooms of political science or global sociology students. Such systems are necessarily complex and even the best scientists hardly understand the complete details. But the notion that natural climate systems are linked to political agendas, economic forces, labor markets, consumption and production is pretty basic. It is a wonder that it is not part of everyone's basic education from an early age.

And so Pima—like the rest of us—is left with simplistic views of climate change. If we recycle, plant a tree or walk a mile for the environment, then something might change. But we lack the fundamental understanding of the overlapping processes that surround us on a daily basis. If we had such an understanding, that very understanding would begin informal conversations, dialogues, curiosity and exploration that would raise our own awareness and create momentum toward collective solutions. Collective learning is a powerful force, as this book will demonstrate, but it begins by understanding that we live in a dynamically linked world where learning is one of our most powerful forces. Learning is not just the facts we learn in school, but the dynamics of exchange, knowledge-building and dialogue we engage in every day, formally and informally.

So, another link between global warming and global systems is the inadequate manner in which we are educated about them. A further link is the way in which our education changes labor markets. Pima's education creates a demand—even a need—for increased consumption of products she is not growing on her farm. She joins a world of consumption dependent upon fossil fuels. Her labor, if it moves to a factory, links her into a labor force that is forged around low education levels and semi-skilled people who get their jobs because their region has low-cost labor. But once more and more of her neighbors get an education and the factories expand, her government can begin to collect more taxes and attract more industries.

If the government is like Korea in the early days of industrial expansion, it will use this increased tax revenue to expand education and gradually increase educational quality. Once this is done, it can attract somewhat better quality industries that pay better wages. The quality of life improves for the people and the mean income rises. Gradually, the standard of living rises along with the educational level and the country moves toward the middle-income range. Soon, the country joins a higher income level of countries, which shifts competition, globally, for middle-income job markets.

So, Pima's education is the beginning of the shifting of labor markets. With that shift of labor markets comes a shift in consumption because the new middle class wants more goods, more electricity and more cars. So Pima's education also shifts the problem of global warming. Her education is not neutral for global warming; it is a dynamic in the full spectrum of global warming.

Development approaches to complex problems

These complex, overlapping, systemic issues can and are tackled effectively and admirably by global organizations. Polio has effectively been nearly wiped off the face of the earth. I was in Bangladesh when a polio team came into the small breakfast room of the hotel. They were the last of the polio detectives, young medical students or graduates from France, Denmark and the United States. They spent days in the most remote areas of the country, in village after village, asking "Is there someone in your village that has been sick for a long time?" If the answer was "yes," they asked to see the person and they assessed their illness. If they found a polio victim, they vaccinated the entire village and all surrounding villages. They carried with them, in Styrofoam containers, live polio vaccine. Through one village after another, laid out on a grid of the country, they were hunting down the last polio carriers in Bangladesh.

As humans, we have enormous capacity to develop systems that counter or destroy bad systems—human or natural. We can even fund the enormous planning, costs and strategies that wipe out a world crippler like polio. We have computer viruses that can destroy my capacity to write this book, to get it to a publisher or into your hands. Such viruses can destroy everyone's ability to write, to publish and to read. But our lives continue largely as if they didn't exist. Our lives are protected by the ingenuity of humans to create. There are free virus scanners that one can download off the internet. For most of us, such a virus scanner works in the background as we type. As new viruses are invented days later, our software updates automatically and cleans out the problem before it disables our typing. We never know. We don't have to know. Someone else is managing this part of our world.

In other words, we are capable of developing systems that work on our behalf. These systems work without our managing our every move, our ever action, our every purchase. Such systems can be motivated by a shared sense of welfare (eradicating polio), by profit (keeping computer systems working so we buy more computers and software) or contributed to by valued civic action (tweeting the latest news out of Iran about its election results).

Knowledge itself is a powerful tool. As we have seen in the recent Arab Spring or the containment of the SARS epidemic, getting the word out, equipping people with information, allowing people to create conversations, raise awareness and find ways of educating each other is a powerful force. Being aware, seeking understanding and finding small ways to participate in sharing that knowledge created momentum in and of itself. Knowledge has power, and collective knowledge has momentum.

It begins here with eliminating the myth that one is educated if one has spent time in a classroom. Facts are not an education: it is simply the basis upon which one can build learning. Learning is dynamic. One has a continuing responsibility to be continually educated. The world is globally linked; possibly the most powerful of these linkages is that of learning. Passing information through global channels, whatever they may be—blogs, emails, groups, networks, articles, websites, videos, news, etc.—created the momentum for global learning. All peoples have the right to participate. Development comes to an abrupt halt at the edge where such exchanges cannot exist—where people cannot participate. So our obligations are to participate, to learn and to be advocates to ensure that all can do so.

Is it possible to view development as growth in markets and trade as the World Bank has defined it? The question must be asked by narrowing the field of the question down from a global dynamic to a single, isolated incident in a particular country and a particular case. Could it be true for a school in Pima's neighborhood? Would that be a good investment? It would be easier to answer the question in this way. What is the future of learning? How will people be learning in five years? Likely, even her area will get hooked to 4G internet speeds within that time. Would it be better to invent a new system of learning for her? Maybe think of technology solutions that could give her some basic understanding with a tutor (possibly from a distance) and then have one teacher who comes for two months a year who can do the work that needs collective learning. How do people learn best and what investment makes sense? How do we get Pima and her village linked to a world that is outside their walking distance? A village center with a big screen and then link in a teacher? It might be cheaper, more effective and provide more opportunities for the whole village. But we need to start with the broader question of learning rather than the narrow question of schooling.

So, how is it that we are still stuck with the narrow national question of individuals, schooling and investment? Why hasn't this been replaced by notions of learning on a global scale with dynamics and global systems? To answer that question, we have to trace back again to another long-held theory—that of human capital theory.

2b Shifting views on development

Although international development as a global concept emerged from the ravages of the Second World War (Arndt, 1987) and was most widely propagated through the coordinated efforts of the Three Sisters of the World Bank, the IMF and the GATT, the large amounts of monies came from other sources. Prominent among them was the Marshall Plan of the United States, which got the ball rolling. Between 1948 and 1995, some $13 billion was sent to Europe to reconstruct its war-torn economy and ultimately create the markets that would maintain the United States on its economic growth path. But even this rather successful foreign aid strategy shifted over the years. It began with a focus on physical infrastructure investment and shifted to major investments in education and health. The thought was that the infrastructural investment did not grow markets without brainpower. Even education and health investments eventually gave way to a period where government restructuring became the primary focus of foreign aid (at least for the moment).

Beginning in the 1990s, as some Asian nations began to emerge into middle-income countries, the foreign aid strategies took a major turn. Rather than unilateral policy implementation, some countries were given the "invest in private markets" treatment while others were given a more welfare/poverty approach to foreign aid (Ilon, 1996). Human development, as a concept, emerged as a viable alternative view (UN Development Programme, n.d.).

But none of these evolving views prepared the field for a networked world. Such a world was gradually emerging from simple cell-phone technology, underwater sea cables, satellites, expanding transportation corridors and globalizing production markets. What had been, throughout world history, a world divided by distances, gradually became a world that was fundamentally linked through something whose power rivaled that of money (capital). That power was knowledge and its networks. In such a world, distance, continents, even language and culture were no longer a natural division of people. The development paradigm of fixed and static rich worlds/poor worlds, so long an apparent truth, would begin to give way. The power of creativity, connectivity, ingenuity and, inevitably, new theories would attempt to explain it all.

Traditional structures

Most of the foreign aid still comes from the wealthiest countries in Europe and North America. Countries in Europe contribute over half of the country-to-country foreign aid (bilateral aid)—about 57 percent in 2012. The United States and Canada contribute about a third (30 percent). Emerging countries in Asia (including Australia and New Zealand) contribute about 14 percent of the total bilateral aid. Figure 2.1 shows the contribution of major foreign aid contributors in 2012 by country. Five countries contribute over half of all the bilateral aid in the world. About two-thirds of all foreign aid comes from bilateral donors. Some of this aid, however, is targeted at specific countries for designated purposes. For example, the United States provides aid to Israel, which amounts to about $3 billion US a year (Harvard Kennedy School Shorenstein Center, 2012).

Table 2.1 shows how the share of foreign aid is distributed across major contributors. The OECD Development Assistance Directorate (OECD, n.d.) keeps track of development assistance (also known as foreign aid, international aid and overseas development assistance). It reports that about two-thirds of current assistance is "concessional." That is, it is either given entirely as a grant

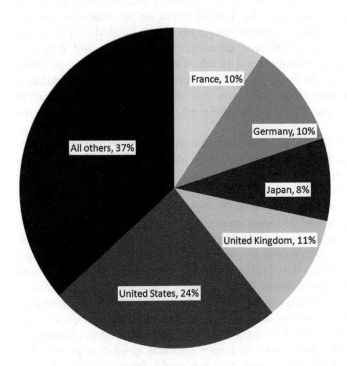

Figure 2.1 Relative share of bilateral foreign aid donors in 2012

Source: Organisation for Economic Co-operation and Development (OECD) (2013)

or, if given as a loan, at least 25 percent is given as an outright grant. The rest of the foreign aid is given as a loan. Some loans are given at very low interest rates or may even be, ultimately, forgiven and never paid back (Ilon, 1996). In the 15 year period measured, there has been about a 75 percent increase in foreign aid worldwide (inflation adjusted). This represents an increase of about 4 percent per year. Notably, the major sources of foreign aid have remained rather stable over the years with the United States and multilaterals gradually increasing their share and Japan having recently receded as a share of aid. A closer look at the multilateral aid, however, reveals that the two UN agencies that are growing faster (in budget) than the average rate of growth of foreign aid are UNRWA (UN Relief and Works Agency) and the IMF. Both, arguably, are responding to a global crisis in instability—emergency aid for people displaced and financial aid for countries in trouble.

Table 2.1 Major foreign aid sources 1997 and 2012 (current $ million US)

	1997		2012	
United States	8,128	11.2%	30,460	16.8%
World Bank	7,519	10.4%	16,774	9.2%
EU institutions	5,778	8.0%	16,173	8.9%
United Kingdom	3,316	4.6%	13,659	7.5%
Germany	6,729	9.3%	13,108	7.2%
France	6,879	9.5%	12,106	6.7%
Japan	9,399	12.9%	10,494	5.8%
Other multilateral	7,121	9.8%	22,682	12.5%
Other bilateral	17,751	24.4%	46,084	25.4%
Total	72,620	100%	181,540	100%

Source: computed from OECD (2013, Table A4)

The World Bank—formally known as the International Bank for Reconstruction and Development—is the largest multilateral donor with about 30 percent of all foreign aid for multilaterals and about three-quarters of all foreign aid for all UN agencies. As Figure 2.2 shows, the amounts of monies devoted to foreign aid from multilaterals derives primarily from the World Bank. Beginning in the 1990s, many European countries began to combine some of their bilateral aid into a common package of foreign aid and that package is now viewed as multilateral aid. This combined package now rivals the amount provided by the World Bank—growing over the years to 30 percent of all multilateral aid.

Evolving purposes of foreign aid

From its inception as the Marshall Plan, foreign aid was viewed as beneficial to both donor and recipient. How the interests of wealthy and poor nations coincide is not always clear. For example, a perusal of the World Bank's website would lead one to believe that poverty alleviation is a primary focus of the

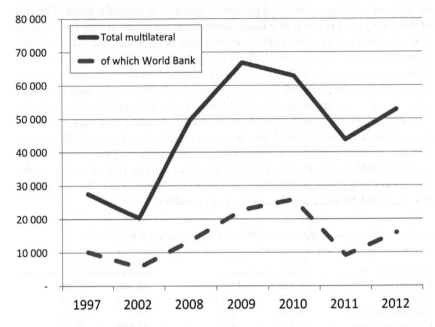

Figure 2.2 Multilateral foreign aid 1997–2012 (constant $US 2009)
Source: OECD (2013, Table A4)

institution. But, in fact, its official purpose makes no mention of poverty alleviation. In its Articles of Agreement the World Bank declares three purposes, all of which are linked to the furtherance of global markets:

(1) To assist in the reconstruction and development of territories of members by facilitating the investment of capital for productive purposes . . .
(2) To promote private foreign investment by means of guarantees or participations in loans and other investments made by private investors . . .
(3) To promote the long-range balanced growth of international trade and the maintenance of equilibrium in balances of payments . . .

(World Bank, 2012)

Bilateral aid is often dictated by the strategic and economic interests of the donor country—at least as much as by the needs of the recipient country (Alesina & Dollar, 2000; Maizels & Nissanke, 1984).

Foreign aid has gone through many phases where different types of assistance have been emphasized. Initially, loans and grants had been given in the area of infrastructure but by the 1970s the World Bank was turning its attention to education and health sectors. The 1980s marked a period where much of the multilateral foreign aid was linked to policies whereby governments were asked to restructure their budgets and agencies—a policy that, arguably, later led to a downturn in economic growth for many poor countries (Stewart, 1991; Streeten, 1987). In recent years, much of this foreign aid has been coordinated between donors such as the "Education for All" effort (UNESCO, n.d.) and the "Global Fund," which has been established to fight AIDS, tuberculosis and malaria (GlobalFund.org, n.d.).

Throughout more than a decade of official development assistance, much of the effort has focused on poverty alleviation—the thought that poor people are not only an issue for social justice but efforts to alleviate poverty also build markets, stabilize governments and create consumers. This is something for everybody—donors, recipients, global corporations and multilateral institutions. But, what comprises poverty alleviation has been a continuing debate.

The standard approach of most development lending has been directed toward economic growth. The unheralded march toward economic growth, especially accompanied by structural adjustment policies, appeared to work against the very equity and poverty alleviation that stabilized many of these countries. Was it possible to pursue both growth and stability? A new set of literature began to emerge that suggested social sustainability was a better goal for development.

Growth, as traditionally defined, is not sustainable. A new theory was brewing —knowledge economics. In 1990, at a small, elite World Bank conference on development, Paul Romer introduced a theory that posited it was the human ability to create ideas that led human progress (Romer, 1993). The theory hinted that ideas (or knowledge) were an infinite resource, were a resource that came before industry (led industrial growth) and could strengthen societies without using raw materials. The theory could encompass growth, possibly overcome the problems of the measures of GDP, and likely manage sustainability issues due to the characteristics of ideas (knowledge).

Societal progress is built from human intelligence, invention, creativity and ideas (Heeks, 2010; Thompson, 2008). It is an emerging theory of development that is built around the world's linkages rather than its divides.

References

Alesina, A. and Dollar, D. (2000). Who gives foreign aid to whom and why? *Journal of Economic Growth, 5*(1), 33–63.

Arndt, H. W. (1987). *Economic development: The history of an idea.* Chicago, IL: University of Chicago Press.

GlobalFund.org. (n.d.). The global fund to fight AIDS, tuberculosis and malaria. Retrieved from www.theglobalfund.org/en/

Harvard Kennedy School Shorenstein Center. (2012, April 26). US foreign aid to Israel: 2012 congressional report. Retrieved from http://journalistsresource.org/studies/international/foreign-policy/u-s-foreign-aid-to-israel-2012-congressional-report

Heeks, R. (2010). Development 2.0: The IT-enabled transformation of international development. *Communications of the ACM, 53*(4), 22.

Ilon, L. (1996). The changing role of the World Bank: Education policy as global welfare. *Policy & Politics, 24*(4), 413–424.

Maizels, A. and Nissanke, M. K. (1984). Motivations for aid to developing countries. *World Development, 12*(9), 879–900.

OECD (2013). Net official development assistance by DAC country and multilateral donor; Table A4. Retrieved from www.oecd-ilibrary.org/development/development-co-operation-report-2013/net-official-development-assistance-by-dac-country_dcr-2013-table60-en;jsessionid=3fms02qm6jklq.x-oecd-live-01

——. (n.d.). OECD Development Co-operation Directorate website. Retrieved from www.oecd.org/dac/

Romer, P. (1993). Two strategies for economic development: Using ideas and producing ideas. In L. Summers and S. Shekhar (eds), *Proceedings of the World Bank annual conference on development economics 1992* (pp. 63–92). Washington, DC: World Bank. Retrieved from http://documents.worldbank.org/curated/en/1993/03/699081/proceedings-world-bank-annual-conference-development-economics-1992

Stewart, F. (1991). The many faces of adjustment. *World Development, 19*(12), 1847–1864.

Streeten, P. (1987). Structural adjustment: A survey of the issues and options. *World Development, 15*(12), 1469–1482.

Thompson, M. (2008). ICT and development studies: Towards development 2.0. *Journal of International Development, 20*(6), 821–835.

UN Development Programme (n.d.). About human development. Retrieved June 30, 2014, from http://hdr.undp.org/en/humandev

UNESCO (n.d.). Education for all. Retrieved from www.unesco.org/new/en/education/themes/leading-the-international-agenda/education-for-all/the-efa-movement

World Bank (2012, June 27). IBRD articles of agreement; purposes. Retrieved from http://go.worldbank.org/5R3OHEHQ40

3a The value of an education

If Pima had grown up in the early 1980s, her path toward education would have appeared to be a simple one. During this time, the major donors thought they had the world largely figured out. Simply educate the world's children in a manner similar to the way European and US children had been educated and, in the next generation, they would create the economic opportunities that Europe and North America enjoyed. It all followed a logic that had revolution-ized the economics profession—something called human capital theory.

Far from the world of carrying water each day, tending to the baby sister or ensuring that the rats did not eat the rice her mother had gathered and stored in the woven structure next to the house, human capital theory seems to put all human activity into a simple formula. It was a formula that economists had been struggling to find for generations. Seeing the miracle of growth that industry wrought, they could see that human labor was a major component. But unlike land, electricity, machines, iron ore, timber or vehicle transportation, human labor could not be bought, sold or wagered, or discarded when worn out. It could not be put into the accounting that both accountants and economists needed in order to account for its productivity as a "factor" of this productive machine.

The growth in educational aid could not have occurred without a strong set of logic that couched the loans as "good investments." After all, the World Bank is in the business of loans. Other donors such as the United States and the UK, most notably in the early days of education assistance, were not giving out loans and faced no such restriction. But these bilateral donors still couched their general policies in terms of the benefits to their own countries. The loans were a way of building markets and market linkages that would benefit their home countries at some point. The key was to link the growth of market and trade with the notion that the recipient countries would also benefit from concomitant increases in "the good life."

The good life

Neoclassical economic theory begins with a simple question—what is a good life? Essentially, the answer that forms the basis of economic theory is that the good life comes from having the maximum resources and the freedom to use those resources however one might wish to use them. If you wish to consume all the corn you grow, so be it. But, if you are tired of eating corn, you can trade it for apples or carrots or new shoes or new shingles for your roof. You can keep trading until the options for things to buy don't appeal to you anymore, that is until everything you currently have is more appealing to you than anything you could trade for. Once you've done that, then you have used your resources to maximize your happiness to its fullest—at least given what resources you have.

So, how does a society maximize its happiness? First, it maximizes its resources. It makes sure that the most resources it can possibly produce are being produced. That is the first condition. Once it has its maximum wealth, then everyone has the ability to trade their resources freely so each individual can maximize their individual happiness given whatever resources they individually have. Once each individual is satisfied in the way they chose to spend their resources (money, energy, leisure, brainpower), then the society has reached maximum happiness. Add up all this happiness and one can calculate the total happiness of the society. Since it is hard to add up happiness but somewhat easy to add up the value of at least some resources (like income, which is equated to resources), then the national income is used as a proxy for national happiness or societal well-being.

No one has to regulate this trading process. The process operates silently with a lot of people making independent decisions on their own behalf. Their actions operate collectively into a large system of exchange. No one is really in charge; no policy makers are regulating this system. Because this system is vast and powerful but goes on silently behind the scenes, economists have named this system "the invisible hand."

The invisible hand works because, as people trade, the prices change and the price changes cause people to change their desire for the things they want. When Pima has too much rice and someone else needs rice but has extra shoes that Pima wants, they agree to a trade. But, how much rice must be traded for the shoes? The shoemaker has three pairs of shoes to sell. He will sell each pair to the person who will give him the most rice. Yesterday, he was able to sell a pair of shoes for four bushels of rice. So, he tells Pima, that the "price" of a pair of shoes is four bushels of rice. But Pima also wants to buy a cooking pot and some pens for school. So, she decides that, maybe, she will not buy the shoes because she needs a cooking pot and pens more. The shoemaker, meanwhile, is having a difficult time selling shoes today and he really needs to contribute rice to a wedding feast for his nephew by the end of the week. So, he tells Pima that he has lowered his price for shoes to three and a half bushels. Pima decides this is a good price and she makes the exchange.

The price might have been lowered if a lot of people in the village needed shoes—the price would have gone up. The price might have been different if the shoemaker had a lot of shoes for sale and had not been able to sell them for a while—the price would have gone down. The price is determined by the supply (how many shoes there are around to be sold by all the shoemakers) and by demand (how many people want shoes immediately). While Pima is trying to trade rice for shoes, a trader in Chicago is trying to buy pork bellies (that give us bacon) by the hundreds of thousands. Iowa farmers are willing to sell their pigs if the price is right. Depending upon the supply of pigs and the demand for bacon, the price of pork bellies will be agreed up. Pima's shoes and hundreds of thousands of pork bellies are all having their price set by "the invisible hand."

I was teaching this concept to my Korean students when a great example presented itself. An unusually wet summer meant that fewer cabbages were produced for the all-important ingredient for Korean meals—kimchi. It was a national crisis for Korea. This was the season for making kimchi and stores were raising the prices of their cabbages, but shortages still persisted. In fact, the demand for the right kind of cabbages now moved to China where, according to the newspapers, prices for cabbages had risen 12 percent in a week. House-wives who prided themselves on their annual output of kimchi had to wait for days or in long lines to capture the prized cabbages as they came into the local stores. Prices had quadrupled. Not only was the supply low, but there is no good substitute for the right cabbage, so demand was very high.

Of course, few of us live in a situation where markets function so well that they reflect completely accurately, at all times, the perfect price for maximizing everyone's happiness. The price of diamonds is manipulated by constraining its supply so that people will pay higher prices and the supply will keep the company in business for a long time. The price of oil is set by a group of country representatives who meet regularly to decide on a world price, although some oil is not controlled by these countries. So, the price of oil varies but, neverthe-less, does not truly reflect supply and demand. Countries build trade barriers to imports, which raise the price. I can buy a Samsung computer in the United States for about half the price I do in Korea where, in principle, it is made (although it is likely made in China). Why? Because the United States is a huge, largely open market for technology whereas Korea still has laws that raise the price of imported technology. But, when one considers the big picture—across all goods, across all global markets, and considering the billions of trades made each day, whether from Pima's village market or computer chips bought and sold—the notion of an invisible hand is a powerful metaphor; the invisible hand regulates supply, demand and prices and can reveal what societies value. This invisible hand idea has many problems but none so much as when it is applied to labor.

The value of labor

The theory is a good one, but economists have to be precise in their definitions to turn theory into good research. Productivity is a big problem because it is relatively easy to define and really hard to count. The simple definition of productivity, for economists, is that productivity is the value of what is produced for a country or an industry or a person. How much did Bayer produce this year? Take the value (price paid) for all their pharmaceuticals and subtract the value (price paid) for all the things they had to buy to produce those pharmaceuticals (chemicals, equipment, electricity) and one has the amount Bayer produced this year. Add that all up for all other things made and produced in Germany in one year and one has a measure of Germany's productivity.

Want to know how much Pima produces from her education? Find out how much she earns when she goes to work and subtract what she would have earned if she did not go to school. That is the value of her production. Want to compare the value of labor in one country against another? Add up the value of everything produced in each country (Germany and Nepal) and divide that value by the total number of people working in each country. Now you can compare. The average working person in Nepal produces about $1,200 (in 2008, US dollars). The average working person in Germany produces about $87,500.

There are a lot of problems in this comparison. What, for example, is "working"? Is Pima's mother who tends to the rice paddies working? Is Pima's father? And, what about Pima herself who comes home and collects the firewood and cleans up after the family meal? Is a poet working? Pima's father, Pima's mother, Pima herself when she comes from school and most poets do not get paid, so it is hard to put a price value on their labor, so most economists would not count the value of their labor. Is a father who stays home to take care of the children working while his wife is "at work"? Those who fought for the end to apartheid in South Africa were productive—giving up time, energy, dignity, freedom and even lives but ultimately successful in bringing a legal end to apartheid? But lives lost, dignity and energy are not counted. A young woman who has given birth generally uses her time more judiciously in order to tend to a baby who needs feeding, bathing and nurturing—something she didn't have to do with her time before birth. Is she now more productive than before giving birth? All of these uses of time, energy, political capital, social networking, nurturing and human sacrifice can lead to additional productivity.

But this is terribly messy data. In fact, how do we count the productivity of the poet or the young mother or of Pima? Economists would, in fact, acknowledge all these uses of our time in the theoretical definition of productivity. But, in actual fact, virtually none of it is actually counted in the statistics. What is counted is the labor that is either paid directly or turns into something that can be sold in a formal market (Pima's mother's extra rice if the rice is sold in a formal market where the government can count its price/value).

In order to be counted in the usual working definition of productivity, it must be of a special kind—it must be labor that adds to the value of markets. Labor that goes into building an automobile, writing a commercial computer program, making a new law, educating children or tending cattle that will be sold for their meat are all productive activities under the narrow definition of human capital. That is, productivity as referred to by human capital theory (indeed, generally by neoclassical economics) does not encompass the production of all human energies. Rather, it captures only energy that results in additional *market* value—things that get sold in the market place.

The concept of productivity is enormously important in measuring the progress of a society to meet the basic needs of its residents. But, in so doing, it is important to remember, in all societies, some of the labor is not being captured by measures of productivity. It is important to remember because improvements in the lives of many of the lives of the poorest do not get registered in national income accounts and so, literally, *do not get counted*. If one year you are eating well and the next year you are starving due to a local drought, there is no change to the national income accounts because your food was never counted in the first place. Your welfare is, effectively, of no concern to your national welfare (income) measure. It never shows up in the statistics. Local donor programs will show no progress at all—whether you ate or starved. Programs that use such measures to show progress measure progress *in markets*, not necessarily in the well-being of people—especially the poor (because their productivity is less likely to be measured in markets).

In societies that are largely based on home production or on informal markets (street food sold from one's harvest, for example), the measure of productivity can be particularly inaccurate. How can such an inaccurate measure of labor value be used by economists for years?

Investing in education

The reason why Pima wants to buy pens for her schooling is because she believes these pens will help her in school and school will provide her a better life. She may not even like school. Her parents may suffer greatly because she cannot give them labor all day long. Walking to school might mean a long walk in hot sun each day and the teacher may not be very good. So, clearly, schooling is not always a joy in itself. But suffering today may mean a better tomorrow. In effect, Pima and her parents are deciding to forego some benefits today in order to get more benefits in the future. The pens are an investment in the future.

Thank goodness we have Pima and her family, because economists had no idea, formerly, how education could possibly fit in their equations. No one doubted that education improved the quality of industrial labor. But industry did not pay for education—Pima's parents did or her government did. So, Pima's education could not be put into the equation for profit maximization that economists are so comfortable with in explaining how industry works.

We also knew that more educated populations seem to help a nation grow. But an educated population was not something a nation owned like land or rivers. Nations could build a population of educated people just as they could build airports and electrical grid systems, but they could not force them to work or even to work in the field for which they were trained. Education was placed into the pile of consumption goods—things we choose to buy for our own purposes for the moment. We pay for movie tickets, vacations and education— it is valuable to us as a way to spend our time.

But the theory of human capital gave an answer. Although—unless one wanted to revert to slavery—human labor could not be compelled to work, could not be bought or sold and was not as reliable on a scale as, say, a machine, it could be thought of as an investment. People did get an education in order to improve their income, and this investment had returns, not just in the short term, but throughout their life. So, people invested in their education in order to have pay-offs throughout their lives. This same investment concept could also be applied to whole countries. Investment in the education of citizens could raise the productive level of a country and have returns in the raised productivity of the country as the educated citizens became productive workers. After all, productive workers raised GDP—the nation's accounting of its income flow.

Thus, Pima's education had only to conform to this new logic that was emerging from the economic theorists. Raise her education level and the level of education of her neighbors and, surely, she and her neighbors would find that their productivity would increase and, along with it, their incomes. As their productivity and incomes increased, so too would the productivity of their country. It was a simple formula, a simple logic, a simple idea with huge power, huge influence, huge implications and enormous influence over development lending and loans from the 1980s until today.

The theory is a strong one and helps us understand why governments spend billions of dollars each year taking taxpayers' money away from them and reinvesting it in public education. Those reinvested dollars make countries wealthy. It is the reason why I went into debt to put my son through college and why Koreans spend decades making sure their children get the best private tutors and go to the best colleges. If all goes well, national, family and personal incomes increase as a result of those well-invested dollars, won, kwacha, rubles and yen.

But the theory is anything but perfect and its imperfections hurt both the poor and our understanding of how to help the poor and how to stabilize a globally linked world. A primary problem is the assumption that price is equal to value. Remember the example of Pima's rice and her desire for shoes? Price made good sense in that example. But price did not make good sense when it came to valuing her mother's labor. Her mother worked hard all day but the economist's "price" put on her mother's labor was "zero." So, if the price of some valuable labor is "zero" then calculating human capital—which depends upon a really accurate measure of the value of labor—is obviously a problem.

Just like the shoe seller in Pima's village, economists assume that one sells one's labor for the highest price one can get. If you can find a job that pays you more, the theory says, you will go to that job. You will continue to seek out jobs that pay you more until you have found the job with the highest pay. If you are a structural engineer and you are paid more than a structural engineer across town, we can assume you must be more valuable. When all employees are engaged in constantly seeking higher wages and all employers, conversely, are constantly minimizing costs, then they arrive at a price that satisfies them both. This is just like Pima and the shoemaker finding a price that satisfies them both. The seller tries to maximize price and the buyer tries to minimize price. In this way, economists believe that your wage is equal to the value of your labor.

The problem is that some people might actually choose a job not just for the salary. It might be close to their home; they might like the working conditions or the hours. As a professor, I am sure I could earn more in the private sector, but I love what I do and do not want to trade the pleasures of my work for more money and different working conditions. Some people would be happy to work in a different job if they had the money to move or had the information about a different job or had the money to invest in the training or the connections to be interviewed. So the entire value of a job is not fully captured by the income. A parent may choose not to work or to work part-time or at a lesser job in order to help raise the children. There are numerous problems in trying to put an accurate "price" on human labor that are not encountered with shoes or rice, and each of these problems causes the robust theory of human capital to be very difficult to apply in practice.

There are nearly as many problems when we try to calculate human capital gains on a national scale. The traditional way to do this is to add up the differences in salaries between different levels of education. For example, how much does the typical secondary school graduate make compared to the primary school graduate? Do this for all levels. Then calculate the costs of schooling at each level and compare the costs to the benefits. The math is a bit complicated but, properly done, one could figure out whether the national returns to investments in education were worth it. Generally, when these calculations have been done, they have shown that education is a very good investment for countries.

There are lots of problems with these calculations. One big problem is that drop-outs and the unemployed are not part of the equation so only those in employment are considered. Leaving them out of the calculation raises the apparent returns. But a much bigger problem is a recent one. How can one calculate the value of knowledge? If knowledge was a regular input into industry, we might be able to make such a calculation, and early attempts took such an approach. Brilliant statisticians took large categories of industry such as computer industries, communication industries, travel, manufacturing, etc. and did estimates for each category of the percentage of knowledge production that went into each industry. For example, one Boeing executive once told me that 70 percent of the value of a new jet was now attributable to knowledge. When you buy a new jet, 70 percent of the check you write for the new jet goes to the brains that designed the jet. Some other percentage of the check went to the seat covers, the aluminum, the wires, the landing lights and tires. So, once you could figure out the knowledge value of each category for each industry, you could figure out how much each country's productivity depended upon knowledge production. Effectively, you could calculate how much of the country's value depended upon knowledge work and knowledge workers.

Here's the problem and why they gave up. What do you do with Google? I probably use it ten times a day. Now, when I use Google, that value never appears in a market because I don't pay to use Google. Whatever Google reports as transactions (to the government for tax purposes or to the statisticians to keep track of national growth), they certainly do not report my transactions in using Google services because I do not pay Google to use their services. And, if Google actually did report the value of my transaction, would the value of my transaction belong to the United States or Korea (where I currently live)? Because, although I received value from Google when I used it, they actually received value from me (my search improved their search engine and, possibly, improved their ability to create new products). So, actually, there was an exchange of value—part of the value came from Korea. But neither the value from Korea to the United States nor the value from the United States to Korea went through a market. And, possibly, maybe it never went to the United States at all. Possibly, my English-based Google search really goes through Australia and, anyway, maybe Google pays its programmers in India and has most of its data neatly tucked away in some other country. So although knowledge creates tremendous value, it just does not really have a country or a nationally-based market and cannot easily be counted as a product. It is a flow—as technology people like to call it: something that moves around.

And, as to the value of my labor, whose value is that anyway? I'm paid by Korea and human capital theory would, therefore, place my human capital within Korea. But, that assumes that knowledge is a product that is owned. What if it is a "flow" that keeps moving and growing? Then, the value I transmitted to Google may have begun with my formal education in the United States, been added to when I worked in 20 countries throughout the world, was added to when I used vehicles and trekked off-road to rural areas where the world's poor educated me (as this book will amply show) and then allowed my highly diverse students to raise amazing questions that caused me to rethink what I thought I knew and, lastly, moved to Korea, which caused me to reassess my view of the world. So, whose knowledge is this anyway, that was transmitted to Google? The problem with human capital theory is that it does not tell us where and how to value an idea and its spread. It only says that your value is exactly equal to what you are paid, where you were paid at the moment you create the knowledge.

But, even within the narrow confines of neoclassical economic theory, not all of education's value can be captured by labor value. There are ways that societies benefit from education that are not monetary, that do not go to market and, indeed, are not directly connected to traditional resources—time, energy, psychological costs and money. Educated societies can sustain democracy cheaper and more easily. Educated societies tend to absorb knowledge of better health care, better environmental practices and better ways of sharing information (which is different, necessarily from their willingness to act on this information). Information is often cheaper to distribute and cheaper to gather when people can read and write. Laws can be contemplated and understood, news can be consumed and ideas can be spread through the written medium. Economists have a concept that captures these kinds of benefits.

Externalities are benefits derived by others from the purchase or consumption by another—from someone else's education, for example. When Pima goes to school, her neighbors benefit because she can read the information that comes to the village or inform them about important events about which they need to know. Her education may bring in better information on farming techniques—which will be adopted by her neighbors—or better health information. So, areas where more educated people live are generally better places to live, even when a specific person, family or household is not educated. The surrounding area may be cleaner, more organized, more productive, have better political connections or have better services. These benefits to education that accrue as a result of the education of others are known as externalities.

Governments may well emphasize education because it raises the level of national income directly. It allows government to provide more services to their citizens through higher taxes, thereby increasing government popularity and raising national prominence in an international arena. But, in so doing, governments have also unleashed the forces of civic engagement, pressures for democracy and the desire to link and understand a broader world. In so doing, it also makes some functions of government easier and cheaper. Printing information is cheaper than having to spread it through community organizations; laws that can be read are more likely to be enforceable, for example. For this reason, most governments and societies have a collective interest in seeing that a basic education is attained by most citizens. But, in order to do so, they often need to provide for this education free or relatively cheaply.

Private costs to education

Pima's education may actually appear free to her parents. The government may provide the schooling free of charge. It may even provide the textbooks and school supplies to little Pima. But even if this were the case, Pima's school results in a very large cost to her parents. This is known as an opportunity cost.

Opportunity costs are the value lost from engaging in an alternative activity. School costs little Pima's parents, not usually in out-of-pocket costs, but in the labor foregone when Pima attends school. There is value in her labor at home and, in losing that labor, the family has less to eat. Attending college almost always involves an opportunity cost because it means the income one could have for working during college hours is foregone.

In poorer communities, opportunity costs tend to be higher than in wealthier communities—at least in the primary school years. During these years, parents in wealthier countries are often engaged heavily in other activities during the day—working or maintaining a complex lifestyle. If their children were not in school, they would face a larger babysitting cost. So the public provision of schooling, even though costing them additional taxes, also reduces their household expenditure. In poor families, children contribute to household incomes at an early age—either by helping tend animals, cooking, watching younger siblings or earning small income through their labor. Parents forego this income or value of labor when they send their children to school. Furthermore, even at a young age, adults are around to keep an eye on them so there is no alternative babysitting cost. Thus, the provision of free, basic education still has high costs for the world's poor. Ideally, if education pays off in the long run, parents could borrow the money today to educate their children and pay it off years later when the child increases their productivity.

Imperfect capital markets impact education when the benefits of education cannot be easily paid for by borrowing the money. Of course, in the case of Pima, her parents likely have no bank and do not access credit for any expenditure. But, even if this were not the case, worldwide, parents can rarely borrow money to pay for their children's schooling. This is partly because it is difficult to know the value of Pima's future increased productivity or even if she can attain a job or be a better farmer. In cases where loans involve such high risks, the costs of borrowing rise, but are not generally unavailable. But a bank has no way of forcing Pima to pay back her loan. They cannot force her to work at a job she does not want (i.e. slavery) nor does it make sense to put her in jail if she chooses not to pay—doing so removes her ability to pay.

We don't usually think of the efficiency of a school as a private cost of schooling, but it can be a private cost. If a school is run poorly, then the cost of school—whether it be the tuition that parents pay or the opportunity cost (Pima's labor or the salary we forego to go to college)—has less value than it might have. So, what is the optimal efficiency of a school?

School efficiency is the measure of how close a school comes to accomplishing its goals for the least cost. Many schooling efficiency measures assume that the goal of the school is to raise test scores. But schooling has lots of goals for the individual, her family, community, nation and the world. We want people who are honest, who can complete standard forms and manage their money properly. We want people who can work with others, who have a desire to contribute to society and who appreciate a variety of social goods such as sports or art. If we measured test performance and put everyone who did poorly in a room and just entertained them while high scorers received a good education, we could reduce costs and raise average test scores (restating only those who are getting an education), but we would end up with a society we did not like. High test scores, absent other values, would mean aggressive, self-centered, dishonest, poorly socialized and uncooperative students and, later, adults.

Thus, schools that target only high test scores may actually be inefficient in accomplishing the total package of goals a society really wants. In fact, in many Asian countries, equality of schooling opportunity appears to support growth in national incomes over many years, so there is some evidence that equality of schooling may actually be efficient. Some of the most equitable national schools systems actually score the highest in international tests. So, it is important to think of the entire spectrum of national goals when considering what an efficient school system is. All too often, efficiency is wrongly confused with cutting budgets or maximizing one element such as test scores rather than considering the full spectrum of goals. When the poor use their very few resources, such as their precious opportunity costs, it is especially important to consider what their full set of goals might be.

Communities have many goals that are worth spending time asking about. For individuals, we want them to have personal, social, collective and intellectual skills. For societies, we want people who think collectively, understand environmental sustainability, understand public health initiatives, are engaged civically, obey laws, challenge unethical or immoral norms, sacrifice for shared values and contribute to the society beyond their work. Thus, an efficient school begins with defining all the goals of the school—individual, work, community, national and global. Once they are defined, there must be a generally agreed balance between these goals. Only once these are defined, can schooling be measured on an efficiency scale. Achieving this balance, for the least cost, is the mark of an efficient school and good schooling system.

There is nothing in this definition of efficiency that neoclassical economists would argue with in theory. Costs and benefits include all costs and benefits—individual, family and community, collective, national and international. The problem, once again, is applying in the theory because application means putting all these values into a number. Since the easiest numbers are monetary, if the value does not equate to a monetary value or a test score, it is often left out of the formula. The practical effect of human capital theory applications is to reduce this extensive network of costs and benefits to those that can be easily monetized or, in the case of schooling outcomes, measured in terms of tests.

Human capital theory applies the value of investment of one person to one income. In an interlinked world of innovation and learning where a lot of value never goes to market, human capital theory just does not have the power to capture the dynamism of global learning. The notion that education is worth investing in is still a powerful idea and the theory has some robust qualities. Taken at face value, the primary criticism of human capital theory is really a criticism of its application—the tendency to narrowly define schooling costs, benefits and outcomes. Because the theory has been so predominant in justifying national expansion and international financing of schooling, it has tended to be viewed as the singular definition of schooling—all about incomes and testing. It is time to move beyond old development and human capital theories to theories and ideas that capture global dynamism, the links that bind us all, acknowledge our joint interests and help us all learn together.

3b Human capital theory

Human capital theory was effectively launched with a speech to the American Economic Association by Theodore Schultz in 1960 (Schultz, 1961). Human capital theory posits that education can function like an investment. Education has costs (in time, energy or lost work hours) but it has long-term future benefits in increased productivity. The value of that increased productivity can be captured by the worker (through increased wages), a nation (through increased nation income and taxes) or even by a community (through its ability to conduct public business more efficiently or effectively). Gary Becker later explained how this value was captured by employers even when they had to pay higher wages for educated workers (Becker, 1964).

The birth of the theory provided a means of documenting these contributions, tracking them, putting monetary value to them and, as a result, planning for them. The theory remains powerful today even as it is receiving its biggest challenge—the notion that innovation may be at the heart of economic growth. DeYoung (1989) puts the birth of human capital theory in a historical context: he believes that the industrial setting was right for the theory. The economic needs of the United States emerging from the Second World War were ready for such a theory:

> Historically speaking, then, political economists from the late eighteenth and early nineteenth century saw little utility for economic productivity in public schooling. Neoclassical economists first ignored and then began to flirt with academic and abstract notions of people as possessors of skills that might be considered a form of capital. But following World War II, economists began to argue for the practical utility of viewing people as resources.
>
> (DeYoung, 1989, p. 91)

The new productive needs of industry required that people be moved from their farms to factories.

Basic concepts

The relationship between education and productivity is fundamental to human capital theory. Nothing within human capital theory requires that its value be measured in monetary gains. Yet, as a matter of practice, the returns to invested educational monies have generally been measured in monetary income. Monetary gains are viewed as a way of measuring the worth of the increased productivity (see Figure 3.1).

Figure 3.1 Human capital logic of how education affects society's well-being
Source: Author

But investments are often difficult to make in human capital. Unlike machinery, buildings or raw materials, human cannot be owned. So loans cannot be bound to the ownership and retention of the "goods." Banks are generally unwilling to loan monies for education. Thus, governments often have to provide incentives or guarantees in order for students to get loans for their education—even when it can be shown that the investments are likely to have positive returns.

Most societies, however, provide some free public schooling. This is because education has *externalities.* That is, the education of an individual has benefits both to the individual and to other people (external to the individual). If most people in the society have an education, democracy is enhanced, productivity is gained and civic society works better. Thus, education has some aspects of what makes a good public investment—public goods. How much a society ought to invest collectively and at what point an individual ought to take over and invest individually is always a debate within the society. Different countries have different points where public funding ends and private funding must take over if the individual wants to continue education.

Education is critically important as a tool to mitigate poverty, but among the world's poorest, a sizeable proportion does not have the means to contribute to the cost of their children's education. Many exist in non-market, subsistence economies where production moves directly from the field to the household in the form of food, clothing and shelter. In such countries, even a small cost of education can be prohibitive. When families live on the edge of existence, all energies are, essentially, devoted to survival. Time and energy devoted to schooling is a drain they sometimes cannot afford.

This is closely related to the concept of opportunity costs. The notion of opportunity costs is that a student who is sitting in school or studying is foregoing some sort of other activity. In many instances within both wealthy and poor communities, the productivity lost when a student is in school is a bona fide cost of schooling. That other activity could have value. So, the value lost when a student is not participating in the alternative activity is a bona fide cost of schooling. In market economies, these opportunity costs are frequently determined by estimating the value of wages the student might earn if he/she were not in school or studying at that moment.

Human capital theory does not work very well if people cannot accurately assess the likely benefits of the education in which they want to invest. The value of education is often hard to determine. One of the primary problems in assessing the value of education is that the value we expect to derive is far removed from the time when we make the investment decision. Thus, an MBA degree may have had very large returns when one entered graduate school in 1995, but considerably less value when one completed the degree (part-time due to continued employment) and entered the MBA job market.

Analysis

Production functions

The first attempts at measuring the value of human capital modeled an economy and added education into the model. This is known as a production function. National output was the dependent variable and education was one of the independent variables. Several authors undertook research that applied production functions to the study of education contributions to national production—most notably Denison. Estimating the contribution of formal schooling to economic growth, he calculated that about 23 percent of economic growth within the United States could be attributed to the contribution formal education had made (Denison, 1962).

An early favorite model along these lines was the Cobb-Douglas production function. The particular specification of production has two characteristics that appeal to theorists (Hanushek, 1979). It allows for a very general specification of national productivity (resources, human capital and monetary investments) and it has mathematical properties that can smooth such returns over time so that the investments made early have less influence than those made later.

Rate-of-return analysis is another common measure of the value of human capital and this came later. It answers a different question: whether the benefits obtained from that additional productivity due to education justify the additional expenditure. This return rate can then be compared with the returns of other types of investments (capital investments or investments in the stock market, for example) or can be compared with the costs of borrowing the money to determine whether an investment in education is a good idea.

Although rate-of-return analysis was already well established in the early years of human capital research (Schultz, 1961a) it was Psacharopoulos' work, beginning in the early 1970s, that brought substantial policy focus to the research (Psacharopoulos & Hinchliffe, 1973). He continued to update the findings for many years, his most recent work being 2004. He summarized findings from 23 countries: national investment in education had returns that ranged from as low as 8.5 percent for higher education in wealthier countries to 25 percent for primary schooling in sub-Saharan Africa. Family returns to investments in education were even higher (Psacharopoulos & Patrinos, 2004). The findings are astounding. They indicate that investments in primary schooling are very high for a country—much higher than for nearly any other investment it can make.[1]

Note

1   However, these methods of rates-of-return are often an overestimate as they do not include those who are not employed or who are employed in an informal sector. That is, the returns to education are only considered if one has obtained a job in the formal sector and, the calculations assume, one retains that job and follows a trajectory of advancement throughout one's working life—a fairly large error in poor countries. See Weber, 2002.

References

Becker, G. (1964). *Human capital: A theoretical and empirical analysis, with special reference to education.* Chicago, IL: University of Chicago Press.

Denison, E. F. (1962). *The sources of economic growth in the United States and the alternatives before us.* New York: Committee for Economic Development.

DeYoung, A. J. (1989). *Economics and American education: A historical and critical overview of the impact of economic theories on schooling in the United States.* Boston, MA: Addison-Wesley Longman.

Hanushek, E. A. (1979). Conceptual and empirical issues in the estimation of educational production functions. *The Journal of Human Resources, 14*(3), 351.

Psacharopoulos, G. and Hinchliffe, K. (1973). *Returns to education: An international comparison.* Amsterdam: Elsevier.

Psacharopoulos, G. and Patrinos, H. (2004). Returns to investment in education: A further update. *Education Economics, 12*(2), 111–134.

Schultz, T. (1961a). Education and Economic Growth. In N. B. Henry (ed.), *Social Forces Influencing American Education* (pp. 46–88). Chicago, IL: National Society for the Study of Education.

——. (1961b). Investment in human capital. *The American Economic Review, 51*(1), 1–17.

Weber, B. A. (2002). The link between unemployment and returns to education: Evidence from 14 European countries. *Education + Training, 44*(4/5), 171–178.

4a Education and development

There is much evidence that education does, indeed, often result in increased earnings and growing national economies. But, there is also considerable evidence that educational investments can sometimes have few rewards or are costly without much to show for future income. During the final 20 years of the twentieth century, industrial output in sub-Saharan Africa (except South Africa) grew by only 2 percent annually even though education investments by the World Bank and others increased from $24.5 million US to $61.5 million US—more than doubling in the same 20 years. On the other hand, in Korea during the same period industrial output grew 7 percent annually and educational investment increased at the same rate. Why the difference?

No one, it seems, really knows. Political scientists posit that bad governments and unstable regimes were the underlying cause of poor growth in Africa. This may be the case, but bad government and unstable regimes occurred elsewhere and still resulted in growth. Korea experienced a military dictatorship at a time of rapid economic growth. Eventually, though, the Korean people rose up, overturned the dictator and replaced him with a democracy. Inherent values of the people—such as the message of social conformity and personal responsibility for education—are often cited as a partial explanation for Korea's advancement. But Asian scholars see the contemporary Confucian influence as much in Japan and China, and both of these countries had divergent development paths.

Does culture matter? To be sure, there are striking regional patterns of development that might lead one to believe cultural similarities are at work. Imagine, for a moment, what you know as East Asia: China, Japan and Korea, primarily; we think of these countries as rising rapidly, from being (largely) non-participants in a world economy, to countries where cheap production occurred, to skilled industrial labor forces, to an increasingly important place in the knowledge economy. Think of sub-Saharan Africa: much of it has been mired in unstable governments, low levels of education, substantial dependence on raw material exports and huge numbers of people living on the edge of existence. Of course, Africa is a huge continent and these generalities apply only broadly, and no two countries have had an identical history. Nevertheless, we view them as only marginal participants in a global economy with few who are educated to the point of leading their industries into rapid productivity gains.

We could make similar generalities for Europe, for Canada and the United States, for the Middle East and for Latin America. Seemingly, culture might matter along with a shared history. But, many economists now believe regions have a path that grows particular industries. The theory goes that, if labor, government, infrastructural and civil society conditions are optimal, a particular industry may move to a location because it provides a good environment for production; examples might be the IT sector in India, the auto industry in East Asia. Then, once a new start-up or foreign investment spawns a success, there is good reason for similar industries to move there or grow there. The same conditions for success prevail and now there is a workforce that is partially ready for the industry and the supportive infrastructure. As time goes on and more companies move there, a real benefit begins to accrue. People with the particular skill are attracted to the area, residents change their skill set to match, universities build competence in the area, suppliers move capacity in. So, is it this location impetus that defines regions, or is it culture or something else?

None of these trends, regional patterns or shared history can be explained by human capital theory. What is clear is, if conditions are right, then investment in some form of education for some members of a society can result in good investments that provide a better life for the educated person and a higher income for the country. For many countries, such investment continues to pay off and their growth rate is phenomenal. But no study has yet determined just what conditions must prevail for this investment to take off.

The importance of a new idea

Economists are currently trying to grapple with the notion that sometimes a brilliant idea can change the lives of huge swaths of humanity. We can understand, for example, how the pharmaceutical industry has researched and brought to market the many drugs that have changed our lives—antibiotics, insulin, high blood pressure drugs and chemotherapies. These are, in fact, ideas. We can also call them new knowledge or innovations. They took considerable investment to produce profitable results. Companies set aside or borrowed the money for the research phase and had to fund many failures on the way to one success. But patents protect their profits once they do achieve success, so it produces an environment that rewards investment. In such an instance innovations lead to tremendous advances.

But the invention of the polio vaccine, although profitable at the beginning, became a public good rather than a market good. Governments and the World Health Organization (WHO) took over the administration as a public program. The eradication of polio is a product first of a vigorous drug industry but the profits from this research were not enough to provide for the optimal public good. Rather, a public process of policy making and government intervention took over to develop the means to get it to the poorest people in the world. And what of Bell's invention of the telephone or electricity? Although profits have been made worldwide on these inventions, it is also true that such inventions have improved the lives of people who could never have afforded to buy the product at cost. These inventions had widespread benefits far beyond their original narrow industrial production. Sailing ships and compasses are also inventions that affected the lives of many—far beyond those who sailed or explored. The printing press—while making the written word accessible to those who could pay—also changed the nature of civil society because many could get the news or educate themselves without personal contact with those in the know.

Human capital theory does not explain how such innovations changed the lives of many. Those with changed lives are not those who invented the new idea. Many who had an ancillary idea—such as the iPhone—never paid for the idea of electricity, telephones or the written word. Here, several issues deviate from the notion of education simply paying back the educated. The inventors are not always the beneficiaries. Many ideas have value far beyond anything the inventor could have profited from—witness the idea of Wikipedia. Now there is a "how to" website with a similar idea spawned from Wikipedia. Further, Wikipedia never paid for the understanding they derived from precursors—encyclopedias. In fact, they largely put encyclopedia publishers out of business.

The idea seems to spread from the original idea to many applications and across a wide range of people, and the idea itself is free even if the invention is not. The idea of the telephone has changed the world in all its spaces, but the inventions of Bell and his company are only a small fraction of this benefit. Pima's mother may well benefit from a microloan, which gives her the money to start a small, home-based business. The "idea" of microloans was started in the neighboring country of Bangladesh in the 1970s and has grown to billions of dollars; they have changed the life trajectory of thousands, perhaps millions of people worldwide. The small enterprises are in many countries, but the idea itself was "free." Once it was invented, many benefited.

There is a specific theory now that explains the economic gains of such ideas although the theory is so new that it still has many names and is not fully accepted by mainstream economics. It will be discussed in a later chapter. But, suffice to say it poses questions not answered by human capital theory.

Collective knowledge-building

Another problem with human capital theory is that it does not explain the progress of society as it learns together. Democracy is a concept born from the experiences of generations of people who live under dictatorships, kingdoms or other forms of governance where decisions were made for them. As societies grew, as collective experience was gained, people began to believe they had the capacity to rule themselves—that a good society could result from the decisions of the people. As this knowledge grew, people became more restless to have this freedom and, eventually, were willing to fight and put their lives on the line for such freedoms. It is the knowledge, not of just one person, but of a collective of people who decided the conditions were right and their experiences supported their conclusions that a form of democracy could work.

This can most easily been seen by the progress very suddenly being made by the changes in Tunisia, Egypt and Libya during 2011, even though those changes will have to be followed by years of social, political and civic building of institutions, which will not be an easy process. But people have been building collective knowledge for generations. Culture is a collective knowledge. The ways we organize ourselves to ensure that large numbers of people have the necessary water to drink, that people follow the laws and norms of a society or learn jobs and structure their lives, are all examples of collective knowledge. When scientists found a vaccine for polio, it was collective knowledge that got the word out on how valuable it would be to have everyone participate in the mass polio vaccination program. When there is a national census, it is collective knowledge that convinces us to participate because our collective well-being is raised. Global warming, disease management, global welfare and terrorism—to say nothing of the issues in one's neighborhood—all depend upon collective knowledge to tackle the issues.

Originally, collective knowledge was spread from person to person, each group learning from the experience of others, understanding how it works, experiencing small opportunities for local democracy and, eventually, clamoring for democracy themselves. In one sense, it is an idea—an innovation. That is, it is a piece of knowledge that changed the lives of millions without going through a market, without being sold and—once the idea was spawned—it was free to be used by others. The more the idea was used (the more people living in democracies) the more widespread the idea—moving from place to place seemingly effortlessly. At least the idea's spread was easy and cheap, even if the fight for it was costly. But what sets something like democracy apart as an idea that moved societies forward is that it was born of a collective.

Although the workings of a democracy may have emanated from the collective conversations and dialogue of a few people working to make it happen, the notion that self-governance was possible and desirable emanated from the society as a whole. Many people talked about it, debated the idea, talked about the possible consequences, problems and possibilities. People began to change their views and started to contribute to the notion of possibilities. Eventually, the society was ready, pushing for some form of democracy: they took action. There is a relatively new theory that explains this collective knowledge, which is dealt with in Chapter 8b. But, for now, it is worth noting that human capital theory cannot explain the benefits of social progress that builds from collective knowledge.

Pima's education changes labor markets

The current theory assumes that Pima's education allows her to join a world that is under way. There are markets, the ability to sell to people in neighboring villages or to a buyer who comes to her village. If she has enough education, she can go to the town and get a job as a semi-skilled laborer. Perhaps she can work in a shop or get a job packing the dishes that are made in a local factory and shipped elsewhere. If she goes even further, she can work in the big city of Katmandu and get a top job as an accountant, a computer expert or a lawyer. If she gets a top education, she can go to another country (often the best qualifications are difficult to find at local universities) and return as a professor, scientist, surgeon or pilot. Or, she may choose to stay abroad and live the life of many global professionals who circulate around the world. These possibilities exist. We can find someone in a village near Pima's who did this (unfortunately, this person is unlikely to be female; such opportunities almost always are provided first to males).

But what is not part of the theory is that Pima's entry into this world of markets, skilled employment and global professionals actually changes that world. In my first job in Malawi, I was assigned a young man named Chris Moyo to work with me. The team consisted entirely of PhDs from the United States, and each of us, if I remember correctly, was given a young Malawian to work with. Chris was clearly intelligent and understood quite a bit about education and policy. He also served as an excellent translator and cultural guide. But there was no expectation that he would or could understand my analysis. There was no expectation that he would participate, in any fundamental way, in the construction of the analyses and reports the team produced. He was an informant—albeit rather well trained—and a translator.

A few years ago, I returned from Zambia having headed a small team for two years. That team was helping the Ministry of Education build the systems that would guide policy and strategic planning into the future. My team had the following professionals: one African American who had an IT background; one Canadian of Sri Lankan ethnicity who was a programmer with an excellent database background; one Tanzanian who headed our HIV/AIDS initiative for teachers; one young Zambian who was in charge of the computer network at the ministry and in charge of overseeing the wiring of provincial education units; one Zambian who developed policy procedures in the ministry; and one Zambian who was the policy analyst for the team.

Each of these people was equally skilled. In fact, of all this professional team, the one I thought I was at greatest risk of losing was the young Zambian who was the IT guy. He was so bright and skilled and hard working I thought the chances of him staying in that job and in Zambia were slim. I immediately raised his salary as much as I could and asked him directly how I could keep him. I told him that I was worried about losing him. He told me that he wanted to keep learning and that, if I allowed him to take short courses in South Africa, he would be happy at the job. Learning was the "currency" that motivated him to stay.

The earlier team I worked with was in Malawi in 1991; this later team was in Zambia in 2005. In those 15 years, enough young people had received enough high-level education and experience that they were able to fill the slots of a highly professional team and work side-by-side with global professionals. It is true that only the salaries paid by the top development agencies could attract this small, highly skilled labor force. Their level of skill was rare and we tried to employ the best in the country. Nevertheless, the environment had changed. It was not just that these Zambians had entered a skilled workforce, but that their entry changed the nature of the workforce.

First, their entry changed the nature of knowledge used in such a team. Although each had particular, rather high-level knowledge in their area, each also had local knowledge. They knew how to get something done in the city. It wasn't just the local professionals that I depended on for local knowledge. I had several support staff as well who possessed valuable local knowledge. The driver for the team could, it seemed, solve just about any problem we threw at him, for example, getting my personal vehicle registered and through the maze of bureaucracy and offices that seemed bewildering to me. He knew the process, knew where there would be a hitch, knew where there might be someone who wanted to be paid off and how to put pressure on them, knew how to phrase things and who worked where. But the local professionals knew a lot about the local environment as well. We all knew that putting sustainable systems in place meant working with the local understandings, processes and people. We counted on their local knowledge to guide our system's development so it was integrated and made sense.

Although Chris Moyo in Malawi also knew the local systems, he did not know what the team needed or wanted. He did not have the experience or education to understand that: the melding of local and global-professional was incomplete. But, given the knowledge of our local professionals in Zambia and many at the Ministry of Education who knew even more, we were a well-integrated team that could build top, sustainable systems that were useful, used and added to the quality of educational planning and policy development.

Local professionals change the quality of applications to local sites, but they change the nature of the profession as well. They grew up in a different world, with different values, different perspectives and different ways of learning. Necessarily, they tackled a problem differently. We might ask why teachers are not getting tested for HIV and, therefore, getting free treatment. They might ask why their home villages are breaking apart because AIDS is devastating the social networks. But it is these very social networks that we need to use to get teachers tested. In other words, we outsiders look at the problem through the eyes of individual actions and they look at the problem as a social network: same problem, different ways of analyzing it. When people who grow up with different values, different forms of social organizations, different core beliefs and assumptions, they bring more varied thinking to the problem. They make this global workforce more innovative, more flexible and better learners.

It used to be that if a young woman from the United States wanted to work in a non-Western country she needed to get a job as a manager who would head a foreign division of a US firm. My brother headed the Japanese division of a US robotics firm in Japan. Such professionals were given extra money to school their children in international schools, to relocate and, sometimes, to live in "hardship" conditions. Today, such a job would be done by a Japanese professional who is bilingual (my brother spoke Japanese) and understood international standards (as well as local standards) of management. She would be paid a local salary (increasingly, globally competitive) but receive no extra benefits for living abroad or special schooling for children.

The young American who wants such an experience abroad now, can do so, but they are not too likely to be heading the overseas division of a US company; those jobs usually go to locals now. They might, instead, be working for a foreign company that wants to globalize its workforce or wants people who can represent them in a globalizing world. I do such work now; I was hired by Seoul National University to globalize its faculty and to teach young Koreans about global development perspectives. The entry of young professionals from around the world to world-class professional status has changed the nature of the global workforce: it is more creative, learns faster and has more breadth of knowledge. But it also is leveling the opportunities. We all compete with each other—not just Western countrymen who go abroad.

Pima's education changes global production

Several years ago, the United States faced a severe shortage of nurses. Nurses' wages increased substantially as a result and hospitals and clinics found themselves severely understaffed. The result: nurses were brought in from other parts of the world to take the jobs. Nurses from the Philippines were sought because they often spoke good English. The IT sector faces frequent shortages of high-quality computer programmers and has provided jobs for a large number of Indian computer programmers who now work in the United States. The same phenomenon can be found in a number of industries. These professionals can be brought in because their training is fairly similar to that in the United States, so they can adjust to the work relatively easily.

The shifting of particular professionals from one country to another is a result, essentially, of the education of Pima. As educational levels rise throughout the world, some pockets of society begin to get a higher level of education. The same tax base or personal income base provides the means to raise the quality of education for enough people such that their skills begin to approach world-class standards. They find that they can sometimes compete against people throughout the world for top jobs. This often raises their pay, provides them with increased opportunities and provides further incentives for those back home to get a better education and to push for higher quality.

One result is that some countries have seen a "reverse brain drain." Whereas the first people to be college educated stay abroad to take professional jobs and raise a family in a wealthier country and send money back home for aging parents and younger siblings, the next group reverses this trend. They find that opportunities are expanding back home. They return home to build new businesses and raise the quality of production in their home country. Many from

Japan, Korea and China are returning home to take good jobs or be entre-preneurs. At the same time, virtually all countries experiencing rapid growth find that there is a willing migrant group that will take jobs at the bottom of the economy—those jobs requiring few skills and paying low wages. As an economy moves from low-skilled and poor pay to improved skills and elevating pay scales, they have incentives to keep wages low at the bottom end. Thus, many countries have immigrant communities at the lowest end of the pay scale.

Each of these migrations, at the top and at the bottom, is labor related and is a result of rising levels of income and education in previously poor countries. Pima's education, and that of her neighbor, changes the mix of people in a country and also changes the mix of professionals in an industry. It also changes the nature of the profession. The Filipina nurses may prefer certain kinds of foods from the cafeteria, which might result in a change of menu. They might have been trained to bathe a patient differently or to engage with patients differ-ently. The patients receive somewhat different care. If that care is beneficial to patients or is more efficient, then it might be adopted into routine protocols at the hospital or clinic. Nursing becomes a mixture of Western protocols and Philippine protocols.

Those IT specialists from India may have different ways of communicating when there is a problem with the software. Or, their means of dividing and sharing collaborative work may reflect Indian patterns of communication, social hierarchy and power rather than Western patterns. If a creative solution is required to a particularly vexing problem, the Indian workers may approach the problem differently and have an alternative plan for its solution. Educating Pima changes the nature of how we work and live. New ways of seeing things, of organizing people, of solving problems and doing work and designing new procedures not only expand when people of a different culture become colleagues, they expand our own thinking. Professionals exposed to this new thinking may well begin to ask themselves "is there another way to see this problem?" when encountering a challenge. They might do so because their experience tells them that others have different ways of tackling problems and finding another way to see the problem might produce a good alternative. Professional teams may find they seek a mixture of cultural inputs as a way of being more innovative and competitive.

At the low end of the labor market it is unlikely that professional protocols will change as a result of the unskilled labor market of migrants. Viewed as uneducated and untrained, they will be given a particular way to do a job and expected to follow orders. Nevertheless, their culture will change their communities. They have different social service needs, different language and food needs and different ways of organizing their social life—church, schools and leisure activities. Their music, customs, foods and crafts will leak to the surrounding community. It may take a generation, but the overlap of cultures and social life will produce people in both communities who seek out interactions, even marriage. Inevitably, the community will become a reflection of both cultures.

Of course, not all migrant community influences are positive. The threat of seeing jobs go to migrants makes the host community feel under attack with their livelihoods at stake. Some colleagues will welcome the differences and recognize that this new community adds strength in a situation that was unstable. But prejudices and distrust also grow. Resistance at work to the differences of the new workers will grow between some. Political milieus might change to be more conservative, more liberal or more divisive. Tensions can grow in such situations where such tensions were not evident before.

These days, no one has to move or migrate for communities and workplaces to change because of Pima's education. There are thousands of IT workers living in India and working for overseas firms. Many countries are developing industries in "medical tourism" where expensive operations can be undertaken for a fraction of the cost elsewhere and with highly skilled medical staff. The way of organizing work, medical protocols and medical record-keeping can be standardized throughout the world to reflect new global standards. The global standards are a result, often, of practices worldwide. One's closest colleague or part of one's team may well be halfway around the world. Working virtually does not eliminate the cross-cultural, creative influence of an increasingly diverse work force.

Pima's education changes Pima's world

Wherever there was a formalized system of education, it began as a system to educate a select few for jobs that required a particularly high level of knowledge accumulated over years. These selected few were removed from the productive workforce and allowed to study in order to give service to the larger community or to the rulers. Whether among scholars of ancient Egypt, monks in Buddhist Asia or the gentry of Europe, education was the province of a few. But, as industry began to take hold, increasing numbers of people found time to study and become part of what would be a middle class. Becoming middle class became, increasingly, a function of education, at least in part. The trend continued whereby even lower classes began to receive education; as a result, the middle class raised their skills such that the level of education required rose with it.

Wherever this spread of education is in play, it is possible, generally, for a few, select people to rise above their origins and move up from one class to another—from illiterate to literate, from poorly educated to modestly educated, from modestly educated to highly educated. In such a movement it is also possible to jump through levels—to go from illiterate to highly educated, from lower class and destitute to well educated and stable. But Pima's world does not change much when she—and she alone—gets educated. In the case of a single individual or a few select individuals, their education truly gives them entry into another world—that of the educated. Generally, they have to move in order to join this group.

But what happens when Pima is part of a larger group? When Pima goes to the new school created in her community, she goes with many of the other children her age—perhaps most. What happens is that most of the kids her age go to school in the local school, become literate, learn how to calculate and some become skilled enough to read a newspaper or read the signs in the town nearby. The children will grow to be adolescents and be curious about the larger world that is now accessible. They may feel freer to move back and forth from their village to the town, taking the local bus. They may be more comfortable taking excess produce to the local market and might wonder how others in similar markets manage to make their produce look particularly appealing. They might listen carefully to someone who brings outside knowledge of medical care or crop planting or opportunities for water pumps.

In short, their world has become larger and their opportunities have expanded, not just because they are somewhat more skilled, but because the written language and numeracy skills they have learned are a kind of "language" that links them to a larger world. They have been given a window into this larger world. They can look at a newspaper, a poster or an outsider and understand that they bring knowledge from a larger world. Their own world appears linked in some fashion. Their reality has expanded beyond the confines of their small world to that of a broader realm.

I have a Korean student right now who is preparing to go to Zambia. As far as I know—and anyone at my major Korean university knows—she is the first Korean to go independently to an African country, without a group or sponsorship. She will have my own connections in the country, but she will largely experience it on her own. She is scared, as I once was on my first similar trip to Zimbabwe, although I was going for a job that would ensure my stability. Her parents are scared as were mine. She does not know yet, that *that* world— of Zambia—is organized in a way like her own world, with apartments and houses, bedrooms, bathrooms, roads, traffic lights, grocery stores, internet cafes, coffee shops, banks and post offices. Of course, she can be told all this, but it isn't part of her reality.

When she goes, even if she were to stay one week, her life will be transformed forever. She will know how life is organized there, how toilets flush, how people get from one place to another, that ATM machines are in English, that cell phones work much as they do in Korea, that people will help her if she gets lost. Simple exposure will teach her a life lesson. If she later goes to Uganda, she won't be nearly as frightened because she would now have a window into sub-Saharan Africa. She will have a kind of "literacy" known quite well by people in my field—the knowledge that you can find a taxi, bottled water, a friendly stranger, a place to eat and a good conversation wherever you go. Over time, of course, you also learn to assess dangerous situations that you've never encountered before, because those situations also begin to form a pattern.

So, too, will Pima's contemporaries be forever changed. Their "window," albeit through books and a teacher, exposes them to a larger world. And, they assume, there are even larger worlds beyond that might not seem as foreboding. Nepal provided me with the opportunity to meet Pima's mother when the US AID office asked me take a look at a literacy program they had. Many women were taking the program and learning, but they were too shy to take the final exam. Lacking this test result "evidence" of success of the program, the program administrators feared they would not be funded again. They asked me for assistance in devising a system that could show their progress in light of the poor turnout for the final exam.

When I asked them how they knew the program was making a difference, they told me of very clear changes in the local villages that had been running the program. One difference I remember was that the women who had participated in the program became more politically aware and engaged. As evidence of these changes, they told me that when they went to a village they instantly knew if the village had been running a literacy program. The women in the village would come out to greet them if they had taken a literacy class, but otherwise would stay in their huts. It wasn't the reading, per se, that changed the women, but the window to the larger world: they gained confidence and curiosity about this larger world and the people in it.

So, Pima's world changes as her neighbors get educated. They begin to use and understand the health clinic in the next village. They begin to integrate knowledge of agricultural techniques brought in by agriculture workers. They begin to integrate aspects of a cash economy by selling excess produce and bringing it to market and, in turn, buying shoes. The few that went on to high school now have jobs elsewhere and send money home and provide their parents with cell phones so they are connected to larger cities. They live in a modestly connected world, where outside ideas penetrate—but so too do the forces of disease, pollution and construction.

But what happens when an entire country begins this process? Some will go on to be employed in the local factories, which are the first to employ the modestly educated workforce. They congregate in towns and cities and move away from a farming life to a monied life. Their lives could well be extremely poor—earning just enough to feed and shelter themselves and to send a bit home. But they are entirely products of a global system of production. They earn money which, in turn, buys their everyday needs. People moving up this ladder have a different reality to their rural friends: they are exposed to mass media, advertising and large stores. They know some of the latest trends but, perhaps more important, they understand the concept of trends. They understand that there is a larger world out there, bringing in new ideas and possibilities. They may be too poor—or even too exploited—to ever have a chance of accessing most of these opportunities, but their awareness changes their world forever.

They are not, in a sense, held in a particular time or space. They recognize they live in a world that is vast, where decisions and ideas get made far outside their realm and have an impact on their daily lives. They know, somehow, that they have a government that provides the roads and schools. They understand they are part of a larger economic system of which they are either beneficiaries or victims. They may or may not feel powerless, but they are aware that this larger system is human-made and that it changes and responds to pressure. They have begun to see themselves as connected to a world that impacts their lives in a fundamental way.

This is quite different from seeing oneself as interacting primarily with a seemingly invariant natural world: your existence defined by whether it rained much this year and whether you can stay healthy enough to be a productive farmer. Now, at least some of your world is defined by the way humans organize their world—decisions about production, politics, schooling policies, environmental protection and commerce. You may be a small player in this system, but you understand that it is human-made. You are close enough to the production system, for example, that you understand the decisions of your employer—how it affects you and the products they produce. This is the awareness that causes, given the right conditions, people to rally for better working conditions, more schooling opportunities for their children or attempt to halt environmental destruction around their homes. It is also the force behind terrorist recruiting as well as local initiatives in media and markets.

Although it is useful to understand that an investment in education, simply put, can result in a wealthier society, it leaves unexamined the system's nature of education and economics. It is a system that changes the very nature of society. It also changes the ways humans interact with their world. It creates a more dynamic, diverse and creative workforce. It adds to the labor pool at the bottom (unskilled, semi-skilled) as people move away from family farms. It creates an ever-spiraling level of skills, knowledge and creativity at the top of the labor market. It changes the nature of economic life and it changes what physical, psychological, knowledge-based and spiritual needs and wants people have. In its simplest form it is just a matter of one more human joining a more modern world. But, in its dynamic, global form, it is a matter of changing the very way we live our lives and organize our societies.

4b The knowledge economy

Although powerful in concept, human capital theory has a fatal flaw: it does not take into consideration that the world—taken as a collective of inter-linked societies—has limited resources and also has limited ability to heal from ecological shocks. Yet, the global world operates, in many cases, as a global unit. The very fact that the World Bank and bilateral donors are involved in education is an indication that investment in education has been globally linked for half a century. This investment set the stage for linking global labor markets and has been part of a huge globalization process that began in the 1990s.

Global spread of education and skilled labor

Education expanded rapidly after the Second World War. From 1950 to 1997 primary school enrollment more than tripled, from about 200 million to 670 million worldwide (UNESCO, 2000, p. 41). These educated people were able to change the way they lived: people with basic education tend to make better farmers (Jamison & Lawrence, 1982); educated women tend to have fewer, more educated children and healthier families (Schultz, 1993); people with a basic education take advantage of basic health care, live longer and healthier lives and make better health choices (World Bank, 1993).

All of these decisions have an effect on the communities in which they reside and on the larger world. People who choose to have fewer children reduce the pressure on the world's resources. People who get their children immunized and get help from clinics are less likely to spread disease. They are much more likely to move away from subsistence farming into formal labor markets. Thus, there was a worldwide push to increase global enrollments of children. The opportunities were created by global investments but the impetus also came from the day-to-day efforts of millions of parents who wanted a better life for their children. Table 4.1 shows how secondary school enrollments increased worldwide from 1950 to 1997.

Although the worldwide expansion was about ninefold, in Africa—where secondary enrollments had started small—enrollments increased from about 1 million to 34 million. Expansion in all of the poorer countries far outstripped that of Europe and North America. Children were accessing secondary schools at ever expanding rates and this opened up the potential for new labor markets.

Table 4.1 Secondary school enrollments by continent, 1950 and 1997

	1950	1997	percentage increase
Africa	1	34	3300%
Asia Pacific	15	241	1507%
Europe	16	70	338%
Latin America and the Caribbean	2	29	1350%
North America	7	25	257%
World Total	41	399	873%

Source: adapted from UNESCO (2000, p. 60)

A few years later, one can see what happened to global labor markets. Figure 4.1 shows the expansion of global labor markets over the following decade. Asia's expansion of secondary education enrollment of over 200 million people resulted in a labor force market expansion of 271,000 jobs in the following decade, just in the formal-sector labor market. Overall, the growth

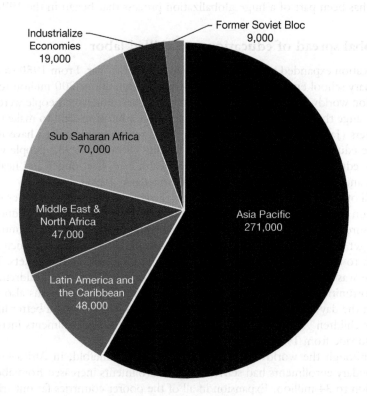

Figure 4.1 Number of new labor force entrants, 2000–2010

Source: adapted from International Labour Organization (2003, p. 4)

in labor markets patterned that of education expansion. Where the educational expansion occurred in the 1980s and 1990s, the job markets grew in the beginning of the next decade. Although education is not the full explanation for labor market growth, it is likely a necessary condition for investment in jobs.

Global markets and global labor

As more education, management and experience was accumulated abroad and as it became easier to move production away from high-income labor locations and to the emerging labor markets, production markets dispersed worldwide. The three examples below show just how integrated production, labor and financial markets have become.

Integrated multinationals

One of the first signs of international integration was that complex industrial products, such as automobiles, computers and airplanes, began to outsource the manufacture of various parts and have those parts shipped in to local factories to be assembled. This allowed for the cheap manufacture of some parts, although the final product was often assembled in a major market country where quality control could be monitored.

These kinds of integrated production markets have many forms. Sometimes, manufacturers develop strong ties with other companies who are nearly wholly dependent upon their businesses and supply them exactly according to their specifications, timing and demand. In other cases, the parent company may own or control the manufacturing, even though the supplier is wholly independent. Figure 4.2 shows how global production networks have grown in recent decades. The chart reflects the amount spent on trade (international) production in three sectors: textiles, automotive parts and information communication technology (ICT). In all three sectors, international production began to take off in the early 1990s. Although all three sectors continue to grow, the knowledge-intensive industries—automotive parts (which often include some knowledge components) and ICT (which are heavily knowledge)—have increased sharply over the last 15 years in the chart. This type of integrated global production is increasingly complex, more common and is often tied to the regional or bilateral trade agreements between nations (Orefice & Rocha, 2014).

Transient labor markets

When manufacturing moves to the place where it is cheapest to manufacture, it affects labor markets. Boeing sought out highly skilled labor markets and markets that offered various types of skills. But many industries sought out countries with the cheapest labor and moved several times to seek out such low-waged labor. An example of such an industry is the garment manufacturing industry, which continues to shift countries. Each new country, as it comes

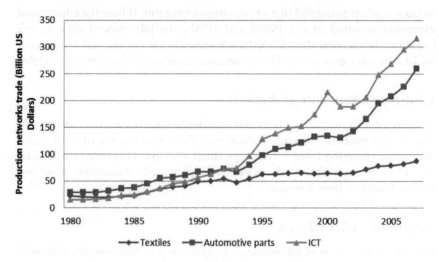

Figure 4.2 Global production networks patterns in three industries

Source: Orefice & Rocha (2014, p. 116)

on-stream, has the potential to offer cheaper, adequately skilled labor along with the basic national infrastructure. Such an infrastructure includes reliable utilities, stable governments and services such as banking, communications and transport. Table 4.2 shows the distribution of US garment imports in 1995 and 2005. The third column shows how much of the share of total (US garment industry) value was gained or lost during this ten-year period. The top part of the chart lists the countries that gained relative share of the garment manufacturing for the US market. Their average per capita income was $1,843. Those that lost market share had an average per capita income of $14,254 US. This shows that, increasingly, garments were imported from poorer and poorer countries while countries with higher incomes lost the garment manufacturing business.

Viral financial crises

Linked production means that the world investment network and global finances are now vastly interlinked—the third example. One of the best illustrations is the global financial crisis of 2008. The 2008 downturn of the US economy had an unprecedented effect on the entire world's economic prospects (Claeseens & Forbes, 2009; Scott, 2014). The IMF, surveying the rapid change in the world financial outlook, asked "How did things get so bad, so fast" (International Monetary Fund, 2009, p. 2).

A study done for the Overseas Development Institute, which looked at the impact of the financial crisis on 11 developing countries, found all but one had experienced negative national (GDP) growth rates relative to what the IMF had predicted just one year before. Two of the developing countries (Cambodia

Table 4.2 Value of US garment imports: 1995 & 2005

Country	% of total garment import value			GDP per capita 2009 US $	avg. per capita
	1995	2009	gain/loss		
China	14.9	39.1	24.2	3,749	
Vietnam		7.4	7.4	1,232	
Cambodia		2.7	2.7	735	
Indonesia	3.3	5.8	2.5	2,272	1,843
Bangladesh	2.8	5	2.2	598	
Pakistan		2	2	987	
Jordan		1.1	1.1	4,027	
India	3.3	4.3	1	1,147	
Thailand	2.9	2.4	−0.5	3,979	
Sri Lanka	2.5	1.8	−0.7	2,057	
Malaysia	3	1.8	−1.2	7,278	
Mexico	7	5	−2	7,690	
Canada	2.2		−2.2	40,764	
European Union	4.8	2.3	−2.5	31,368	14,254
Philippines	4.1	1.5	−2.6	1,832	
Dominican Rep.	11.9	8.9	−3	4,703	
Korea	4.6		−4.6	18,339	
Taiwan	5.5		−5.5	8,086	
Hong Kong	11		−11	30,697	

Source: adapted from Gereffi & Frederick (2010); The World Bank (n.d.)

and the Democratic Republic of Congo) had an 8 percent drop in expected annual GDP growth rates (Willem te Velde *et al.*, 2010, p. 24). Of the six countries for which they were able to estimate the impact on poverty, they estimated that overall rates went up an average of 12 percent—affecting nearly 14 million people in Bangladesh, Bolivia, Cambodia, Kenya, Uganda and Zambia.

While the costs of transportation and communication are declining, the price one pays for any given commodity or good is converging toward a single globally competitive price. But knowledge still varies by location: people are educated at different levels. The concentration of knowledge, knowledge exchange, ability to create new knowledge, ratio of quality of knowledge to labor costs and ability to adapt new knowledge is both location specific, but also sensitive to culture, government policies and history (Audretsch & Feldman, 2004; Jaffe *et al.*, 1992). Further, markets, production, tastes and demand were also sensitive to history, culture and regional/national/cultural/ethnic trends. Different peoples have different skills, mindsets, abilities, ways of putting their logic together, working together in groups or separately with different access to human and technological resources and differential abilities to put creative groups together and mold them to a new task at hand.[1] So, knowledge became the new competition—the new value creator.

Technology assisted this trend by providing the ability to create knowledge in a way that had not previously existed. Whole industries began to develop that were knowledge based. Older industries quickly added knowledge as a primary input. A decade after the fall of the Soviet economy, the Organization for Economic Co-operation and Development (OECD) estimated that a third of OECD national incomes were derived from knowledge[2] (Figure 4.3).

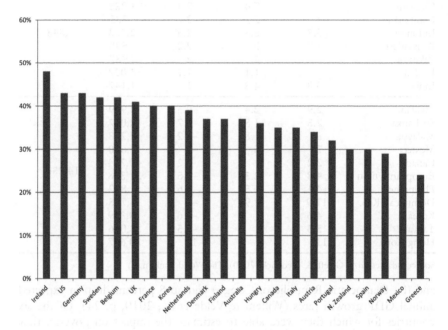

Figure 4.3 Share of national income from knowledge-based industries, 2002
Source: Brinkley (2008, p. 50)

The growth of the knowledge industry was only beginning to be formed and shaped. Because creativity no longer had to move through industry, because knowledge is a freely available resource, knowledge value is now being created in unexpected places. This creativity takes many forms. The spread of ideas is facilitated by people who both have ideas and now know how to use the social networks as a powerful tool to communicate. Such was the case with the Arab Spring (Lotan *et al.*, 2011). Poor countries are also becoming innovators themselves, such as Kenya's innovative use of cell phones for passing money between people without a bank (*The Economist*, 2013). A young generation that knows how to get the latest information and how to create online communities to build new ideas together has become a powerful resource, a resource that is not only being rapidly developed and exploited, but one that is becoming a major world force and is changing the face of global power.

Notes

1 The work spawned a growth in the "New Economic Geography" of which the hallmark work is that of the Nobel Prize-winner Paul Krugman (Fujita & Thisse, 2009).

2 Their definition of knowledge-based industries was high- to medium-tech industries, financial services, telecommunications, business services, education and health services.

References

Audretsch, D. B. and Feldman, M. P. (2004). Knowledge spillovers and the geography of innovation. In J. V. Henderson and J.-F. Thisse (eds), *Handbook of regional and urban economics* (Vol. 4, pp. 2713–2739). Amsterdam: Elsevier. Retrieved from www.sciencedirect.com/science/article/pii/S157400800480018X

Brinkley, I. (2008). *The knowledge economy: How knowledge is reshaping the economic life of nations.* London: The Work Foundation. Retrieved from www.theworkfoundation.com/Reports/41/The-Knowledge-Economy-How-Knowledge-is-Reshaping-the-Economic-Life-of-Nations

Claeseens, S. and Forbes, K. (2009). *International financial contagion: An overview of the issues.* New York: Springer.

The Economist (2013, May 27). Why does Kenya lead the world in mobile money? Retrieved from www.economist.com/blogs/economist-explains/2013/05/economist-explains-18

Fujita, M. and Thisse, J.-F. (2009). New economic geography: An appraisal on the occasion of Paul Krugman's 2008 Nobel Prize in Economic Sciences. *Regional Science and Urban Economics, 39*(2), 109–119.

Gereffi, G. and Frederick, S. (2010). *The global apparel value chain, trade and the crisis: Challenges and opportunities for developing countries* (Development Research Group). World Bank. Retrieved from https://openknowledge.worldbank.org/bitstream/handle/10986/3769/WPS5281.pdf?sequence=1

International Labour Organization. (2003). *Global employment trends 2003.* Geneva, Switzerland: ILO. Retrieved from www.ilo.org/wcmsp5/groups/public/---dgreports/---dcomm/documents/publication/kd00041.pdf

International Monetary Fund. (2009). *World economic outlook 2009: Crisis and recovery.* Washington, DC: International Monetary Fund. Retrieved from www.imf.org/external/pubs/ft/weo/2009/01/pdf/text.pdf

Jaffe, A. B., Trajtenberg, M. and Henderson, R. (1992). *Geographic localization of knowledge spillovers as evidenced by patent citations* (working paper No. 3993). National Bureau of Economic Research. Retrieved from www.nber.org/papers/w3993

Jamison, D. and Lawrence, L. (1982). *Farmer education and farm efficiency.* Baltimore, MD: Johns Hopkins Press.

Lotan, G., Graeff, E., Ananny, M., Gaffney, D., Pearce, I. and Boyd, D. (2011). The Arab Spring| The revolutions were tweeted: Information flows during the 2011 Tunisian and Egyptian Revolutions. *International Journal of Communication, 5*(0), 31.

Orefice, G. and Rocha, N. (2014). Deep integration and production networks: An empirical analysis. *The World Economy, 37*(1), 106–136.

Schultz, T. P. (1993). Returns to women's education. In E. King and M. A. Hill (eds), *Women's education in developing countries: Barriers, benefits, and policies* (pp. 51–99). Baltimore, MD: Johns Hopkins Press.

Scott, H. S. (2014). *Interconnectedness and contagion: Financial panics and the crisis of 2008* (SSRN Scholarly Paper No. ID 2178475). Rochester, NY: Social Science Research Network. Retrieved from http://papers.ssrn.com/abstract=2178475

UNESCO (2000). *World education report 2000*. Paris: UNESCO. Retrieved from www.unesco.org/education/information/wer/PDFeng/wholewer.PDF

Wilem te Velde, D. W., Ahmed, M. M., Alemu, G., Bategeka, L., Calí, M., Castel-Branco, C., *et al.* (2010). *The global financial crisis and developing countries: Phase 2 synthesis*. London: Overseas Development Institute. Retrieved from www.odi.org/sites/odi.org.uk/files/odi-assets/publications-opinion-files/5856.pdf

World Bank (1993). *World development report 1993: Investing in health*. Washington, DC: World Bank.

——. (n.d.). GDP per capita. Retrieved from http://data.worldbank.org/indicator/NY.GDP.PCAP.CD

5a Learning goes global

If education links the world together so fundamentally, why did a theory like human capital escape this scrutiny for so long? How did our view of development and of education as a global system remain tied to a linear view of the change process? That is, people get educated, assuming a stable world around them, they join a modern world, this raises everyone's income, the world gets wealthier and the poor world becomes less poor. Now we know there is a feedback loop—a global system at play. As people join the "modern world," the nature of that world changes and with it the lives of all participants—rich and poor. The rules of the game change along with the education of Pima.

As with many "truths" that seem self-evident in retrospect, one has to be able to see through historical eyes to answer the question—if this is so true, why wasn't it obvious before? When Galileo proposed that the world was spherical, the church was angry. If this was so fundamental a truth, how could the church have been wrong for so long? The church—at that time, the ultimately arbiter of truth—had access to God and so the legitimacy of the church was being challenged. But, just before Galileo's time, there was no real reason to spend much time considering the shape of the earth. Travel was limited to the land and navigation to the extent of the land that an eye could see. New sailing ships challenged this belief and provided the means to test it.

The realities of the industrial revolution and subsequent rebuilding of Europe made it clear that people needed an education to take advantage of industry. Moving people away from family farms and into factories meant that basic skills would need to be widespread—telling the time, following simple directions, mastering basic literacy and numeracy. As a middle class began to form and industry began to progress, the gulf between the designers/entrepreneurs and the unskilled began to close. Now, factories needed managers and people to fix the machines and people to design the factories. Opportunities expanded for those with enough education, and with this expansion, the wages of the newly skilled also expanded. It was just after the effects of European reconstruction began to be linked with an educated labor force that the so-called "human capital revolution" occurred.

Schultz's view that education is a form of investment that raises value (capital) is now widely accepted. But it does not go far enough. As Schultz implies, the evidence of human capital benefits is seen "in Western societies." He is Galileo, looking through a lens of the Western, industrialized world. Many ancient societies had formal education, but it was in the West that massive growth in industrialization was centralized. It was in these societies that the results of education of the masses could first be observed. It made sense that, understanding the world of Pima many decades later, one could view her education in a similar manner. If she was educated, she could join this world. If she was not educated, she would be like the farmers' children and not benefit from an investment in education.

Acquiring the skills of industry

In order to fuel the labor for industry, many people needed an education. When wealth depended largely on the ownership of land, some modest skills were required of the landowners, but none by the people who worked the fields for them. Control of land, whether through personal ownership of a farm or control over a people of a land (such as a kingdom), was the source of wealth. "Landlords" were wealthy; workers were largely poor. A few skilled artisans who made shoes or metal tools were also needed. But wealth shifted during the industrial revolution. Ford may have owned the land upon which his car factories were built, but his wealth came from production—not land. His workers made enough money to attract many of them off the land and into his factories.

But this kind of production could not be sustained by illiterate workers. They needed to not only use tools, but also to follow instructions, to understand how parts fit together and how to buy goods in a monied economy. It was just at this time that the "common school" began to form. Instead of small farm schools, whose teacher was hired by local farmers, large schools began to form near places where industrialization was growing. Children gathered together in large schools with a centralized curriculum and schooling was paid for by taxes. Schooling became compulsory, not just to ensure children had the right to the education that gave them access to these jobs, but also to ensure that the growing industry had a large pool of educated labor from which to draw.

What does a factory worker need to do to be a successful employee? Much more than basic reading: the math skills one needs to be able to stick to a schedule, to do what one is told to do and to follow a sequence of prescribed instructions. One did not need to invent new procedures, to ask for variations in techniques according to individual strengths or to question the production system of which one was a part. So, schools began to look very much like the factories in which their graduates would work. Teachers stood in front and issued instructions and gave the necessary knowledge. Students sat dutifully in their seats and followed instructions, memorized the material and knew the rules of schooling. If one wanted to go to the bathroom, one raised one's hand and asked for permission. In order to ensure that the correct material had been mastered, children were given exams. Exams were scored and children ranked according to the extent they had mastered the material.

Curriculum was increasingly established at higher levels whereas once it had been the province entirely of the classroom teacher. It began to be sequenced and each sequence was linked to a grade and an age of the child. Multiplication was third grade; algebra was seventh grade. Curriculum has become increasingly complex so it is not enough to learn basic information: now one needs computer skills and consumer skills so the curriculum of upper levels has become complex. Administrators struggle to find time in the week to schedule all that is needed. Although students now have computers from which to receive their information, we have not varied much from the lock-step, industrial-based notions of schooling. What one can learn is largely prescribed by one's age, by a curriculum and is overseen by a teacher.

For most of the last century, curriculum has come increasingly from the top of the education chain, often decided by curriculum specialists who exist at the state or national levels. Even sanctioned texts are often prescribed or come from a recommended list. This is all in keeping with the notion that knowledge devolves from the top of the education ladder. Those with more education and more specialization know more than those at the bottom who are termed "the learners." Students don't invent algebra so, logically, they cannot decide to put it into the curriculum or when and how it will be taught. If an engineer wants a job, she ought to have taken physics, but the principles and math behind the physics is not hers to decide.

For decades, the only sources of information for this curriculum were the teacher and the textbook. If one needed further information, one might have access to a library. That was it. Increasingly, though, people have access to the internet. Children go home from school and do their homework using the internet. While writing this chapter, I quickly looked up two pieces of information: I made sure that it was Galileo who was attributed with promoting the view of a round earth and I checked to see whether there was a good quote from Schultz's speech that I could use. Each took me only a couple of minutes before I could begin writing again.

The internet has, indeed, changed the nature of sources of information. But in schools it has just become a reasonable substitute for books and teachers as sources of information. In large part one still needs to master prescribed subject material; teachers organize one's learning; curriculum is established at the top; one's grade is determined by one's age; and progress is managed through progress reports, rankings and "schools days." The internet has added a new source of information and made facts available on a more informal basis, but the school factory, in large part, worldwide, still looks and operates like an industrial-age factory.

In this structure of schooling, human capital theory had little to question itself about. People passed through a prescribed curriculum, became skilled in the manner determined by industry or experts, passed tests to demonstrate their mastery and were likely rewarded with a job that matched their demonstrated skills. One began schooling as an unruly, freewheeling child and emerged as a practiced, skilled, refined worker. One was given entry into the "modern" world where industry paid you for your skill levels. Investment in your education meant investment in a higher level of productivity, which meant both you and your employer benefited. That is, until the computer revolution . . .

Acquiring the skills for innovation

In 1995, IBM acquired Lotus Development Corporation for $3.5 billion US (termed an "astronomical" sum by the *New York Times*) (Keegan, 1995). At the heart of this acquisition was a team of four developers who were located a mile away from the headquarters. Their brains were widely considered to be the true value of the corporation. Some industry insiders thought the price was too high, especially since the core value of the purchase was assumed to be the small team behind Lotus Notes: "Speculation was fueled anew that Ozzie and his crew might walk, taking most of the $3.5 billion in assets—that is, their brains—with them." (Keegan, 1995, p. 50). Yet the team worked continuously, collaboratively through their shared computer interface.

> They don't like being interrupted by phone calls and knocks on the door. Meetings are infrequent. . . . "the common areas makes it clear why Iris [parent company to Lotus] has been called a developer's Shangri-La. There's a big-screen television surrounded by couches, video games scattered on the floor, a pool table."
>
> (Keegan, 1995, p. 51)

How could four developers be worth the $3.5 billion US (in 1995 dollars) purchase price? Human capital theory would tell us that you are worth what you are paid. But these four were paid nowhere near this price. Nor, as the *New York Times Magazine* article implies, was it even considered that they, individually or collectively, would be replaced by equally skilled people. The $3.5 billion US deal went through with a guarantee that the team would remain and, in exchange, the team were promised continued autonomy.

The answer would not be forthcoming soon. It would take many, largely technology-focused companies with fundamentally relaxed work conditions and environments to begin to understand what was going on here—or at least know enough to replicate its value. The value was in the collaboration. It was not only the skills of the individual employees, it was their collective ability to innovate—to work together. They were not simply applying the engineering skills they may have acquired in university (in 1995, it is just as likely they acquired them on their own, in their parents' basements, hooked to a desktop computer). They were using the raw skills, building on those skills daily, and working together to build a new product. The fact that meetings hardly occurred and the common area was set up for play helped that creativity. When working, their own software helped them collaborate and stay focused. But creativity is hard on the brain, so they needed to take breaks—to play. They set up an area for socializing. Their apparent physical distance from their parent corporation gave them a chance to build an optimal collaborative environment away from the rules, dress codes and formal work structures of the parent company. Creativity—not quite productivity—was being maximized. Or rather, creativity became productivity.

It must be fun to work like this—in fact it is half the fun I have as a professor. I get paid to exchange ideas and try out new things. The resource I need most is at hand: other intelligent people who work in related areas who are just down the hallway. I can always ask for an opinion or get a new idea. My inspiration often comes from students whose minds have not been fully structured in my field, so they ask unusual questions—they think about things I haven't thought about. Working through these problems with them helps me think better. Finally, what would I do without the internet to fill in the missing facts, check an occasional source and build on an emerging theory? All are collaborative experiences—I learn because I am connected.

But this kind of learning is not fully defined by formal schooling. None of the Lotus Notes crew was applying just what they had learned in high school or college.

> By funneling most of the daily office work through Notes, Iris tried to prove that a company can scatter its departments all over the world. And it can draw important people from the outside—suppliers, subcontractors, consultants—into its cyberspace office.
>
> (Keegan, 1995, p. 52)

No one had taught Ray Ozzie to think about this. It was his idea and he was using the software developed by the team to test the product. Their work was their creation and their creation was their work.

Innovation works much the same worldwide, although there is a misconception that Asian approaches to work are less innovative. I have been continuously amazed by my Asian students' creativity in class assignments because their work frequently moves far outside the parameters that I originally imagined. Yet there is no one apparent "innovator" or, necessarily, an "individual-oriented" innovation context. Rather, they take my lead. They watch and observe the parameters I lay out and first make sure they understand them thoroughly. Then quietly, without fanfare, they work collectively to build on the original idea. They frequently tell me they will work more effectively in a group. They challenge each other, try out new ideas and build new notions. An idea that started as an unformed idea in my head finds its expression in innovative ways I never imagined.

The Western world frequently underestimates this creative atmosphere because we imagine that innovation comes from a spirit of individualism and rebellion. We underestimate the power of collaborative groups that work together to build the parameters for innovation and test out new ideas collectively. We see what appears to be a passive face when, in fact, groups are working hard at new ideas behind the scenes. We imagine an uncreative worldview when, in fact, an energetic group atmosphere creates a safe environment for experimenting and fostering new ideas. What we imagine as a rigid environment is truly a creative atmosphere that has a public face or order, routine and hierarchy. They see our world while we fail to see theirs. They can draw from both traditions while we often draw from only one view of innovation. There are many ways to innovate and, worldwide, many of these approaches are collective.

There are at least three kinds of knowledge being used here: the programming skills people had learned elsewhere (school, basement); the experiences they had about an optimal work environment; and their collective thinking to solve problems and suggest new ideas. That is, the knowledge acquired through formal schooling or study; the awareness of the environment and its opportunities and problems; and the collective knowledge of the group, knowledge being built in real-time—built when it was needed. The sources of this knowledge are equally diverse. School and skill knowledge comes, generally, from outside sources, which communicate known facts, information and procedures—programming language, chemical compounds, recipes for Mom's chocolate-chip cookies. Awareness of environment is a kind of culture; it is knowledge of the systems of how things operate—within an office, a country, a gender group, a language group or a particular community. Finally, collective knowledge must be built layer by layer—each person adding something, the group understanding the new layer, integrating it into their thinking and using this new layer to build something they uniquely understand.

A common misconception is that innovation is only important for a modern world—not for Pima and her classmates. But let us imagine that her community is facing a particular threat to their existence caused by the impact of an outside world. Let us say that the water used to irrigate the rice paddies are being reduced because of a factory upstream. How can Pima's education help if it is geared toward innovation? Under the definition used here, innovation skills involve moving beyond just knowledge acquisition to building and using networks, working collaboratively and applying general knowledge to specific situations. This worked for Lotus Notes, now can it work for Pima and her community?

If their water is being reduced, using Pima's traditional education she will have little to help the community. She is learning the "big" skills and theories. Industry, in this view, is a necessary and possibly welcome input to development. Moving people away from subsistence farming and toward formal-sector employment does not help the water problem, but it does move people away from communities and into factories.

But Pima, having been shown how innovation works, will not stick with the old knowledge—the old approaches. Rather, she will think of how to use networks and collaboration to build a solution that works for her community. She can use and build networks to the region or national experts and people who have investigated this issue. She can explore how other communities approached the problem and present possible solutions to her community. She can study the needs of the industry, how it works nationally and where the decision base is for the industry. She can bring this knowledge to her community and educate them about the industry, politics and economic parameters.

Then, using this knowledge and the knowledge within the community, they can define an approach that might work. The community knows the parameters of its situation so can decide if they have the means of adapting (possibly switching seed varieties or types of plants to grow) or whether they cannot adapt enough to the poor water supply. If they cannot adapt, possibly they can access a program that will build the community a well. Or, they can find a way, through local networks, to have a conversation with the industry or political leaders who have influence. By building the community understanding of the outside force (industry, economics and politics), the community is in a position to adapt and also influence the outside force.

In the meantime, Pima's education is richer. She has learned to build and use networks to help collaborative learning and knowledge-building and to find solutions that work in a unique environment—her community and the encroaching industry. This is the framework for many local innovations and for communities that are resilient, healthy and growing. It is also the framework that builds ties to the community for Pima and builds her skills as an innovator whether the context is her community or IBM—her future employer.

Acquiring an education

Only one of the sources of knowledge possessed by the Lotus Notes team is acquired in schools—that of mastery of particular facts and procedures. The ability to integrate the strengths and problems of one's environment or to work collaboratively to solve complex problems by using the diverse understandings of individuals within the group—both of these knowledges were acquired elsewhere. So, given that the original insights of Lotus were correct—that collaborative work would be of immense value, that groups could work at a distance and that creative construction added at least as much value to production as old-time efficiency—was their learning formula proof of the success of industrial-based education, or a fluke that proved that industrial-based education needed to be rethought?

Could the learning practices of many generations that brought countries from war-torn poverty to industrial powerhouses really be the wrong education to bring emerging economies to the fore? Could the education system that launched me really be wrong for Pima? It is easy to see that the people who succeed in this world have, in large part, mastered the skills necessary for full engagements—reading, writing, math, professional skills. Korea is a particularly good example. Coming out of the Korean War, the peninsula was one of the poorest countries in the world; today it scores at the top of countries taking an international achievement test. It is the country I live in today and from where I write this book. A friend of mine, who works in the Ministry of Education in the section of science and creativity, recently sent me an abstract to read and to correct any English errors. She is writing a paper on how the ministry is beginning to broaden students' exposure to science through the integration of museums and other community/civic resources to bolster students' interests. So, even as Korea is the top scorer on international tests, they continue to innovate and strive for higher achievement.

The Korean system is largely regulated at the top: the curriculum is established by the ministry. There is strong competition to become a teacher and only about half of those who complete the degree will do well enough on the national exam to qualify to be a teacher. From an early age, children's work is directed toward the all-important high-school achievement test, which is really a university entrance exam. This one exam—and the exam only—determines which university one can attend. Those university relationships determine the network of people who will work with you for the rest of your professional life, who will help you find jobs and connect you with others in the field. Generally, the top universities are thought to be the best trainers in any given field. In short, education is directed toward an individual achievement test that measures mastery of curriculum. This rigid system is kept in place because one's future opportunities are determined by the test results.

The problem for Korea is that, while it has perfected the means to have children master the knowledge needed to score well in an exam, it has, in the process, given up the focus of the other skills that made Lotus Notes so successful—innovation around one's environment and collective learning. The OECD report on Korea's prospects to be a leader in innovation puts it this way:

> The high school curriculum is tailored to prepare for the [university admissions] test; it relies heavily on rote learning and leaves little room for the creative thinking and exploratory spirit which are essential for [science and technology] education. The result is that while Korea's total spending on education is one of the highest in the OECD area . . . much of this investment is inefficient and wasteful.
>
> (OECD, 2009, p. 150)

The problem for Korea can be found in the Lotus Notes example. Although mastering skills and knowledge is a tremendous source of knowledge for creativity and innovation, it is not the only kind of learning that goes into innovation. And, since it is innovation and human thinking that is increasingly driving money, and because—more or less—we've gotten pretty good at providing the means to master skills and knowledge, it is the other two types of learning that will begin to make a real difference. To be sure, the computer will become ever more helpful in assisting in skill and knowledge-mastery.

I've always been pretty good at math and statistics and was bored in classes on these topics all my life. I understood the material in the first few minutes and had to sit through another 40 minutes of explanation and repetition (until I progressed to advanced econometrics where everyone in the class was like me . . . then I had to pay attention). Had I been given a computer, which would have allowed me to go through lessons quickly, I could have learned faster. On the other hand, I was the kid in elementary school that took forever to read something, but once I read it I had good comprehension. Teachers tried to help me learn to read faster with some new method for doing so, but I found it painful. My mind just didn't want to move forward until each line was well mastered. I needed a slower approach to reading (which I've now gotten pretty fast at). A computer program would have been less frustrating for me.

Whereas mastery of material and skills may well become more efficient through technology, the human race, in general, has gotten pretty good at learning to master material—whether in school, on a computer or just through rote memory. What we're not so good at—at least in a formal, structured way—is learning to collaborate and learning to be creative within specific environments. We are not taught these things at an early age as we are taught facts and skills. To be sure, we might be taught to share and work together, but collaboration is not generally built into a curriculum. We are not taught these important skills because, in an industrial age, they were not very important. And, as you will recall, the common school and mass education arose from an industrial need.

Learning to learn

It is tempting to view education through these industrial lenses. It is also tempting to argue one of two stances: either that education ought to follow a path of generating wealth (individual or national); or the converse: that education ought to have little to do with the generation of wealth. Either way does not make sense. Wealth is a means to an end. At the bottom end of the human wealth spectrum, poor people need to generate wealth to get off of the daily treadmill of finding enough food, water and shelter to survive. Wealth, in its simplest, smallest, most humble form, is their answer to survival. Once survival, dignity and freedom have been attained, wealth becomes only a vehicle for possibilities. Humans desire to explore, learn, create, build, be challenged and enjoy. A measure of wealth provides them an opportunity to do so.

Education is a means for helping the poorest to survive and helping others to broaden their opportunities. That education does not necessarily have to go through a corporation, turn into salaries or national income to increase opportunities. My access to the internet and the desire of all people to be heard, to exchange, to engage in dialogue, to share and to increase income, makes the internet grow. This very impetus increases my opportunities every time I turn on my computer. I get paid the same amount (actually, I might get paid less if I didn't use the internet often). My desire to solve a problem on my iPhone and use the internet to tell me what is wrong delayed my writing this morning. But it solved a problem, made my access to streaming news easier, enabling me to write sooner.

Because mass education derived from an industrial need, we still tend to think of it as driven by industry. Even the clear evidence that it has many other meanings—it became a rallying cry for those seeking personal freedom (in South Africa, in China, in Afghanistan) and later took on the status of a human right—we still think of organizing schooling around industrial needs. But, largely, we organize schooling because our citizens demand it. It is not just the harbinger of wealth, it is the carrier of dignity, freedom and empowerment of peoples.

The industrial history of education makes us look at education as a means of creating good workers. And workers, it is assumed, work for industry. It is through industrial production that we get our wages. Those wages allow us to buy new things that increase our opportunities. But in today's world much of this logic is simple-minded: it holds in a narrow sense, but only begins to tell the story of education in an innovation/learning driven world.

There was a young man named Barrack Obama who had dared to think that he could become the president of the United States. His campaign derived much of its energy from the use of social networking strategies, which engaged a large online following and raked in dollars from people who agreed to contribute relatively small amounts monthly as long as he stayed in the race. This strategy used the thinking of Chris Hughes, who was the former CEO of Facebook. He actually quit his position as CEO of Facebook to head the internet team for Obama. Hughes and team created momentum for Obama that soon overwhelmed his opponent, Hilary Clinton. Clinton originally had not only the lion's share of Democratic money behind her campaign, but, early on, was 20–30 points ahead in the polls.

Of course, the internet strategy cannot be attributed as the sole reason why Obama moved ahead in both the polls and in fundraising, but there is pretty general agreement that his internet strategy was a major part of his ultimate success in the election. Yet, the skills and innovation behind the strategy did not get developed by, nor were they ever owned by, industry.

The social networking brains behind the Obama campaign honed their skills in Silicon Valley and in garages and college dorm rooms and at home computers. But, mostly, it was their own knowledge. They brought with them no proprietary software, hardware or patents. They brought with them their knowledge and abilities to build collective knowledge. This understanding was transferred to the Obama campaign. Social networking required not only knowledge, but a keen understanding of the environment (how people connect socially and online, for example) and how to solve complex problems using the skills and thinking of a range of people.

These social networking skills were successfully deployed for Obama. Many of the high-tech strategists for Obama's campaign used skills learned in a similar manner. In this instance, the innovation-learning abilities used on the job or in entrepreneurships were borrowed from the workplace to further a social cause—getting Obama elected. Unlike an engineer who designed a car in the 1960s, or a refrigerator assembler where work skills could be applied mainly at work, today's knowledge workers learn at work and often apply what they know in their private, social and civic lives.

Even at the most basic levels of education, social network skills spread to personal, social and civic lives as well as the ways in which it is turned into money through employment. Education, sometimes framed as a means of linking one forever to a corporate machine, is increasingly the means by which one opens opportunities far beyond money and far beyond employment. In today's innovation/learning world, what one learns everywhere can often be used and applied throughout one's life, to improve it. This is not to say all education, in all situations, is always a good thing—it can also misinform people. Rather, it is to say that the days are dwindling when education's primary benefit to society is its contribution to formal-sector production. The contribution to production still exists but learning now contributes to family life, civic life, social relationships, entertainment, leisure and political engagement. Also, learning can come through social networks as much as through formal schooling.

This new kind of generalized knowledge is derived as much from "the bottom" as it is from the "top." Whereas new vaccines, cell phones and jet planes are designed by highly skilled, innovative teams working at the top of industry, other kinds of knowledge are gleaned from the bottom. If you use Google, you are the constant beneficiary of the knowledge collected from the bottom. Its search is directed by the utility that previous users have gotten from similar searches. In this way it "guesses" what you want. Yahoo became popular from a huge effort to categorize "from the top." Each web entry was put in a particular category . . . San Francisco . . . professional services . . . dentists . . . Nob Hill, for example. If you were a dentist in Nob Hill with a website, you would want it to appear in Yahoo's category for Nob Hill dentists.

Google used a different strategy. It analyzed sites' picks of people who put "Nob Hill" and "dentists" in their search. It turned out that a novel written about dental records and a news article about a murder in Nob Hill weren't that popular; most people did not click on those links, so those links went to the bottom of the list. Whereas a guide to Nob Hill dentists was often chosen, so that rose to the top of the list. Every time you use Google and click on a link, it improves Google's search engine. This is not knowledge from the experts, but rather knowledge collected from the masses—the bottom.

If one tests positive for TB, one has to take a drug weekly for months in order to get rid of the bacterial infection in one's body. If one starts the drug and stops prematurely, the body responds by reproducing the bacteria that weren't first killed by the initial drug use—that is, the strongest of these bacteria. This allows new strains of TB to form that are harder to treat. Thus, it is important that one takes the drug regularly through the entire treatment-time period.

In South Africa, health workers found that many patients were not taking their drugs regularly. This was because, when these drugs ran out, the patients found it time-consuming to visit the clinic; they lacked symptoms so there did not appear to be any real urgency to take the drug. TB became a major problem and new strains were evolving. The scientists had done their job—the drug was effective. Health-care workers were doing their professional job—prescribing the correct drug and telling their patients how to take it. But the social system and education levels of the patients did not fit into the predicted scheme. It took those who understood the community, knew the lifestyles of the patients and understood the social structure of the people to solve the problem. Local people were employed to take the medicine to the patient on a weekly basis and watch them take the medicine. These local workers had a good supply line for the drug and had a regular schedule to ensure that each local patient took the drug. This problem could not have been solved in Atlanta where the Centers for Disease Control and Prevention (CDC) is located. Nor could it be solved in Geneva where the WHO is located. Rather, it was people familiar with local social structures, practices and lifestyle that could design this treatment plan. It is knowledge coming from the bottom up.

Although this sounds like a donor aid project, in fact it is anything but; it has similarities to the Lotus Notes story. The solution involves high levels of expertise (researchers and public health specialists), awareness of a particular environment (culture, social structures, opportunities and constraints of local communities) and the ability to combine various types of knowledge to solve a complex problem. Whether one is designing the next big passenger jet (engineers, sociologists, marketers, cultural experts), solving a global health problem or waging a success-ful political campaign, the education that results in success goes far beyond the rote learning of facts. It moves into the realm of understanding the particular environment (whether it be global networks or local culture) and in working across professions and peoples to solve complex problems.

In an industrial age, the big gains that improved people's lives came from mastering industrial production. It created opportunities for many individuals and helped move millions from the margins of existence to a stabler, sometimes more prosperous life. But the thinking about education that evolved from this success has stayed with us even when it is beginning to be a problem. The fear of many educators and academics that education is "owned and controlled" by industry hinders us from being open to the possibilities emerging from learning networks that are often created from communities.

The opportunities that technology has created along with globally linked systems are changing the nature of education. The value of local knowledge for the human race is being overlooked. It is just this local knowledge that provides a new perspective in innovation, that provides the solutions to problems that come from global linkages and provides the means to link local people with an outside world and, thereby, increases their opportunities. The ability to combine knowledge from all these perspectives to tackle complex problems such as the elimination of polio, the quelling of rogue regimes, the invention of local processes for development, reside partially within local communities that are linked to thinkers from various fields and interests around the world.

References

Keegan, P. (1995, October 22). The office that Ozzie built. *New York Times Magazine*, 49.

OECD. (2009). *OECD reviews of innovation policy: Korea*. Paris: OECD.

5b Networked learning

The impetus for educating the world's poor since the Second World War was the notion that bringing countries into a modern system of industrial production was good both for poor countries (recipients of foreign aid) and for the wealthy countries (donors of foreign aid). But the new growth of global markets is not driven by donor/recipient relationships—rather it was driven by the competitive nature of global markets. Once freed to compete on a global scale, the barriers to trade, investment and movement of capital were quickly reduced. The one most important input to production—labor—while still largely immobile, has become globally accessible because production can move to labor markets.

Although labor markets globalized all the way from low-skilled to high-skilled jobs, this globalization process was ushering in another change that would change the nature of work itself. The differentiation of knowledge became the most valuable and dynamic part of the private market. The value of knowledge inputs to industrial production and services increased rapidly as a percentage of total value and new globalized knowledge industries began to appear. Amazon, Google, Twitter and Facebook are now joined by their Chinese, Korean, Middle Eastern and Japanese counterparts. These industries did not follow the laws of traditional industries—they worked differently, built value differently, affected societies differently and changed the way people chose to learn. The need to understand knowledge as an economic unit became important.

Changes in knowledge

We used to know what knowledge was—or at least we thought we knew what it was. It was something that we learned from the pool of what was already known. What was already known was stored: in other people's brains, in books, in forms of art, music, architecture, culture, procedures and practices. Sometimes, this known information could be re-formed into new knowledge either through analysis, creativity or happenstance. But, mostly, one had to begin by building the tools for studying what was already known—by learning the tools from which one could access what was already known: reading, math, science and the arts. Once that knowledge was mastered, one could produce new writings, paintings or music.

But all this began to change when knowledge could be digitized. It was not so much that what was known went away or became less valuable, but its form moved from a physical form to a digital form and, with this transformation, it moved from something someone had to physically access to something that could be delivered in electrical pulses. A digital format could be made available around the world at little or no cost to millions of people. Suddenly, the "cost of entry" to begin to be creative, to begin to invent, to begin to rethink and build new ideas, was vastly reduced because the cost of access to the knowledge base was vastly lowered. It was all available quickly, easily, in an accessible form and, furthermore, in a way that could be sorted, organized and rethought in unlimited combinations.

The "economics of knowledge" has changed. When Paul Romer first introduced his theory, which would later often be called "knowledge economics," he understood that one of the most profound implications was that this highly valuable resource had very different characteristics than did physical resources (Romer, 1991). The notion that ideas drive human progress was accompanied by the beginnings of the profound thinking that knowledge had properties that would change our thinking about resource allocation. Contrast these properties with physical products. Knowledge can be spread and duplicated cheaply; many people can use knowledge simultaneously; the supply of knowledge grows as it is used. These "economic" (resource/value) properties of knowledge are discussed in Chapter 7b and form the basis for a knowledge revolution.

Social network theory

As the world became more interconnected through its growing population, transportation, communication, trade, financial and political systems, its natural systems also became more linked, such as its ecology and disease systems. Researchers began to view these linkages through systems theory and, eventually, applied the same logic to the study of knowledge. Whereas academic disciplines were, almost necessarily, rather isolated by separable departments, conferences and research networks, the internet made their knowledges more accessible to other disciplines. It became not only possible, but necessary to view problems in their full complexity—linked across boundaries and disciplines. The complex problems facing the world—global disease, ecological degradation, terrorism, political instability, financial destabilization—now had a method for study.

Complexity theory emerged as an explanation of how such problems could be understood and studied. Complex systems evolve over time in ways that are not planned. As they evolve, they affect other systems around them, causing these systems to change and adapt. In turn, the initial system then changes and adapts to the surrounding systems' changes. This is known as "uncertainty" or "co-evolution." These two properties cause all complex systems to be self-organizing. They do not require a manager to plan the system, organize it and keep it going. The system will organize itself and, if healthy, keep going and adapting and growing and changing on its own (Chan, 2001; Proctor & VanZandt, 2011).

A good example of a complex system is the World Wide Web (WWW). It is clearly complex, is constantly evolving and organizes itself. As new links emerge, it changes the environment and older sites change to accommodate the new sites, links, opportunities and possibilities. These properties show how knowledge grows, builds, evolves and is distributed. It is known as social network theory. The theory explains how people spread knowledge, information, ideas and thoughts through networks—especially using new media.

Barabási is credited with the book that first brought the most fundamental principles of networks to the general reader (Barabási, 2005). Social scientists had previously built their ideas about the distribution of human behavior and characteristics around what was known as a "normal curve"—the notion that there existed a "typical" behavior around which behavior spread, both diminishing and increasing in approximately equal proportions.

Network theory found no such typical or "normal" behavior. With networks, such as the web, some pages were highly linked whereas some were hardly linked at all. About 20 percent of the websites accounted for 80 percent of the links. This distribution was named the power law distribution. Network theory also explained that some networks were constructed so that any given place (node or website) was not far from any other place—through their linkages. They were connected through very few links. This principle is called "small worlds." Some of the properties of networks made them very resilient to shocks; because they were so interlinked, if a particular node or set of nodes fell away or died, the entire network survived. Conversely, however, if a virus hit the network, it could spread rapidly.

These basic principles and others began to form the basic logic of studying how information spread. Social network theory was born (Borgatti *et al.*, 2009). Table 5.1 shows how network theory concepts have been adapted to social network theory. The theory can be used to analyze how information is spread; who, in a network, has the power to spread the information the fastest and has the most influence; and who, in a network, has the most marginal position.

Figure 5.1 is an example of a social network. It shows the co-authorship network of 555 scientists (Krempel, n.d.). Using the diagram, one can clearly see the strong (hubs) and weak (marginal) authors and see how actors and relationships work.

The ability of information to spread easily, be self-organizing and evolve through its own power became apparent as people began to use the networks to build new knowledge. The theory of social networks provided a basis for understanding how these networks worked while the theory of knowledge economics provided a basis for understanding the incentives for why people would build, trade, exchange and share knowledge. The actual power of the resource people were creating could not have been predicted by either theory.

Table 5.1 Social network characteristics

Network theory	Social network theory	Social network example
Node	Actor	Individual scientistis working together; Facebook members; co-workers in an organization
Link	Relationship	Sharing academic findings; Sharing photos; organizing events; building learning sites
Hubs	Strong ties	Scientist with many co-authors; Facebook member with many linked friends; co-worker with many people referencing throughout the day
Weak links	Weak ties	Early career scientist with few professional connections; Facebook member with few friends; isolated co-worker

Source: Author

Figure 5.1 Network of co-authors

Source: Krempel (n.d.)

Learning networks

Social learning theory tells us that human beings have a natural propensity to want to share their knowledge (Bandura, 1977; Haythornthwaite & De Laat, 2010). Only some of these incentives are economic. Other incentives include personal gains such as notoriety, their own learning, building networks, power and recognition for their expertise. There are also collective gains such as building collective sharing networks, furthering humanitarian or collective goals, adding to collective values or goals, working toward a cause or building collective knowledge. The gains in collective knowledge accrue to the person, his or her community, future generations and the linked world. Amartya Sen advanced a theory of collective knowledge gains to society in his Nobel Prize-winning work (Sen, 1995). His view was that societies increase their overall value if the people within the society can collectively and freely (1) discuss major issues facing the society, thus building new collective understanding and (2) act on this new understanding. This new collective knowledge, he believed, allowed the society to avoid or mitigate major disasters.

The web is a tool that allows for such free flow of information, sharing of knowledge and building collective understanding. If allowed to flow freely, it also allows people to take collective action. The impact of this collective action could not have been anticipated. It has changed the way all kinds of knowledge are being created, probably the least of which is the knowledge that flows through industry. But the power of collective and collaborative knowledge, however, has meant that even formerly competitive businesses such as Sony and Samsung now need to build knowledge together in order to stay competitive (Gnyawali & Park, 2011). Scientists have also been quick to adopt social networks for collaboration (Liebeskind *et al.*, 1996; Norgaard, 2004; The Royal Society, 2011) although universities are still having a difficult time marrying the concept of "expertise" with social networks (Rogers *et al.*, 2007; Wegerif, 1998).

Organizations are quickly learning to adopt social networks and learning systems as a means of building new ideas (Bingham & Conner, 2010; Sawyer, 2007; Wenger, 2000). A whole new way of thinking about international development is beginning to emerge. Conley and Udry talk about the use of social learning in Ghana's agricultural sector, for example (Conley & Udry, 2001), while Davidson-Hunt talks about the enhancement of indigenous knowledge systems of native communities in the United States (Davidson-Hunt, 2006). Clearly, social transformation has been assisted by the use of social networks in the Arab Spring or in building disaster relief networks (Fine, 2008; Gao *et al.*, 2011; Lotan *et al.*, 2011).

Many of these uses require people to build a kind of trust, a sense of common purpose and belonging—known as "communities of practice" (Lesser *et al.*, 2000; Wakefield & Poland, 2005; Wenger, 2000). These communities are called "communities of practice" because they work together—they "practice" together. The understanding is not so much that they are *goal* oriented as they are *practice* oriented. They learn together and build together. Through this practice, they build new strategies, ideas and innovations. The practice requires sharing, openness, integrity and trust. It is an ongoing and dynamic process.

The very essence of the new knowledge age is not so much schooling or learning in the traditional sense, as it is collaboration, sharing, creativity, openness and interdependence. Although schools will likely have a role in this new world of learning, one of the major stumbling blocks will be to overcome the old definitions of education embedded in the "educated" elites from when they built educational institutions. Such formal systems prepared them for the jobs at the turn of the last century, but the learning required now to take advantage of opportunities being created is inherently open and accessible and empowers human characteristics to learn collectively. It is a knowledge resource that is ever expanding, free, self-organizing and more valuable when it is shared than when it is owned.

References

Bandura, A. (1977). *Social learning theory* (Vol. viii). Oxford, UK: Prentice Hall.

Barabási, A.-L. (2005). Science of networks: From society to the web. In J. K. Nyiri (ed.) *A sense of place: The global and the local in mobile communication* (pp. 415–429). Vienna: Passagen.

Bingham, T. and Conner, M. (2010). *The new social learning: A guide to transforming organizations through social media.* Berrett-Koehler Publishers. Retrieved from http://books.google.com/books?hl=en&lr=&id=fQexuZjX8IAC&oi=fnd&pg=PR9& dq=smartphone++%22higher+education%22++%22learning+2.0%22&ots=pVXx-53aiy&sig=H-QDhdY_wn3GufxKj-zcVQZw9s4

Borgatti, S. P., Mehra, A., Brass, D. J. and Labianca, G. (2009). Network analysis in the social sciences. *Science, 323*(5916), 892–895.

Chan, S. (2001). *Complex adaptive systems.* ESD. 83 Research seminar in engineering systems, MIT. Retrieved from http://web.mit.edu/esd.83/www/notebook/Complex%20Adaptive%20Systems.pdf

Conley, T. and Udry, C. (2001). Social learning through networks: The adoption of new agricultural technologies in Ghana. *American Journal of Agricultural Economics, 83*(3), 668–673.

Davidson-Hunt, I. J. (2006). Adaptive learning networks: Developing resource management knowledge through social learning forums. *Human Ecology, 34*(4), 593–614.

Fine, M. (2008). Women, collaboration and social change: An ethics based model of leadership. In J. L. Chin, B. Lott, J. Rice, and J. Sanchez-Hucles (eds), *Women and leadership: Transforming visions and diverse voices* (pp. 177–191). Hoboken, NJ: John Wiley & Sons.

Gao, H., Barbier, G., Goolsby, R. and Zeng, D. (2011). Harnessing the crowdsourcing power of social media for disaster relief. *Intelligent Systems, IEEE, 26*(3), 10–14.

Gnyawali, D. R. and Park, B.-J. (Robert). (2011). Co-opetition between giants: Collaboration with competitors for technological innovation. *Research Policy, 40*(5), 650–663.

Haythornthwaite, C. and De Laat, M. (2010). Social networks and learning networks: Using social network perspectives to understand social learning. Presented at the 7th International Conference on Networked Learning, Aalborg, Denmark. Retrieved from http://celstec.org.uk/system/files/file/conference_proceedings/NLC2010_Proceedings/abstracts/PDFs/Haythornwaite.pdf

Krempel, L. (n.d.). A huge coauthorship network. Retrieved from www.mpi-fg-koeln.mpg.de/~lk/netvis/Huge.html

Lesser, E., Fontaine, M. and Slusher, J. (eds). (2000). *Knowledge and communities.* Woburn, MA: Butterworth Heinemann.

Liebeskind, J. P., Oliver, A. L., Zucker, L. and Brewer, M. (1996). Social networks, learning, and flexibility: Sourcing scientific knowledge in new biotechnology firms. *Organization Science, 7*(4), 428–443.

Lotan, G., Graeff, E., Ananny, M., Gaffney, D., Pearce, I. and Boyd, D. (2011). The Arab Spring| The revolutions were tweeted: information flows during the 2011 Tunisian and Egyptian Revolutions. *International Journal of Communication, 5*(0), 31.

Norgaard, R. B. (2004). Learning and knowing collectively. *Ecological Economics, 49*(2), 231–241.

Proctor, R. W. and VanZandt, T. (2011). *Human factors in simple and complex systems, second edition.* Boca Raton, FL: CRC Press.

Rogers, P. C., Liddle, S. W., Chan, P., Doxey, A. and Isom, B. (2007). Web 2.0 Learning platform: Harnessing collective intelligence. *Turkish Online Journal of Distance Education, 8*(3), 16–33.

Romer, P. (1991). *Endogenous technological change* (Working Paper No. 3210). National Bureau of Economic Research. Retrieved from www.nber.org/papers/w3210

Royal Society [The]. (2011). *Knowledge, networks and nations: Global scientific collaboration in the 21st century.* London: The Royal Society. Retrieved from http://royalsociety.org

Sawyer, K. (2007). *Group genius: The creative power of collaboration.* New York: Basic Books.

Sen, A. (1995). Rationality and social choice. *American Economic Review, 85*(1), 1–24.

Wakefield, S. E. L. and Poland, B. (2005). Family, friend or foe? Critical reflections on the relevance and role of social capital in health promotion and community development. *Social Science & Medicine, 60*(12), 2819–2832.

Wegerif, R. (1998). The social dimension of asynchronous learning Networks. *Journal of Asynchronous Learning Networks, 2*(1).

Wenger, E. (2000). Communities of practice and social learning systems. *Organization, 7*(2), 225–246.

6a Becoming creative

What does the learning economy have to do with Pima's education? Unless she is some kind of superstar student, her education will only serve to move her up one level—from an illiterate existence to one where minimal skills allow her to participate in local markets and modern institutions within her region. The innovation economy and the learning it implies may be important for Nokia or Bayer Pharmaceuticals or Ikea world franchises, but how much does it affect Pima's education?

Money moves education. We may all be learning a great deal by using Wikipedia when we want to know something quickly, but the technology behind it thrives because it provides the means for new ideas, new wealth and new voices to be formed. It is there because there is a demand for this service. Increasingly, this demand arises from civic voices, social interplays, environmental circumstances and cultural impulses. But a major force behind much of education—whether it be the growing sources of internet information, the state-design curriculum, the tests that sanction new teachers, the international comparative exams or the educational technology that is showing up in classrooms—is the economic force. It comes, not as we often suspect, from policy makers; it stems from the money generated by graduates.

Parents, worldwide, make educational decisions, for their children and for their tax dollars and private expenditure, in order to further the future of their children. They create demand for particular schools, teachers, educational policies, educational opportunities and educational technology. Students, when they get old enough, are a constant source of information for parents about where to invest, what to buy and how to vote. This demand translates directly into dollars, tax expenditure, purchases and tuition and from there into salaries, profits and markets. As education widens to include the vast array of learning resources—internet, social groups, adult education, informal learning at work, adult learning at home, kid's play that results in learning and leisure that is also learning—the nexus of this demand for learning spreads.

The source of today's education, though, can be traced, in large part, by following the money. It is industrialization that created jobs, that rewarded education, that created schooling demand, that put in place today's schools and their large systems. To understand how these systems are being revolutionized, to understand how education is rapidly moving away from schools and into global networks, to understand why anyone would invest in Pima's schooling, we have to trace how money influences schooling—although this influence is waning as social networks become major sources of knowledge.

A global economy emerges

When the second-world economy of the Soviet bloc collapsed, it set in motion changes in how countries trade that would ultimately lead—along with a technology revolution—to changes in what is valued and, in turn, changes in the means by which countries progressed. In a world of two economic systems, one's trading partners were determined by one's alignment within these two economies. The United States had "most favored nation trading status," which was given to a country that followed the rules, politics and networks of the *first* world's economies. This status meant it was favored for trade and economic incentives to buy goods from that country—reduced levies for example. In the United States, one bought sugar from the Dominican Republic, not Cuba. Even if Cuba could, potentially, grow and market sugar at a lower price than the Dominican Republic, sugar was still bought from the Dominican Republic. There really was not a "world price" for sugar, only a price within the first world and another "price" within the second world. These prices might not reflect market prices at all because the incentives for belonging to one economy or the other distorted actual costs of production.

With the collapse of the second-world economy, these trading relationships gradually dissipated. One commodity at a time, or one country at a time, the market for goods began to unify. As they did so, a global price for many commodities began to emerge—for oil, for steel, for copper, for tuna fish and, yes, for sugar. The difference in the price paid for sugar throughout the world gradually began to depend upon ones proximity to the producer—a variation in the cost of shipment. The base price shifted with the weather conditions, sometimes with the political stability of the producing country, but increasingly the shifts were global.

And so, if one wanted to manufacture a home computer, the price of the chips, the copper, the liquid crystals and the power supplies was the same whether you were Dell in Iowa or HTC in Taiwan. The same applies to the manufacture of office chairs, running shoes and power generators. The raw ingredients come largely from a world market of commodity prices. If the item is heavy, say a bulldozer, then location matters because a relatively large percentage of the final cost is in transportation. But if one is talking about pens or computer chips or windshield wipers, the transport cost does not figure as much in the final global price.

So, few countries or companies have a lock on price—they cannot buy their materials at a more competitive price than anyone else in the world. If one wants to compete on the price of a good, one has to chase the lowest cost of labor. But labor is not the same throughout the world. Some populations have a lot of skilled, trained and experienced labor and some do not. Generally, where the labor pool has high skills, it also is costly. Identifying the right labor pool became important—the mix between wages and skills. Countries, trying to attract the new money for manufacturing, pulled down their trade barriers to effectively lower the price of their manufacturing and to allow global companies to move money in and out of the country freely. The unification of global manufacturing followed the unification of global commodities.

This set the stage for a shift in world production. As both commodity and manufacturing began to even out around the world, such that both labor and input prices were increasingly similar, it became increasingly difficult to compete on either quality or price as the same production conditions and prices existed throughout the globe. One needed to shift competition to better marketing, more efficient production processes, new ideas and new products for niche consumer markets. Each of these competitive strategies involved brains—it all depended upon the quality of thinkers one could employ and their ability to think of new strategies and products: an innovation economy.

Technology played a bit role here. At the outset, technology began to reduce transportation and communication costs. Airline travel, phone calls and shipping all became cheaper. As these costs were reduced, commerce became easier. Bank transfers were facilitated worldwide. Phone calls could be made to check on managers in foreign countries. The cost of transport to a trustees meeting in London became cheaper. Doing business in a foreign land became cheaper and easier. In 1990, when I first began to do work in poor countries, we felt so lucky to have actual laptops to take with us. It was a whole new world with computers that could be taken on a plane reasonably easily. My own major research university did not yet have most offices wired for the internet and our library had only months earlier turned its card catalogue into digital displays in the library.

Year later, working in Egypt for the first time, I remember bringing my phone connection cords with me and being able to dismember the phone in my hotel bathroom to hook up my computer. I could send and receive emails that way through a phone dial-up. The quality of the line was quite poor so it took a long time, but I could do some important emails every couple of days. Ten years later, I arrived in Zambia and immediately had my house wired for high-speed internet so I could make internet phone calls to the United States. The high speed was just ok at the time—barely able to get an internet call through—but it existed. As a team, we wired up the Ministry of Education so all provinces could communicate with the central ministry. In 2013, fiber optics were being laid in the country. The speed, effectiveness and efficiency of doing business continue to be reduced worldwide.

Technology goes global

I was one of the first in line in my university department to buy a personal computer. It costs me something like $4,000, but I owned a brand, spanking new Apple 2E. Hard drives had just been invented and I couldn't afford the new Apple hard drive (I recall "Lisa" was the name of the then separate hardware that was the size of a desktop today). But my new computer had two "floppy" drives and, because it was now available, the ability to put 120 characters across the screen at a time. I began typing up my graduate papers. I was a pretty good typist and had learned to write some of my papers by typing them. It was a little strange to "type" them into something that didn't sound like a typewriter and didn't produce a piece of paper as I typed. But I became used to it.

What took some time was learning to edit on the screen. For me, the screen was not the reality—paper was the reality. So, the screen was just an entry point for getting to paper. Once I had input the document, I printed it and, at that point, I could deal with it—edit it, read it, organize it. I'd cut it into pieces and rearrange the pieces on the floor and tape them back together to form a cohesive paper. Then, I'd get back on the computer and input the changes I had made. For many of us who made the transition from typewriter to computer or, before me, from handwriting (with a secretary to type), the computer was simply an efficient typewriter. If there were changes, we didn't need to retype everything again.

I moved from Niagara Falls, New York to Miami 15 years later and moved a large desk and a large filing cabinet with me. When I needed to work at home, I sat down at the desk with its stacks of papers and projects and began to plow through them. Today, I am writing this book entirely from a laptop which is perched on my lap. Not one sentence has seen paper yet. I have one small file drawer with about four inches of paper in it and I'm trying to find a way of getting rid of even that small quantity. Paper is no longer a method of keeping documents. I organize my writing and my work electronically. When I'm finished this morning, I'll close out the file, which will be sent to some remote storage cloud server somewhere in the world via the internet. The file will then appear on my office computer when I get to work in a few hours.

Computers, in the beginning—and for most of us who simply worked on them (not programmed them)—were just a means to do what we had done before but could now do more efficiently. But eventually they began to change the way in which we structured our work. I no longer depend upon paper— virtually no paper goes in my briefcase each day. I don't have to write from beginning to end anymore. Just below what I'm typing now is a list of scattered thoughts of what I don't want to forget to add to this chapter and also things to put in the next chapter. Often, when I write an article, I begin in the middle and work outwards—toward the beginning and end of the article.

When technology first entered our lives, it was simply an easier or faster or cheaper way of doing what we did before—write papers, teach classes, keep track of expenses, find an old document. But, gradually, it began to restructure our lives. I almost can't find the time to recharge my phone because I can't live without it and my recharging stand is in the living room, where it is part of a speaker system that broadcasts radio news when I'm cooking or getting dressed. My iPhone is part of my daily business (calendar, contacts, lists), part of my entertainment (movies, games), part of my civic life (news) and part of my social/commercial life (shopping, the internet). Who knew that I would move from a simple Apple 2E to an integrated, handheld system that could do most anything I had in mind?

But I didn't make a decision to "move to an iPhone." I simply made each purchase carefully, weighing the costs and benefits of each new acquisition and trying to stay sufficiently informed about technology that it served me rather than overwhelmed me. I could not have imagined, as I cannot now, writing this and knowing that my iPhone will be out of date before this goes to press. Can I imagine what the hand-helds of the future will be like?

The change in the nature of education is moving in the same way. At first, we saw computers as simply classroom assistants. Students could type papers or learn some basic lessons using the computer. Early learning programs attempted to teach lessons in ways familiar to a teacher and a classroom. Subject matter was divided into lessons. The "facts" were put on a screen to read. When one thought one had mastered the facts, one could test oneself by taking a quiz and getting a score right away. The lesson would loop back and cover the facts one had gotten wrong. Some children's programs taught some basic skills in an entertaining way—teaching children their alphabet or counting with cartoon characters that offered verbal or visual rewards, much as a teacher would.

Today's "distance learning" generally has not gone much further. Many internet classes deliver materials in the form of the written word (or, perhaps integrating videos), have classroom discussion online, have students submit homework and papers and deliver grades electronically. This apparent e-learning revolution has not changed too much other than we can now study anywhere we like on our own time. Much of the rest of education looks the same—structured classes, structured curriculum, lessons, teachers, grades, mastery. However, silently, behind the scenes, a revolution is taking place, but because we still hold on to the usual definitions of education, we are largely unaware of these changes—or at least unaware that they are education.

We can understand how this might affect my son whose computer exposure started before he could read and is unaware of a world without technology. But let me use an example far from the United States to show how widespread this learning revolution is. A few years ago, I was in Zambia with a pretty sophisticated smartphone that had a problem with the cell-phone network. I went to the phone company who directed me to their headquarters—a small building that likely had once been a house. I was sent to a back room where the engineers worked. I sat with them for 30 minutes or so while I waited for a particular person to help me. I watched these young men (yes, all men) as they worked around this large room. Each was planted in front of a computer, unless they were leaning over the shoulder of someone who was using a computer. I could hear their banter and good spirits as they worked together to solve problems.

The atmosphere in the room was clear to me: these were exceptionally bright young people. They were using their brains at a high level and all were solving problems of one sort or another. Each person had a job to do but the job was integrated into a larger system, so each also needed others to give them ideas or review their progress or build a new component. I was struck by how similar the people in this scene were to my son who, likely, was roughly their age. Each of these young men operated with each other much has I had seen my son do—casually, enjoying each other's company and intelligence, but with laser-sharp focus. I thought, at that moment, that engineers were engineers all over the world. They were all alike whether they spoke a local African language or whether they worked for a gaming company in Seattle and spoke English.

When the young engineer began to help me, I asked him if he would speak to me for a few minutes about his work. I asked him how much time he spent each day just looking around the internet. I knew something of the IT training in the country and knew, absolutely, that what these young men were doing was something they had not learned in school. They might be college graduates in technical fields, but the work they were now doing was beyond what they had learned in school. At first, he was hesitant. My question sounded like I was asking him how much time he goofed off at work. But, eventually, I made him admit that he probably spent two to three hours a day just surfing the web without a specific purpose.

Now I knew their secret. They kept up to date by exploring things on the net. He would naturally gravitate to websites about his field because he was curious and wanted to know things. But this would lead him to explore other related information, then look to see what kinds of new phones were on the market in the United States, then see how someone designed the software for a new smartphone, then check a site that described a solution to a problem he faced last week. Then maybe he'd check his email for something from his girlfriend, but also check an email from a Tanzanian engineer he'd met at a conference who was passing on an interesting emerging technology.

He was learning. There were no lessons, no teacher, no grades, no tests. He jumped rapidly from one topic to another, spending concentrated time for half an hour and then breezing through ten quick sites that only took a minute each. He referenced something he was curious about from last week, jumped to the beginnings of a new idea, went back to research part of an existing problem, took a break to see what his girlfriend was up to, jumped back to his work assignment for the day, and then repeated the whole loop. His brain could store all this rapidly—from the present problem, to yesterday's puzzle, to tomorrow's possibility, to me. All formed a tight interconnection of a base—from which he became one of Zambia's top engineers—from which he learned. Going back to the Lotus Notes example, he used all three forms of learning. He built on his school mastery of reading, math, physics and computer programming. He used the understanding of his environment (physical, work-related and virtual) to frame his work and also to put limits on how much time he spent on each part of his learning/work. His environment told him how much time it was worth spending on each part. Finally, he used a highly integrated network of virtual connections and relationships at work to build knowledge collectively to construct a complex system.

The young engineers of this world are changing and growing. They no more think of themselves as isolated Zambians than does my Sudanese student, or the Chinese student whose review of this book has made me add this particular example, or my own son who was raised by two PhDs albeit having been exposed to a global world throughout his life. But does it apply to the poor youth in rural China or the child in urban Dhaka who is being educated in an under-resourced school? Likely—possibly surprisingly—yes. In the first case, both may well grow up in a cell-phone environment. Cell-phone companies are finding that investment in infrastructure works in most densely populated environments, even when the people are extremely poor. No area in Bangladesh is far from cell-phone towers. My Zambian student tells me that his friends in Zambia use Facebook via their cell phones because it is cheaper than making a phone call. Cell phones are increasingly "smart" in that they have functions linked to the internet and this functionality blends cell phones with the internet.

But, as youths find their access to networks increase, they find they are part of a global network of youth that passes on information and tests out new ideas and technology. Pima's school may not yet be connected, but when she goes to high school, her friends and, possibly, her high school will have the internet. As fiber optics spread, as cell phones become linked to the internet and as computers get cheaper and more resilient and use languages spread into regional hubs, the world's youth is connecting, passing information, hungry to learn trends and able to update their knowledge in a moment. They begin learning at a younger and younger age and will keep learning throughout their lives. Our desire to define learning as the facts learned in schools is increasingly naïve, outdated and illegitimate. It is only a matter of time until the youth grow up and refuse to accept this definition for their own children.

Just as the Lotus Notes group before them, much of what is learned by today's youth is learned outside the classroom. The skills learned in a classroom —literacy, math, electrical engineering, perhaps philosophy—were applied in the workplace. But the real skill of the workplace is the ability to keep learning continuously. The young Zambian engineer had to make judgments on how to spend his time, had to be able to listen to others and integrate their thinking while assessing its merit, and had to imagine a future while also not neglecting the learning that could be gained from understanding the problems still unsolved from the past. The engineer knew his environment, could define it, but also constantly explored its boundaries for new possibilities and expansions.

The learning that took place inside that engineering office in Zambia could not have occurred if there hadn't existed a networked world of technology. If the internet went away, their jobs would turn back to the engineering jobs of the past—to mastery of what was already known plus some limited exposure through imported, selected books to developments underway elsewhere. But technology made the Zambian engineer part of a global network of engineers, of a local network of innovators and of a network of learners that are gradually embracing an entire world. Sources of information, new ideas, possibilities and the ability to combine one's insights and talents with others in a network of innovation, creativity and learning are all possibilities because technology has now linked us, because it has gotten rather cheap and because we have enough people worldwide who know how to use it and contribute to it.

So, just when I originally thought that my computer made writing professional papers much easier, somehow an iPhone has now appeared in my briefcase and pocket (but never announced itself as a whole new way of communicating). So, while we think of schools as teachers, texts, classes, lessons and students, learning is being fundamentally redefined. What type of learning is being used by young engineers in Zambia? It is a network first and foremost. That is, it is a system that connects people not only remotely, but by field, profession, interest and passion. Lusaka might seem to be remote from Seattle, but for my son and the engineers at Celtel in Lusaka, the distance has no meaning. They fully understand each other.

So, learning is also communication. A network might provide you with the ability to learn, but the exchange of information—from formal documentation of a circuit board to casual texts sent over a cell phone—is what we learn from. Sometimes we just transmit or receive information. Sometimes we send it. But sometimes our ways of operating change even our view of our world. With each piece of information, idea or thought exchanged, our world gets bigger, our possibilities increase. We build relationships with people, institutions and networks online or in person that sustain our learning linkages and strengthen them.

Learning is also a system. Wikipedia exists because some people are willing to put what they know on a system. They might think they have special information they want to share or want to highlight something they value. But it keeps building itself and—through a system of self-policing—the quality of information is quite good. It is the system that built the software I use for email, the one that shares questions and answers to software questions, that discusses the latest trends, that sends podcasts from the United States or Africa to my internet radio for free. It is a system of linkages that rewards people for building the system, for using it and for inventing the system in the first place.

In this system, we have learning. We have teachers and learners. We have lessons and new information. We have places to learn and places to put new information. We have ways to check our understanding and to review what we think we've mastered. We have all the elements of education without, as it turns out, any real notion that the meaning of education is being changed. Education is no longer defined by physical boundaries, by the separation of teachers and students, by particular sources of information or by institutional definitions. Education is a vast international system of learning that is constantly changing and is being strengthened daily by new learning linkages, new innovation and new partnerships.

But even this new notion of education is being revolutionized even before it is fully recognized. Although what we know and how we apply it still counts as education, our ability to utilize it is being exponentially enhanced by a new function—the ability to solve problems using the thinking of many people who think differently and who, collectively, solve complex problems. Physicists or medical researchers may have tackled complex problems before and, by meeting each other and exchanging what they know through publications or emails, have pieced together sophisticated solutions. But this ability is being expanded beyond any capability we have had in the history of the human race. Our real-time collaboration across distances with people we've never met who are tied to a common problem allows us to combine knowledge in ways were never could before. It will change education into learning and learning into learning to learn. To understand this, a third trend needs to be explored.

Communities of learning

It may all be well and good for the engineers in Zambia to spent two to three hours each day (likely an underestimation) surfing the web, but who is paying for this? Isn't it lost productivity? Shouldn't they get back to work and explore on their own time? Is this the explanation for Africa's low productivity—no one watching the efficiency of employees' work time? Hardly. It is the very definition of a good engineer these days. Following the money we can understand why this informal learning is important, and also understand why it pays to have communities linked into this global learning system.

When the boom in industrialization started, the challenge for built industry was reasonably straightforward: machines could be made that used electricity or oil and made tasks much easier to accomplish; ships could sail under the power of engines; houses could be heated without fireplaces; electricity could be generated from hydro electrical generators. The race was on to invent a new machine and to develop a production system that produced these machines relatively efficiently and in a reliable, standardized way. Engineers were needed. Clerks were needed. Teachers were needed. Skilled laborers were needed. Each needed to master their job: define it well, carry it out effectively, produce reliable products such as machines, students, designs and accounting books.

The inventors needed to have the ability to imagine a machine and its use. But, after that, the job was all about production and reliability. To educate people for this work, teachers also needed to be reliable producers. The skills needed for work could be analyzed. A curriculum could be determined and pedagogical skills could be refined. What was required of students was organized, managed behavior in the classroom so that the subject material could be mastered. If one was successful, one could apply the skills learned in school to the workplace and be rewarded with a steady job—often with the same company for life.

What people learn is not always about jobs. People learn instinctively. What causes a two-year-old to be so inquisitive and fussy? Often it is about learning—they want to explore something or build something or concentrate on something and the outside world is setting limits or redirecting them. People learn how to dress properly for cold weather even when it is warm inside. They learn to water crops or clean a cut on their finger. We all learn to talk, walk and use toilets. As adults, we learn to manage money, catch a bus, go to the markets and prepare foods. We also seek learning opportunities—discuss politics with our co-workers, watch informative videos, talk with a newcomer to our community, sing with a church choir or paddle a canoe. If we are lucky to have leisure time and exposure to cultural events, we might go see a play, take an art-history class or take a tour of a foreign country to learn a new language— all for our pleasure.

We also learn for civic reasons. We learn about the candidates for whom we will vote. We become informed on important issues and learn how to work collectively in emergencies such as hurricanes or snowstorms. We learn traffic laws and learn to move to the side when an elevator stops so as to let people off first. We learn to participate in civic events by understanding the rules, laws, practices and expectations of others. We try to stay informed and to have opinions and to take appropriate action.

But the education that has economic consequences, the education that prompts many governments to require certain levels of education and that people seek for their children's future, is often linked to economic purposes. It is designed to link individuals to a system of collective production that increases their individual and collective resources and, thus, provides increased opportunities. Even in the case where a modest education opens up a job that is full of drudgery, is poorly paid and even dangerous, the education provides the opportunity to have the jobs, whereas the less educated neighbor has few options.

It is also true that the shift from subsistence farming to factory work is not always a choice for a community. The outside world may have encroached enough so that one has little choice but to live within a monied economy and the choice of jobs is limited. Yet, even in this instance, where industrialization may have created a framework for a poor-quality life, education can increase one's opportunities. Essentially, being educated rarely decreases one's opportunities. This is why people worldwide clamor for education and why it is often considered a human right.

The country and the world get involved in providing free education and, indeed, in requiring minimum levels of education when it is linked to overall society welfare. In an industrial age, this meant work and it was often defined as work within private industry. Private industry, it was assumed, built things, generated products that were not there before. It generated the income that provided for everyone else—government workers, service workers and teachers and psychologists. Without private industry, it was assumed, new value could not be created within society so government and services could not be funded or expanded. Educational systems were targeted to expanding this production and the services that could be offered in a productive system.

The shift to a knowledge-based economy and the growth of technology has changed some of this formula. Whereas an engineer who knows how to design a car is still valued as an employee, that knowledge of design is only valuable when she has collaborators who know about ergonomics, aesthetics, culture, gasoline efficiency, GPS systems, global trends, international finance and the latest models coming out of Korea and India. All of these factors go into a car design. The lone engineer or small engineering team that sat in Detroit and designed the next cars are now a multi-cultural, multi-professional, multinational team that works collaboratively. The engineer who knows only her own world of engineering and works largely in isolation is not nearly as valuable as the one with the same skills who can work collaboratively with people who think differently, and who can learn from them and incorporate their ideas.

In order to design this new car collaboratively, the engineer needs to have mastered a lot of the technology that not only designs cars, but puts her in touch with the rest of the team (social networking systems within the corporation) and also links her to world trends and new ideas. She must learn and use a variety of ideas that create a complex network of possibilities. These possibilities must be examined by each person in the team. These skills go beyond the basic engineering formulas and processes. They involve good learning skills, good communication skills including computer-aided communication, good skills in managing information and time and good computer skills. When the engineer wants to volunteer for her child's parent-teacher organization or for president of a social group she belongs to, all these additional skills are relevant. Essentially, her work skills are portable—free to be used in personal and civic life even though they were honed in her work life. She is the owner of this skill set and it can be applied in many realms—not just her work.

The generic skills that are valuable in this interconnected world, that apply in all realms of life, are the ability to generate and use networks, the ability to listen to and learn from diverse perspectives, the ability to take in a variety of information and sort it out to apply to a specific situation and the ability to manage one's time given all these inputs and opportunities. Essentially, the massive movement of money throughout the world, its increasing productivity and its networks of linkages in finance, community and education mean that the entire spectrum of education has changed. Although mastery of basic and even highly specific skills such as engineering are still required, one's ability to use them effectively depends upon the mastery of another set of skills involving collaboration, networks and learning.

So, as Pima goes to school, mastery of basic skills and information will continue to be as important as it always has been. But until she and her fellow schoolmates also learn to make use of the networks within their region, country and globally, they will remain largely isolated and largely without the possibility of moving from subsistence farming or low-wage factory jobs to something more satisfying or better paid. Their opportunities, while larger than before, are quite limited in a world where networks, ideas and learning keep changing the environment just outside their village. The concept of the "one room schoolhouse" whether applied in Dubai or rural Mali, is no longer enough to join a modern knowledge economy.

This shift is not dictated by Pima's needs. It is not Pima who decided to put the factory upstream or created an internet from which her counterparts in

Holland are learning math. It is, rather, the reality of a very changed environment. It has meant that low-skilled labor has very little value on a global scale whereas knowledge-savvy labor continues to see its value increase. And this impetus will not stand still. As knowledge continues to bring in value and, especially, as that knowledge-learning ability can be applied to a wide variety of sectors and aspects of our lives, the value of collaboration, networks, learning and information management will continue to grow. It is not a matter of raising the knowledge-mastery of existing schooling; it is a matter of rethinking schooling entirely.

6b From global production to digitization

Although Paul Romer's notion that ideas drive human advancement was beginning to draw the attention of development economists as early as the 2000s (Warsh, 2007), the concepts underlying this theory were not the only threat posed to human capital theory. A major, but related challenge, was the notion that the world was connected—that development, per se, was not something to be viewed as one country's isolated goal or even one country's goal vis-à-vis other countries. But, rather, the development of a country was highly linked to a world of interdependencies. Given that all peoples and countries live on the same globe, these interdependencies are, at some level, obvious. But in the 1990s a set of systemic human-driven changes converged to make the human-driven interdependencies all the more obvious.

Foundations of global linkages

Three events happened in parallel to bring about a new focus on global interdependencies; these involved rapid changes of economic circumstances. The first was the break-up of the Soviet bloc as a major world economic (and political) power. Until the 1990s, much of world trade (and foreign aid) had been linked to identifiable partnerships in trade—first (Western) and second (Soviet) world trading alliances. Both first and second worlds attempted to extend their influence by winning over Third World countries and bringing them into one of the alliances. But, with the fall of the second world of trading alliances, this first-world/second-world competition for goods, trading partnerships and labor sharing disappeared. The stage was set for the globalization of commerce.

The second event was almost the concomitant development of the World Wide Web in 1990 (Brugger, 2010). Although the beginnings of the internet had existed for some 20 years, the WWW provided the means for people to create their own sites and link them to other sites. Essentially, this allowed for the natural growth of information on the web. Not only were people and companies able to get their information out to the world, they were suddenly able to get their information out to their own internal networks across the world. Previously, information had to go by mail, difficult and expensive phone calls or someone had to get on an airplane and fly across the world to relay the information in large and complex quantities.

The third event was the understanding of how these two changes would transform how value was created in the world. In a world where goods could now be shipped anywhere, where global competition and technology was reducing the cost of shipping and communication, the race was on for reductions in global commodity and manufactured goods production prices. Localization, marketing and innovation replaced regional markets as the new competition (Audretsch & Feldman, 2004; Jaffe, Trajtenberg *et al.*, 1992). Niche marketing, advertising, innovation and production efficiency are all driven by knowledge—so knowledge became the driving force of commerce.

Global ties

It was around this time—the late 1980s and early 1990s—that the UN Conference of Trade and Development (UNCTAD) began to track global movements of investment monies. In 1989 it issued the first in the series entitled *World Investment Report 1991: The Triad in Foreign Direct Investment* (UN Conference on Trade and Development, 1991). It heralded the global growth in overseas investment. Figure 6.1 shows the growth in foreign direct investment (FDI)[1] in the period immediately preceding UNCTAD's first report. The growth was substantial from about 1986. The most recent report shows that

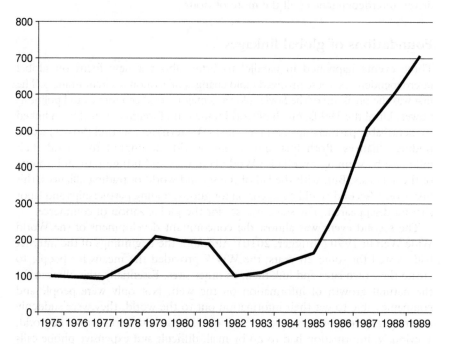

Figure 6.1 Index of FDI outflows; 1975=100

Source: UN Conference on Trade and Development (1991, p. 5)

the growth continued. From 1995 through 2014, FDI outflows have grown by 370 percent in real terms (UN Conference on Trade and Development, 2014, p. 2). Thus, the 1990s heralded the beginning of a substantial increase in cross-border investment where money flowed from one country to another to begin new enterprises or expand existing enterprises, from the countries of source money to new territories.

The freeing of available money created a large enticement for governments to break down barriers to trade and investment in their countries. Countries wanted to attract this money, the jobs the money implied, the governmental largess that much of the money brought and the implied government validity that financial growth often brings. They responded by reducing trade barriers. The 1996 UNCTAD *World Investment Report* focused on this trend (UN Conference on Trade and Development, 1996).

Table 6.1 shows how countries increasingly reduced their trade barriers beginning in the 1990s. By 1995, over 60 countries were implementing policies that freed trade and investment activities within their borders resulting in over a hundred policies that made such investment easier.

Table 6.1 Trade and regulatory changes, 1991–1995

	1991	1992	1993	1994	1995
Number of countries that introduced changes in their investment regimes	35	43	57	49	64
Number of changes	82	79	102	110	112
Of which:					
In the direct of liberalization or promotion	80	79	101	108	106
In the direction of control	2	0	1	2	6

Source: UN Conference on Trade and Development (1996, p. 132)

Some multinational corporations were making huge international investments. In 1994, Ford Motor Company reportedly had about 80 percent of its assets overseas, General Motors, 85 percent and Toyota, 82 percent. Of General Electric's workforce, 64 percent worked outside the United States in the same year, while 60 percent of Volkswagen's workforce was overseas and 64 percent of Royal Dutch Shell had a workforce outside its home country. Even in the emerging economies of the 1990s, foreign investment was growing. The Korean company Daewoo had a third of its workforce outside the country as did Hong Kong's Hutchinson Whampoa. Korea's Hyundai has a third of its assets invested outside the country (UN Conference on Trade and Development, 1996, p. 6).

When there were two competing world economies (first and second worlds), then any given country's trade was largely defined by whom one had as a trading alliance. Whether one bought sugar from Cuba or Hawaii depended upon whether one belonged to the first world or second world of trading partners. The price of sugar was not globally competitive, but depended, first, upon the price within the smaller trading partner market and second, upon the political costs of keeping the country within that market. Price was not always determined by competition, but also on the current politics and the speculation on future politics.

But the dissolution of the second-world alliance meant that a global market rapidly emerged. The price of global commodities and goods rapidly began to converge because of world competition. The expanded availability of global capital had the effect of merging global labor markets because of the removal of trade and investment barriers. Production could move to where the labor, skill and knowledge markets fit best. Labor markets began to globalize.

Table 6.2 shows the resultant shifts in jobs between major world regions. Investments of funds originating in North America, for example, resulted in over 217,000 jobs being created elsewhere. Money coming into North America resulted in a net gain of only 32,139 jobs created within North America. The result was a net loss of jobs to North America of 185,155 jobs. The clear "winners" during this period were the Asia Pacific countries, which gained over 200,000 jobs as a result of net FDI flows. "Global markets" now took on a new definition—from "Western" to "global."

Table 6.2 Jobs created by source of investment, 2002–2005

	Jobs created by source of investment	Location of jobs created	Net difference between source and location of jobs
North America	217,294	32,139	−185,155
Asia Pacific	59,969	273,028	213,059
European Union 15	74,728	33,526	−41,202
Other	15,584	28,882	13,298
Total	367,575	367,575	0

Source: Huggins *et al.* (2007, p. 443)

Growth of data

As economic factors began their onward march toward globalization, the definition of how societies gained momentum, built progress and moved forward began to change. Although the usual ways of measuring progress in terms of industrial output still predominated, an impetus to find a new way to measure social progress began to be built. It followed a trend in how money and power was built. Whereas money had tended to define power, progress and mobility in the last century or so (Berg, 1994) and, before that, land tended to build the new wealth (Brenner, 1976; Wright, 1987). Suddenly, the power of knowledge began to build new structures and possibilities for individuals and societies.

These sources of power and influence did not always go through private corporations or markets. Although powerful media corporations existed, networks of people could also organize and build new information outside such markets. Although corporations could still dominate commerce, networks of people could organize influential protests that changed the political and social environment. Although governments still had control of their institutions and laws, networks of people could organize protests that overwhelmed their governments and caused them to change course, or even toppled them. New forms of action began to form outside official, corporate and sanctioned media circles.

This all began with the linking of internet communications systems and the ability to digitize knowledge. Knowledge, in this instance, is often defined as some form of information that can be digitized (Open Knowledge Commons, 2011). Figure 6.2 shows the growth of storage of digital knowledge in the last decade. Essentially, in 2005, the world stored a small amount of exabytes of information—judging from the graph, something around a 100 or so exabytes. In 2015, the storage had grown to over 8,000 exabytes.

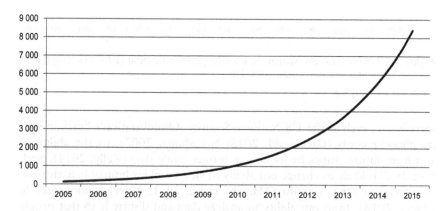

Figure 6.2 World data storage in exabytes (billions of gigabytes)
Source: OECD (2013, p. 55)

The OECD has attempted to measure some of the growth in market value as it impacts traditional corporations and capital markets. As Figure 6.3 shows, investments in knowledge have been steadily rising while investments in physical goods (tangibles) have been declining as a share of GDP.

But most knowledge does not register on capital markets and so does not get measured in the traditional metrics of economic indicators. For example, Google Scholar contributed substantially to doing the research for this book, digital media helps communicate critical information during disasters and social media helps organize global disease control efforts. Virtually none of this value gets registered as national income, corporate profit or individual salaries. But each of these knowledge inputs adds value: to the happiness or productivity or satisfaction of individuals, communities or societies.

This value is not always positive. The ability to collect data in massive quantities leads to possibilities unimaginable a decade ago, from government

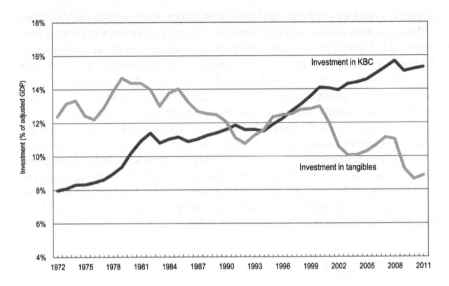

Figure 6.3 US business investment in knowledge-based capital (KBC) vs. tangible capital as a percentage of GDP

Source: OECD (2013, p. 14)

surveillance, such as the US National Security Administration's "vacuuming" up phone records (Greenwald, 2013; Nakashima, 2007), to the ability to anticipate future crimes by looking at former crime data (Kelly, 2014). Such "big data" is likely to change our ability to view complex human behavior and its effects on other systems (Manyika *et al.*, 2011; Mayer-Schönberger & Cukier, 2013). Even our ability to analyze data and display it so that people can visualize trends, track historical developments and find interconnections is improving, as big data becomes available through public databases (Gonzalez *et al.*, 2010).

Note

1   Foreign direct investment (FDI) is the amount of money that is transferred from businesses or investors in one country to be invested in another country.

References

Audretsch, D. B. and Feldman, M. P. (2004). Knowledge spillovers and the geography of innovation. In J. V. Henderson and J.-F. Thisse (eds), *Handbook of regional and urban economics* (Vol. 4, pp. 2713–2739). Amsterdam: Elsevier. Retrieved from www.sciencedirect.com/science/article/pii/S157400800480018X

Berg, M. (1994). *The age of manufactures, 1700–1820.* London: Routledge. Retrieved from http://proxy-net.snu.ac.kr/2b05b02/_Lib_Proxy_Url/books.google.co.kr/books/about/The_Age_of_Manufactures_1700_1820.html?id=M8KHAgAAQBAJ

Brenner, R. (1976). Agrarian class structure and economic development in pre-industrial Europe. *Past & Present, 70*, 30–75.

Brugger, N. (ed.) (2010). *Web history*. Bern, Switzerland: Peter Lang International.

Gonzalez, H., Halevy, A. Y., Jensen, C. S., Langen, A., Madhavan, J., Shapley, R., Shen, W. and Goldberg-Kidon, J. (2010). Google fusion tables: Web-centered data management and collaboration. In *Proceedings of the 2010 ACM SIGMOD international conference on management of data* (pp. 1061–1066). New York: ACM.

Greenwald, G. (2013, June 5). NSA collecting phone records of millions of Verizon customers daily. *The Guardian*. Retrieved from www.theguardian.com/world/2013/jun/06/nsaphonerecordsverizoncourtorder

Huggins, R., Demirbag, M. and Ratcheva, V. I. (2007). Global knowledge and r&d foreign direct investment flows: recent patterns in Asia Pacific, Europe, and North America. *International Review of Applied Economics, 21*(3), 437–451.

Jaffe, A. B., Trajtenberg, M. and Henderson, R. (1992). *Geographic localization of knowledge spillovers as evidenced by patent citations* (Working Paper No. 3993). National Bureau of Economic Research. Retrieved from www.nber.org/papers/w3993

Kelly, H. (2014, May 26). Police embracing tech that predicts crimes. *CNN*. Retrieved from http://edition.cnn.com/2012/07/09/tech/innovation/police-tech/

Manyika, J., Chui, M., Brown, B., Bughin, J., Dobbs, R., Roxburgh, C. and Hung Byers, A. (2011). *Big data: The next frontier for innovation, competition, and productivity*. McKinsey Global Institute. Retrieved from www.mckinsey.com/insights/business_technology/big_data_the_next_frontier_for_innovation

Mayer-Schönberger, V. and Cukier, K. (2013). *Big data: A revolution that will transform how we live, work, and think*. Boston, MA: Houghton Mifflin Harcourt.

Nakashima, E. (2007, November 7). A story of surveillance former technician "Turning in" AT&T Over NSA Program. Retrieved from www.washingtonpost.com/wp-dyn/content/article/2007/11/07/AR2007110700006_pf.html

OECD. (2013). *New sources of growth: Knowledge-based capital key analyses and policy conclusions*. Retrieved from www.oecd.org/sti/inno/knowledge-based-capital-synthesis.pdf

Open Knowledge Commons. (2011, June 10). Knowledge Commons: Activities. Retrieved from www.knowledgecommons.org/activities/

UN Conference on Trade and Development. (1991). *World investment report 1991: The triad in foreign direct investment*. New York: United Nations Conference on Trade and Development. Retrieved from http://unctad.org/en/pages/PublicationArchive.aspx?publicationid=622

——. (1996). *World investment report 1996: Investment, trade and international policy arrangements*. New York: United Nations Conference on Trade and Development. Retrieved from http://unctad.org/en/Docs/wir1996_en.pdf

——. (2014). *World investment report 2014: Investing in the SDGs: An Action plan*. New York: United Nations Conference on Trade and Development. Retrieved from http://unctad.org/en/pages/PublicationWebflyer.aspx?publicationid=937

Warsh, D. (2007). *Knowledge and the wealth of nations: A story of economic discovery*. New York: W. W. Norton.

Wright, E. (1987). *People, cities and wealth: the transformation of traditional society*. New York: Basil Blackwell.

7a The value of knowledge

The scenario of a changing world of learning comes not just from the way that production creates value. It comes from the economics of knowledge itself—an economics that is just beginning to be understood. The particular characteristics of knowledge, how it creates a better world and how it is created and spread makes it unlike any other resource we, as humans, have analyzed before. During the industrial era we were pretty sure we knew how to "create value" as economists like to call it—make something we want out of something we have. Like a car, or a book or a new suit, we take the resources we have at hand (labor, electricity, machines, raw materials) and build something new. We can afford to build this new item because we can sell it. We can sell it because it has more value than the inputs taken separately (more value than the raw materials, electricity, machines and labor sold separately). Each of these steps of logic is fundamentally wrong when we talk about knowledge.

Yet, what we do know is that knowledge does create value. Less than half of people living in Africa have clean water to drink. But research carried out in Beirut, Switzerland and Ireland developed a method of disinfecting water using nothing more than plastic bottles and exposure to sunlight. The idea (knowledge) is saving lives every day in poor countries. It is creating real value. The idea (knowledge) of a smartphone is changing the productivity and pleasure of people at the other end of the economic spectrum. What is this strange economic unit called knowledge and why is it so different than the pen we write with or the mattress we sleep on?

The question is worth exploring because it is the very economics of knowledge that sets the stage for understanding the cost of not educating Pima. Her education directly affects our opportunities in a more direct way than it did when the production of goods was creating most of the new value in the world. It also spreads the benefits of new production far beyond the boundaries of industry into our personal, social and civic lives. As a result, how we direct education, how we invite it into our lives through our lifetime and how we share it with others changes. Education changes from merely an investment in future productivity returns to an opportunity where everyone's education raises the ability of all to improve their lives.

Economic characteristics of knowledge

The notion of an innovation economy has been popular within the technology industry and high-tech industries worldwide. The original iPhone sold 1.5 million units on its first day on the market. Innovation makes money. I suffer from migraine headaches. Years ago when my mother was alive, they did not have effective drugs to manage migraines. She would retreat to her bedroom for three days in utter pain. There was nothing any of us could do and she reeled from pain during those days. These days, when I feel a migraine taking hold, I pop a pill into my mouth and, with a half hour, it has gone—long before it becomes truly painful. That drug sells for about $10 a pill, although I get it much cheaper with medical insurance (or Korea's marvelous health-care system). But, no doubt, it only costs a few cents to produce. Like many ideas, the cost is in the development, but the spread and use is just about free thereafter—ready to either turn into profits or create opportunities and possibilities for us all.

This is the first characteristic of knowledge—it is often expensive to develop but relatively cheap to duplicate. If I want to build new typewriters, I need metal, plastic, ink, labor, machines, a building, electricity, water and solvents to produce them. When I'm finished, I can ship out a number of typewriters. If I want to produce more, I need to buy more of all the inputs—machines, electricity, labor, etc.—but if I want to produce the next version of a word-processing program, mostly I just need brains. I need people who can think of the next innovations, who can test it on different populations and can ensure it will have an appeal when it goes to market. Sure, I need, possibly, a little office space and maybe some computers, but then, again, maybe not. Maybe many of my specialists live around the world and do what I'm doing right now—sitting in my study in my pajamas, typing on my own computer using my own high-speed internet connection. When I'm ready to ship out the new product, I may ship something out, but I may just mount it on a server computer and put it up for download after the sale. If I want to make the next version of the word processor after that, I *already have* my resources. I have my creative team. Not only that, but the input (brainpower for creativity and collaboration) has actually increased in the process of building the previous version. I have, actually, more of the materials (knowledge) needed for production of the second version than I had for the first. My resources have increased rather than being expended as with a typewriter!

Let's examine this production. First, it required mostly people. Although it will have high economic value (possibly make my company a lot of money), it requires virtually no physical resources to produce. Think about it: your iPhone has very few physical inputs—metal, plastic, copper, etc. But you paid a lot of money for it. The physical part of a knowledge product is often relatively small compared to its counterpart in an industrial age. The word-processing program I use now actually has NO physical form. It was downloaded off the internet to my university and loaded onto my computer.

Second, it was expensive to create. Some ideas are cheap and highly valuable like the creative uses of social networks these days. This knowledge is created by a lot of people using their best thinking to apply a new opportunity. The fall of the Mubarak regime in Cairo was not due entirely to Twitter. It was due to the ability of large numbers of people to engage in the exchange of ideas over time. Long before the protests there were lively debates. People were finding information, learning about alternative ways of living and governance. They were talking to each other through emails, networks, blogs and coffee-shop conversations. The internet helped because they could get information rapidly and accurately and exchange information across distances with like-minded people. They could build knowledge collectively with relative ease. When the time came they could take action also using technology to assist. The software and management of these social networks is not cheap—lots of programmers, lots of time, lots of thinking. But it highlights another characteristic.

Knowledge is often cheap to duplicate. In fact, many people studying the economics of knowledge are grappling with the very definition of knowledge. One definition of knowledge (in an economic sense) is that it is anything that can be digitized. This is because knowledge (ideas, art, music) that can be digitized, can be shared and spread at little or no cost and, hence, takes on special economic properties. So, software, the idea of solar disinfection of water, books, music, videos and the notion of vaccines are all information that can be digitized. Some of these ideas must take a modest physical form (the vaccine itself, plastic water bottles, hard drives for storage) but their physical inputs are small relative to the value of the product itself.

So, a third characteristic of the word-processing program is that it is cheap to duplicate. Like all digitized ideas, it costs virtually nothing to get it to others— a small investment in infrastructure (internet, computer, local connections) and little else.

A fourth characteristic is that the inputs needed to make the word-processing program were created during a production process. Unlike the typewriter where you use up resources each time you create your product, in a knowledge-based industry, you actually *create* your inputs as you create your production. The very process of production actually generates additional resources for what you need later to make more. Knowledge actually creates its own supply (of resources) at the same time that it produces the final product.

A fifth characteristic is that it also creates its own demand. As soon as you ship the new word processor out of the factory, it has raised the bar for word processors. People don't settle back with the satisfaction that they "have the latest." Unlike a typewriter that you might generally use until it is worn out, with a word processor you know that, some years down the road, you'll want to or need to upgrade. You look forward to the new version that allows you to insert comments to your co-author or convert to the web page format for your first web page. When a new idea is created, it is the building block for the next new idea and it creates a desire to keep improving. So, knowledge often creates its own demand.

Finally, let's examine how the company makes a profit. It knows that, the minute it releases its new software, all its competitors instantly have all the knowledge embedded in it. All the great ideas, thinking, design and marketing required to make it successful are now public knowledge. If, in fact, that knowledge was the company's competitive advantage, it just lost its competitive advantage by releasing its new product. But this may not be true. What the manufacturing company has is a team that knows how to work together, that has thought through ideas and possibilities, that has a means of seamless collaboration across, perhaps, long distances, cultures and professions. It has a great team. That team has a learning advantage over the competitor's team (if, indeed, the competitor has a team) in that it has learned to learn together. It is the ability to learn quickly and effectively that defines the competitive advantage.

This ought to sound familiar. Let's go back to the Lotus Notes example. The value of that team was not in its individual engineers or their knowledge per se, rather it was in their collective ability to learn and create. Thus, when IBM made the purchase they did not assess the Lotus Notes team as a group where they could replace anyone they lost. Rather, knowing that they were buying a *learning* advantage, they first investigated what it would take to keep the team together—to purchase the learning advantage.

At the moment, patents are supposed to guarantee a company that it owns the rights to the knowledge it created. Apple owns the rights to the iPhone. Pfizer owns the patent for Lipitor drugs. But it is also true that the minute they release these products to the market, their competitors also have the knowledge embedded in these products. They can go to work inventing products that are quite similar. No one can release an iPhone, but Samsung phone can release an Android based on the ideas embedded in an iPhone—apps, touch screens, user-friendly interface, etc. Lipitor can be re-engineered with some of the basic building blocks but enough differences to call it a different drug. Lipitor now has many competitors. The competitors to the iPhone and Lipitor also have the advantage of looking at the originals and avoiding some of the problems. Patents do buy you ownership of a product, but they don't protect you from the learning that builds on the original knowledge.

When Steve Jobs resigned from Apple, no one doubted that the patents for Apple still held. What everyone wondered was whether the learning environment, the creativity and innovation that had marked the company, would remain. Learning, essentially, is Apple's true competitive advantage—not its patents for the iPhone or the MacBook Air.

Setting the global trends of knowledge production

These very characteristics of knowledge have changed the way industry makes profits and, through this change, the way countries build their economies. In turn, parents and voters are beginning to reassess which types of educational systems they desire to support. It has also caused a new demand for a different kind of education—one that affects our lives far beyond our schooldays.

Before the industrial revolution, people accumulated wealth largely through the ownership and control of land. Sometimes this land had agricultural value. Sometimes it was the land upon which houses were built. Sometimes the land had other natural resources of value such as a riverfront. After the industrial revolution, ownership and control of industry created new wealth for individuals, industry and countries. The ability to generate income from industry was a major shift. With this shift, the wealth of nations changed in nature and governments derived their legitimacy through making this new source of wealth available to their citizens. Citizens, in turn, did what they could to be part of this growing wealth—including sending their children to the schools they believe would give them access to the wealth.

It would be difficult to say when, exactly, this shift occurred. There was never a time when industry had no bearing on wealth nor has there been a time when land ownership had no bearing on wealth. Rather, it was a change, over a period of time, from the *primary* source of wealth being land ownership and control to industrial ownership and control. No doubt, as this change happened, it was not immediately apparent to the people living through the period that such a shift had occurred. It was not decreed by a government or marked by an anniversary. Simply, new wealth was increasingly created by industry.

The knowledge economy has caused another shift of a similar nature. Whereas industry continues to be an important driver of goods and profits, increasingly knowledge production is replacing it as a primary means of new wealth. Old industry leaders and old industries die; new knowledge-based production replaces them. Using the definition of knowledge as information that can be digitized (a physical book, for example is knowledge because it can take on a digital form), then the shift toward knowledge production in just 20 years is phenomenal. The OECD estimates that over half of all national production within its member countries is now attributable to the production of knowledge. Over half of the value of old industrial production–such as cars and airplanes—are now knowledge related. Our very credit cards, car keys and rice cookers have knowledge built into them in the form of chips.

All this knowledge and all this wealth is a mixed blessing of sorts for humanity. It does not necessarily bring about happier or more fulfilling lives. It does not necessarily bring about freedom or dignity to those living at the bottom of the world's socio-economic spectrum. It does not guarantee freedom of speech or more humane treatment of strangers in our cities. But it does drive a lot of human effort and purpose. It is sought by countries and individuals worldwide. It satisfies some basic human desire—possibly mostly a desire to have increased opportunities and possibilities. Possibly, it also satisfies a desire to be challenged and to contribute. Whatever the underlying human desires, it moves power, wealth, investment and schooling throughout the world.

Amazon began as a simple bookseller using an online model. At its outset, it did not appear to be a knowledge company any more than the bookstore down the road from you. It simply sold physical books which, when ordered online, would be shipped to you. The advantage of Amazon was that you could generally find just about any book. Your bookstore down the road had the advantage of enticing you with books that you could look at and, possibly, read a few lines before purchasing. Amazon did not try to compete with this. It simply offered you the ability to buy a book of your choice, conveniently, when you were at your computer and would get it to you rather quickly.

It actually faced considerable financial difficulties at first and almost failed as a company; it didn't stabilize until years later. When it did so, it began to realize that it was a knowledge company—not just a reseller of finished goods. Amazon creates value not just in the convenience of ordering a book, but in their website. If one wants to explore a particular type of book or subject area, one can use the search engine to locate similar books. More recently, one can find out what other people who bought the book also bought—likely something else you might be interested in. Now one can often browse a portion of the book and read reviews on the book. Readers can post their own opinion on the book and rate it. It is a great resource for finding books on a particular subject, assessing their merit, understanding how the subject is being treated within the book world and making a decision about whether the book is worth publishing. And, while you are at it, you might as well order it from Amazon since you are on their website anyway.

What Amazon sells is knowledge. You can go down the street and order the book through your local bookstore or, for that matter, directly from the publisher. But if you want to find out what others are reading, what the reviews said, how others rated the book or browse the table of contents or sections of the book, you want to go to a knowledge source that has that information— Amazon. Recently, Amazon also began selling more digital books than it did physical books, so you don't even need to wait for the physical book: you can begin reading within minutes.

A traditionally trained bookseller or bookstore clerk or even librarian would have a hard time finding employment at Amazon, although it is possible that some of this traditional knowledge has value within the company. You are more likely to find employment if you know database management, understand social networks, have built web pages before or have an understanding of electronic marketing. If you are a knowledge worker, in other words, you might find a job at Amazon. The role of professionals, even those highly skilled with targeted educations in chemistry, medicine, engineering, dentistry, or music, is increasingly interfacing with knowledge management.

One of my students diagrammed the ways that people learn to play a musical instrument in these modern times. When she had a diagram that included all the possible sources of knowledge, she began to link them with arrows showing which sources learned from which sources. For example, music teachers were linked with online music chat groups. Once the diagram was completed, it was amazingly complex. Only a small part of the diagram was traditional music classes, although that formed an intensity of linkages to other sources. Much of it had to do with sources found electronically including downloading music, online chat groups on music, videos on how to play certain types of music (she's a violinist and she learned fiddling by watching a video) and databases of music. Music is now often recorded using electronics and is as often written by a computer as someone plays the music on an electric keyboard.

Such a specialized talent that requires substantial individual mastery and practice is still fundamentally enhanced by electronics—knowledge access. Professionals, no matter which type of work they do, are increasingly part of a global network that leads each other to new ideas, sources, opportunities, information, problem solutions and growth. If you want a job at Amazon or want to become an accomplished violinist, you'll need mastery of a specific set of skills, but you'll also need to know how to join with others to create new possibilities and opportunities and how to use the knowledge that others are creating. Imagine the professional, cultural and social networks that build a modern jet plane. An engineer, sitting in front of an isolated, non-networked computer, no matter how skilled, would not stand a chance of employment.

These are generalized skills: learning how to build new ideas and opportunities by sharing thoughts with others who are working in your area or who are working in areas that share some alignment. I've read hundreds of articles and books in the field of technology and business although I'm in the field of education and economic growth. I dare not turn my back to them or I stand to fall behind in my field. I am a voracious consumer of international news and of social trends because I know the new trends come from these sources. As I write this, I am in awe of the power of knowledge to bring about change. The Arab Spring has shown us that the ability of people to build knowledge about alternative ideas, to engage in conversations about new ways of organizing their worlds and to use these ideas to create momentum so powerful it can bring about the downfall of governments that have ruled for decades and have billions of dollars of resources.

In this strange world where new value is created, not by adding something to your living room shelves or your jewelry drawer or the equipment room of your office, but by placing some code on your USB drive that you keep on your key chain; in this world where an engineer is practically unemployable without learning skills built around networks of diverse people; in this world, countries have to rethink their development strategies. And so you and I have to rethink education.

Korea is a good example of this new world of education. When Korea emerged from the Korean War, its people were some of the poorest in the world. It had few natural resources upon which to trade to the world—no oil, iron ore or gold hidden beneath its surface. It began a simple plan. It began to educate its people. At first, it educated people in basic reading and math skills in simple schools. The schools were overcrowded, unheated and had few supplies; teachers were poorly trained; conditions were bad. But the children learned the basics and moved out of the primary schools into the factories, which built simple manufactured goods.

Small industries began to grow in Korea, but the goods were of poor quality. At first there was just a trickle of foreign investment in industry, but the population had enough education and was organized enough to attract some basic manufacturing. This manufacturing base and the income it generated for the country was quickly turned back into education. The quality of the basic education was raised so that primary schools could turn out better quality graduates. Meanwhile, opportunities were opened for secondary education. Although spaces for secondary schools were limited and conditions were poor, such opportunities were available. Now, manufacturers began to open up better plants because the human capital in Korea was of higher quality. In each phase, Korea expanded education, then raised quality of education and then expanded the next level. This was done in tandem with industrial expansion.

Home-grown industries were protected at the same time, but such industries could only have thrived if the population was educated. Essentially, in a country with few natural resources, Korea was growing its own—human capital. And it was doing so in a very smart way. It expanded education with increasing equity. Year after year, educational opportunities expanded for all citizens so that the scope of the resource grew. Today, nearly all young Koreans graduate from high school and nearly 90 percent go on to some form of higher education. This young population is the most educated population in the world. They also score the highest in international testing. Korea has, effectively, grown its own resource.

The old economics that did so well explaining an industrial world is clearly facing challenges as it tries to explain this unusual world. We no longer know what the price is when the cost of an idea can be borne collectively (Facebook or software that is built through a community of developers or users); when the knowledge seller is also the knowledge consumer (Amazon learning from its customers how to build knowledge into its system); when a nation's primary resource is not its industry but its people's ability to learn; when the production of a piece of knowledge creates new demand and supply for knowledge. When markets are networked and global, we need to search for a new understanding of the economics of knowledge.

Knowledge systems

Traditional neo-classical economists can hardly begin reading a paper on knowledge economics without disagreeing on even its fundamental characteristics. Those characteristics tend to violate even the most basic of classical economics. For example, one basic tenet is that supply and demand set a market price (assuming nothing is interfering with the market). But the very fact that your Sunday newspaper is filled with ads for varying prices of the very same product tells you this is not the case. If you want to find the best running shoes for the best price, you do a little research. You might know which stores usually carry your brand or which is likely to have a good price; or your friend told you where they shop for their shoes; or you saw an ad for a good price. You make your selection based on some of this knowledge plus a decision about how much time and effort you want to spend in finding out more information. In other words, you make your decision based on knowledge and information. You are weighing the cost of information (time and energy) as much as the cost of the shoes. Knowledge will guide your purchase.

To understand another way that knowledge works differently as a system than classical economics, let's go back to Pima's village. In classic economics, we would explain the happiness of the village this way: everyone has a certain amount of possessions and income and each one chooses how to spend that income and wealth based upon their own preferences. Maybe I love bananas and you love fish. So I'll trade my fish for your bananas. When we all finish trading, we know that everyone has maximized their happiness based upon their resources because if I could increase my happiness (maybe get more bananas by trading more fish) then I would do so. I stop when it is not worth it for me to make more trades. Maybe someone wants to trade me more bananas for some shoes, but I have more than enough shoes so the trade is not worth it for me. Everyone stops trading because, relative to our incomes and resources, each of us is as happy as we can get. At this point, standard economists would say that the society has maximized its happiness—its overall welfare.

But knowledge economists would say that the sum of each individual's happiness is not always the maximum of the society's happiness. What if the members of Pima's village realized that the rice paddies were beginning to pollute the banana fields? They discover that, by separating the rice paddies from the bananas with another crop, they can yield the same amount of rice and also get more bananas. They work together to experiment for one year and find they are correct. Then they reapportion the land so that they can get more bananas. Knowledge economists would say that this innovation was a product of collective knowledge-building—something now familiar in the new theory. They were able to talk among themselves, make observations, analyze and gradually build the collective knowledge of the village. Then together they found a way to take action and again, used their collective knowledge to analyze what they knew. Based upon this new information, they made an innovation that raised the collective welfare of the entire village. So, the welfare of the village is based partly upon the decision of each member and partly upon the ability of collectives to innovate.

Knowledge production works like a system rather than a physical product. Let's take Google as an example. For those of you who can remember, several other search engines were number one before Google. Yahoo was very popular. Yahoo employed a bunch of librarians to develop a system to categorize all possible websites. If you wanted to post a recipe, for example, you might be in put in a category like, household > kitchen > food > recipes > soups. Yahoo has since given up (apparently) this categorization, but it used to be easy to tell which category you were in. Then, if you wanted more soup recipes, you just needed to go into the soup category. If you had a new website, then you could tell Yahoo and suggest a category. Google based their search engine on another premise: it decided that it would "learn" from its users. So, if I typed in "leek potato soup" (as I did the other day because I had some lovely leeks and needed to use up some potatoes), Google would list first those sites most people had chosen. Maybe the most popular site was a favorite recipe site that experienced cooks who were web-savvy knew had good recipes. Maybe it was a particularly good recipe for such soup. Maybe it was one of only three that actually matched the search—the rest being leek and sweet potatoes or potato casseroles with leek as an ingredient. The combination of the best "fit" for your search (really, I did mean both leeks and potatoes and I specifically wanted soup) and the popularity of the link most people chose, determined which sites Google showed you and in which order.

It was a marvelous idea. It quickly became the first choice for search engines. While Yahoo kept people busy trying to accurately classify an exploding number of websites, Google took advantage of this explosion of knowledge and rather than try to tame it through classification, it used the information inherent in the explosion to create what economists would call "value." It made something that people wanted, used and improved their lives. This amazing value was also free. How a truly valuable economic good was free is the primary characteristic of knowledge economics.

Google is also a good example of how this systems-based economics is not easily explained in the old economic theory. Its price—at least to its consumers —is free, so supply and demand (for the consumer) do not set a price. It also creates value through collective knowledge. If Google only had your individual preferences to guide its search engine, its value would be small. But, because it can use the preferences (knowledge) of the hundreds of thousands of people who have clicked before you, it can create value out of collective knowledge. Broadcast television is another knowledge product (it meets the economist's definition of something that can be digitized) but is a hybrid, somewhat unformed, version of a knowledge product. Whereas both broadcast television and Google derive revenue from advertisements, only Google also gains value directly from the users of its knowledge product.

Google, the internet itself, ant colonies, market economies, climate and nervous systems are all complex systems. They have many pieces that change, adapt and sometime grow according to collective behavior. Google gets better the more we use it and the better it gets, the more it is used. It grows according to some basic principles (it incorporates existing knowledge, it provides good answers) and adapts. When Facebook came along, Google's search engine adapted, so one can find the Facebook web page easily through a Google search. Before Facebook, Google would have had a difficult time trying to guess what you wanted if you typed in "Facebook." Probably, it would have returned some links for books on facial care or facial looks.

Because knowledge is often so valuable, it can be exchanged for other types of knowledge. We know that, when we tell Hotels.com how well we rated our hotel room, the next time we use Hotels.com we'll benefit from similar information other hotel guests posted. So, we agree to rate our hotel rooms. When I first taught at the State University of New York (SUNY) at Buffalo in

1990, I asked for an office that had a connection to the internet (yes . . . that's right, most did not). I was one of the people who helped the vast complex system known as the internet to grow. It gave me knowledge that I valued, so I asked for its access. In turn, my usage grew the network (complex system). Each person, asking for access to this system (usually paying for access) has grown the internet system. Our use—and sometimes our input—increases its value, causes it to adapt and thereby provides the impetus for its growth and sustainability.

It is easy to understand such systemic, interlinked characteristics when we talk about Google or the internet or even Lotus Notes. But just such a system is what results in the factory being built in Pima's township, which provides things as mundane as the writing paper for her neighborhood school and underlies the impetus of her government to compel Pima to go to school and the desires of her parents to make the sacrifice to get Pima educated. We can imagine that knowledge is what makes Google grow, but can we imagine how it reshapes Pima's world? Even more difficult, can we imagine how Pima's knowledge reshapes *our* world and creates *our* opportunities and possibilities? We have to go further into the theories of knowledge to begin to link our use of Google with Pima's classroom, or the creativity of the Lotus Notes team with her curriculum. But the basis begins with the understanding that knowledge is a system; it grows, adapts and incorporates new pieces and its shape, function and linkages bind all our prospects together.

7b The economics of knowledge

Economics is the study of resources. Economists begin by asking how people maximize their happiness (something termed as "utils" in the field of economics) using their resources. Resources can be anything—money, power, influence, time, energy, relationships, physical energy, health, etc. But, because many resources either cost money, can be traded for money or their production generates money, the field of economics focuses on money. Money is also easy to calculate and modern economics is all about formulas.

Knowledge just doesn't fit into these neat parameters. Knowledge turns out to be a resource that leads to a great deal of satisfaction. It helps humans increase their quality of life and raises the well-being of societies and communities. But it does not necessarily need to be built, exchanged or accumulated through markets and, thus, doesn't always turn into money. Even if it did, it does not work in the neat formulas of existing economic theory. As Mirowski's review of attempts to build models of knowledge within neoclassical economics concludes:

> Everyone seems to believe that knowledge is the key to economic success, and yet our most-developed schools of economic thought are mired in the most frightful muddles when it comes to modeling knowledge in an economic setting.
>
> (Mirowski, 2009, p. 144)

Economic characteristics of knowledge

Mirowski's "muddles" derive from the unusual characteristics of knowledge as a resource. Many of these characteristics contrast sharply with the characteristics of physical goods and thus, operate differently "in the marketplace." Several authors have described some of these characteristics (Blakeley et al., 2005; Cortright, 2001; Romer, 1990; Skyrm.com, n.d.). The characteristics are still being discovered. The first were simply a contrast to those of physical goods or services. But another layer is being added—those applying to networking characteristics. Likely there is another layer—dynamic characteristics.

Non-rivalrous

Knowledge can be used by more than one person at a time, unlike a pen or a car for example. Physical goods can only be used by a specific number of people at a time but knowledge can be shared and used by many people at the same time. I can look up a concept on Wikipedia at the same time as anyone else in the world and we can both benefit equally from the use of that knowledge. Both of us can grow and build our knowledge base without harming or taking away the value of the other's use of that knowledge.

Increasing returns to scale

Knowledge is often rather expensive to produce because it requires a valuable resource to produce it—human thinking power, time and effort. But, once produced, it is cheap to spread that knowledge. In fact, the cost of spreading that knowledge is rapidly declining as the cost of digital storage declines. Thus, the first time the knowledge is developed, it is often expensive (like a blog, an experiment, a piece of software), but the next time it is produced (like when it goes up for the world to see or use or purchase) it is cheap. Arguably, the more widely spread it is, the cheaper each viewing, access or item is. This is known as *decreasing* "returns to scale"—cheaper the more one produces or provides access.

Contrast this to a physical produce (or service). Producing many tires for automobiles has the opposite consequence. The more one produces, the more rubber is needed. One must purchase more latex from trees (or oil for artificial rubber). But latex supply is limited and the more one demands, the more expensive it is to produce more tires. Thus, physical products generally have *increasing* returns to scale—they get more expensive the more are demanded and produced.

Non-excludability

It is not easy to exclude people from the use of or access to knowledge. Both the film and music industries have had to adjust to these new realities (Sherman *et al.*, 2014; Tschmuck, 2010). Although patents and copyrights attempt to attribute ownership to knowledge, such laws are increasingly difficult to enforce. In fact, it could be argued that the new profits are in giving away knowledge— witness Twitter, Facebook and Google: they make their money by providing people with access to valuable knowledge and networks.

Cumulative

Knowledge accumulates over time, unlike physical goods, which tend to have a limited supply. This characteristic is also sometimes known as non-depleting. There is only so much oil in the world. There is only so much arable land upon which to grow crops. Although we can replenish the trees we cut down and the world's water supply is annually recycled, in fact the amount available on an annual basis has limits. But knowledge simply accumulates. In fact, it might be said that even when we want it to die or go away it still has a life as, it appears, once it is digitized it is difficult—if not impossible—to have knowledge destroyed forever (Ebert, 2011; Rasmussen, 2012).

Half-life

It is interesting to contemplate that knowledge sometimes has a "half-life." That is, new knowledge that is being developed may have more value than older knowledge (Weinberger, 2011). What we know about the theory of knowledge, for example, is much more valuable today than when the theory began to be formed. New ideas or software on how to create a video are important and interesting to people, more so than older ideas. Nevertheless, new ideas are built on old ideas so the concept of cumulative knowledge is important here. For policy and historical researchers, older knowledge is critically important.

Mobile

Knowledge moves with people and also with the objects that embed the knowledge. Thus, it is hard to hold knowledge within companies or other entities. Human capital theory assumed that people were trained for a given job in a particular company and the value of that training was largely held by the company (Becker, 1964). Knowledge economics assumes, however, that humans carry that value of knowledge and they take this value into various aspects of their lives. Knowledge of how to access information from the web or social networks can be learned at home and applied on the job or can be used in one's social circles or civic participation.

Substitutable

Although knowledge is a virtual (digitized) good, it can, at times, replace the need for a physical good. Digital readers replace books and reduce the need for paper and the trees from which paper is produced. Digital music replaces records or magnetic tape. But other kinds of substitutions are noteworthy. New telecommunications reduce the need for travel in some cases. New fiber-optic cables carry substantially more communications than copper wire and are thus more efficient and reduce the demand of physical resources. All of these examples are a result of knowledge production.[1]

In some cases, knowledge can make an old system more efficient without requiring that a new physical system be put in place. Researchers in Australia developed data-encoding technology that increased the efficiency of existing fiber-optic cable networks. The efficiency increased so much that, they claim, the entire existing internet traffic could be encoded on a single optical fiber

(Quick, 2013). This new knowledge works on existing equipment, but that existing equipment is simply reprogrammed (new knowledge!).

Networked properties of knowledge

Because knowledge is networked, it also has characteristics that derive from the properties of networks sometimes combined with the lowering cost of technology and its accessibility. Some authors have begun to document these properties (Chan, 2001; Siemens, 2006).

Creates its own demand

Knowledge is increasingly easily available and accessible. As more and more people access it, they find they use it more casually, more often and for more purposes (Pew Research Internet Project, 2013). The search for new information increases and more people are willing and able to add new information to the internet. In the last 14 years, internet usage has gone up 5,000 percent in Africa, 3,000 percent in the Middle East and nearly doubled in North America (Miniwatts Marketing Group, 2014).

This contrasts with physical products (or services) where the more one has something the less likely one is to want more. If one has just purchased new jeans, one is less likely to want more jeans. If a city has just purchased a fleet of new buses, it is less likely to want more new buses. Thus, with physical products and services, demand recedes the more it is produced. But with knowledge, the more knowledge is accessible, the more new knowledge is sought.

Creates its own supply

Principally, the raw material for creating knowledge is, in fact, knowledge itself. So, when a piece of knowledge is created, it builds the supply for the next piece of knowledge to be created. In fact, when creating a piece of knowledge, both knowledge and *learning* are created. Individuals and teams learn how to create new knowledge. Teams create a dynamic of learning together. So not only the supply of knowledge increases, but *the ability to create* a new supply increases.

This contrasts with physical goods, which are composed of physical resources. Physical resources are either finite (such as oil or diamonds) or have a fragile renewable quality (such as trees or electricity). Even human labor can be thought of as having a fragile renewable quality as it can only expend so much energy in a given day or space.

Transferable

Any given piece of knowledge is easily moved from one place to another with little or no cost. Even if it is not available on the web, it can be moved around through electronic means at low cost because it is digitized. Most of the low cost is because our data system is networked and digitized. Contrast this with physical goods that must be physically transported: services require either that the service provider go to the new customer or the customer transport themselves to the service provider.

Accessible

The cost of getting knowledge to people is rapidly decreasing (Miller, 2013; Team Smartling, 2012). A characteristic of networks known as scale-free networks helps make knowledge accessible. Scale-free networks are structured in such a way that the links between any source of knowledge and the place on the web where one might begin the search is relatively short—it is not a long path (Watts, 2004). You do not have to go through the internet and click randomly, hoping you will chance upon the information. For example, if you are interested in a particular book, Amazon will not only give you the important information about the book, but will guide you to similar books and books that others who bought the book also bought. The structure of networks means that most information can be relatively easily found within a few clicks (links). Thus, knowledge increases in accessibility because of technology (growing networks of information) and because of the inherent properties of knowledge networks.

Collective

People tend to want to share knowledge and create new ideas together. This appears to be an inherent quality of human culture (Flinn, 1997; Norgaard, 2004). The networked characteristics of the web have afforded people the ability to expand this human quality across physical space. They now have the ability to build new virtual communities based on collective interests (Cortes *et al.*, 2002; Lesser *et al.*, n.d.; Wenger, 2000).

Again, a characteristic of networks assists here: because healthy networks tend to be self-regulating, they require little management cost to maintain. These virtual communities do not need a management structure—their participants can devote nearly all their time online to contributing, learning and creating. Networks also tend to evolve (are emergent) so that what is known and learned changes over time. Participation is continuously rewarded because new information, insights and ideas are generated.

Note

1   Of course, replacing old systems requires investments in new systems and there is still wastage, such as the growing amount of electronic waste (Greenpeace International, n.d.), so knowledge's substitutability does not mean that it has no cost to replace older, more resource-intensive systems.

References

Armstrong, A. and Hagel, J. (eds) (n.d.). The real value of online communities. In E. Lesser, M. Fontaine and J. Slusher, *Knowledge and Communities*. London: Routledge. Retrieved from http://proxy-net.snu.ac.kr/2b05b02/_Lib_Proxy_Url/books.google.co.kr/books/about/Knowledge_and_Communities.html?id=SySuAuY7VLQC

Becker, G. (1964). *Human capital: A theoretical and empirical analysis, with special reference to education*. Chicago, IL: University of Chicago Press.

Blakeley, N., Lewis, G. and Mills, D. (2005). *The economics of knowledge: What makes ideas special for economic growth?* (No. 05/05). Auckland, New Zealand. Retrieved from www.treasury.govt.nz/publications/research-policy/ppp/2005/05–05

Chan, S. (2001). *Complex adaptive systems*. ESD.83 Research seminar in engineering systems, MIT. Retrieved from http://web.mit.edu/esd.83/www/notebook/Complex%20Adaptive%20Systems.pdf

Cortes, C., Pregibon, D. and Volinsky, C. (2002). Communities of interest. *Intelligent Data Analysis*, *6*(3), 211–219.

Cortright, J. (2001). *New growth theory, technology and learning: A practitioner's guide* (No. 4). Washington, DC: US Economic Development Administration.

Ebert, J. D. (2011). *The New Media Invasion: Digital Technologies and the World They Unmake*. Jefferson, NC: Mcfarland.

Flinn, M. V. (1997). Culture and the evolution of social learning. *Evolution and Human Behavior*, *18*(1), 23–67.

Greenpeace International (n.d.). The e-waste problem. Retrieved from www.greenpeace.org/international/en/campaigns/toxics/electronics/the-e-waste-problem/

Miller, M. (2013, October 8). Tech giants turn focus to affordable internet access in developing countries. Retrieved from www.brandchannel.com/home/post/2013/10/08/Tech-Affordable-Internet-Access-100813.aspx

Miniwatts Marketing Group (2014). Internet world stats. Retrieved from www.internetworldstats.com/stats.htm

Mirowski, P. (2009). Why there is (as yet) no such thing as an economics of knowledge. In H. Kincaid and D. Ross, *The Oxford handbook of philosophy and economics* (pp. 99–156). Oxford: Oxford University Press.

Norgaard, R. B. (2004). Learning and knowing collectively. *Ecological Economics*, *49*(2), 231–241.

Pew Research Internet Project (2013, December 27). Mobile technology fact sheet. Retrieved from www.pewinternet.org/fact-sheets/mobile-technology-fact-sheet/

Quick, D. (2013, April 7). Closing the gap to improve the capacity of existing fiber optic networks. Retrieved from www.gizmag.com/cudos-fiber-optic-network-capacity/26969/

Rasmussen, K. V. (2012, November 8). Digital footprints. Retrieved from http://ccc.ku.dk/research/digital_footprints/

Romer, P. (1990). Endogenous technological change. *Journal of Political Economy*, 98(5), 71–102.

Sherman, R., Waterman, D. and Jeon, Y. (2014). The future of online video: An economic perspective. Presented at the Future of Broadband Regulation Workshop, Federal Communications Commission, Washington, DC: Institute for Information Policy. Retrieved from www.indiana.edu/~telecom/people/faculty/waterman/Thefutureofonlinevidefinal6-11-14.pdf

Siemens, G. (2006). *Knowing knowledge.* Creative commons licensing. Retrieved from www.elearnspace.org/KnowingKnowledge_LowRes.pdf

Skyrm.com. (n.d.). Characteristics of Knowledge. Retrieved from www.skyrme.com/kmbasics/kchars.htm

Team Smartling. (2012, May 31). Developing countries driving global internet growth. Retrieved from www.smartling.com/blog/2012/05/31/developing-countries-driving-global-internet-growth/

Tschmuck, P. (2010). *Creativity and innovation in the music industry.* Amsterdam: Springer. Retrieved from http://proxy-net.snu.ac.kr/7a056e7/_Lib_Proxy_Url/dl.acm.org/citation.cfm?id=1952024

Watts, D. J. (2004). The "new" science of networks. *Annual Review of Sociology, 30,* 243–270.

Weinberger, D. (2011). *Too big to know: Rethinking knowledge now that the facts aren't the facts, experts are everywhere, and the smartest person in the room is the room.* New York: Basic Books.

Wenger, E. (2000). Communities of practice and social learning systems. *Organization, 7*(2), 225–246.

8a The power of ideas

In order to understand how complex knowledge systems like Google and Lotus Notes inform us about Pima's education, we need to go back to the mid-1990s. In the early days of my international work in poor countries, one issue many of us faced was the possibility of needing an intravenous transfusion while on the road in a rural location. HIV was just beginning to be understood and no one wanted to get a recycled needle put in their arm. Major injuries could put us on an ambulance jet to South Africa, but to keep us alive until then, we might need a transfusion. If we caught an intestinal bug, we could dehydrate rapidly, so I, like many others, asked my doctor to give me my own needles to travel with—at least I'd have a sterile needle—and usually even remote hospitals had sterile saline fluids.

The problem could not be as easily solved by parents whose young children might dehydrate even faster than my adult body. If one lived more than an hour or two's walk to the nearest clinic, one's child could die of something as simple as food bacteria—something a good antibiotic could resolve symptoms of in a day. But help was on its way. Research done more than a decade earlier was paying off. Researchers discovered that water containing small amounts of sugar and salt were more easily absorbed by the intestine than plain water alone. By drinking clean water that had some sugar and salt mixed in, one could rehydrate pretty fast. It took some more research and then time to get to word out to rural areas, but pretty soon parents began to understand how to save their children's lives; they could hydrate them well enough to get them to a clinic for the antibiotics. Today, it is estimated that about a million lives a year are saved by this *knowledge*.

It is a simple piece of knowledge. You only have to have a rough idea of the right proportions of water, salt and sugar for it to be effective. It was very expensive to get this knowledge (no doubt, the research took some time and some testing), but once it was first known, it could be spread *free of charge* and used to improve the well-being of many a family and society. The knowledge was not created by a market, spread by a market nor bought within a market. It is just good information that needed financial backing that is improving the lives of vast numbers of families whose children are alive today. It is an idea with tremendous value—personal and collective.

How could an idea make so much difference be explained by an economic theory that says value is created through production and that production derives its value through markets?

A new theory emerges

For years, economists and other social scientists had problems with the notion that it was only markets and market growth that produced societal progress. With the whole world starting to build their economies, was it really sustainable for everyone to be on the path to growth? Weren't there real limits to total global growth? Weren't there costs to unconstrained growth such as pollution, ecological problems, political unrest and refugees? Further, some markets thrived when people and societies were under stress. War raised the market production of armaments and put soldiers to work—this raised market values, but could one really say that this was progress? And what of people who lived off their own land? If they had a good year due to rains (or not), since their produce was never sold in markets, the value of their well-being was never measured in national accounts of societal well-being.

But a new theory began to be formed in the 1990s and early 2000s. The theory said that it was the power of ideas—not industrial production—that caused societies to move forward. The idea of how to navigate ships by stars or the invention of penicillin or the experiment of a new form of government called democracy caused the rapid advancement of societies. Some of these new ideas turned into industrial production, some changed the ways societies organized themselves or people learned. But at the heart of these advancements were new ideas. The theory has had several names since it first took hold—"new growth theory," "knowledge economics," and its initial title "endogenous technological change" to name a few. It continues to evolve and develop, but its introduction has caused a revolution in the way people think about development, learning and societal well-being.

Pima's village could serve as an example. For years and years development agencies have been coming into Pima's village with great ideas for developing her village. They've brought lots of ideas. Maybe we can educate the women and teach them how to read. Maybe we can introduce a new kind of crop that has a better yield of rice. This time, there is a better idea of how to get children into school or organize the local school. Now there is a way to get the villagers to think about family planning or to vaccinate their children or to change the method of irrigatation or gathering firewood. Each time, the villagers listen. Sometimes, the ideas seem to have merit. But none of these ideas seems to work out the way they first were presented.

Sometimes, the original idea just doesn't work very well. Although the women were willing take evening classes for literacy, they were not willing to be tested at the end, so the project could not prove it was successful therefore did not get continuing funding. The new strain of rice required villages to change the timing of planting and harvesting; they didn't understand how to do that and also it did not fit with the rhythm of their other village work. Family planning did not conform to the power relationships between men and women. Anyway, no one actually understood all the seemingly complex rules that the outsiders always had for implementing these changes and the projects never had long lasting effects. The projects were only good for short-term resources.

Now imagine a different scenario. What if the villagers worked with Nepalese college students who were being trained in development and in networked systems? The students began to understand the needs of the villagers. Instead of importing solutions, they asked villagers what their immediate problems were. Then they began to build the networks that helped villagers build their own knowledge—links to NGOs, experts, resources, ideas and things that worked in other villages. Instead of importing solutions, they gave villages the tools to build knowledge collectives by building networks. Villagers can build their own ideas and innovations and design their own projects. All those wasted resources for failed projects can be turned into successes with many fewer resources because they now incorporate a powerful new resource—the thinking, creativity and integrated culture of the local communities.

This example is taken from a poor community but I could easily have used a wealthy community just as well. Korea is building learning communities to use the power of the whole spectrum of its people—young and old, rural and urban. All are regarded as necessary participants to improve the quality of life of the whole society.

New growth theory itself is now a subject of much writing and research. Few are trying to put it into mathematical formulations. Rather, the research is centered on trying to discover its basic tenets and the characteristics of knowledge. It has taken on many titles through this exploratory period—endogenous growth theory, new growth theory, economics of knowledge, innovation economics and learning economy. It appears in much of the work being done in the field of technology and, increasingly, it is integrated into work involving economic development. As it grows and develops, the older theories of competition and economic growth also continue to be researched.

The theory is based on two major tenets. First, it posits that a nation's ability to grow its economy is partly based on its ability to create and absorb new ideas (originally thought to be ideas about technological change). Second, it posits that ideas have specific economic characteristics that make them perform unlike other goods or services. The two tenets imply that the old formulations of economic growth needed to include *ideas* as an input to economic growth but also, once ideas were included, they would not operate under the old rules. In short, when Romer first proposed the new theory of endogenous growth in 1988, there was not an awareness that the theory would result in an entire rethinking of neoclassical economics. Such rethinking produced a backlash from critics that asserted its invalidity for the very reason that it did not fit neoclassical economic theory.

What could be the role of ideas that so disrupted economic science? When a society can produce something (like an idea) that becomes quite easy and cheap to reproduce (just put the idea on the internet, for example) and can be used widely by lots of people all at once, then the notion that our economic well-being is constrained by natural resources, our labor and our investment in things we build, necessarily, is challenged. Here is an economic good that never takes physical form and its use by one person does not preclude the benefits it can have for many people. The car you drove home today, the haircut you had yesterday, the vegetables you cooked for dinner tonight do not fit these characteristics. The production of a car, the shorter hair, and the vegetables you cooked are only produced one at a time—one car, one haircut, one bag of vegetables. You "consumed" the use of your car (for that period of time), the haircut and the vegetables. No one else could have it. But an idea, that is another type of thing.

While you drove home, you listened to the radio. While you waited for your haircut, you read a magazine. Before you cooked your vegetables, you found a recipe on the internet. All of these things are knowledge (they could be digitized) and they can be consumed by many people at the same time without taking away your benefit. Admittedly, knowledge, when it takes a non-digitized form of say, a book, can only be consumed by one person at a time. But, none-theless, because it can be digitized (an e-book or an audio book for example), it can be reproduced cheaply (sometimes at no cost) and spread throughout the world for thousands, perhaps millions to enjoy at the same time.

I live in Korea and listen daily to National Public Radio from the United States and the BBC from the UK via either an internet radio or a podcast. I read the Korean news through Google news and keep up on technology using podcasts and a particular website. Things are being digitized fast in this world. I haven't carried a set of keys for years—my home and office have digital keypads on which I enter a number. If I want to enter my building after hours, I use my finger to register on a lock for the outside door. If I want to catch a bus or subway or pay for a taxi, I hold my wallet up to an electronic reader, which records my payment information. My bank totals the charges up on a regular basis and debits my bank account. My entire financial picture—from my paycheck to my rent to my investments to my bank statements—exists only in digital form. My iPhone has more computing power than the computers used to put a man on the moon. My student records are all kept and archived digitally, as is my syllabus, assignments and this book now. When I need new software, it is transferred electronically from its source to my computers. All my phone calls and nearly all my mail are now electronic.

All of these forms of information are cheap to distribute. Although Romer's idea of technological change really involved the innovations that spur an economy, the basic tenet that knowledge had particular characteristics opens up the possibilities of thinking differently far beyond technological produc-tion. The value of technological change is not about modern electronic form of technology per se, it is Edison's idea of the telephone, Franklin's idea of electricity, the ocean-going ship, irrigation and crop rotation. All these ideas improved our world, all could be digitized (the ideas could be distributed through digitization if it had existed at the time) and all had profound effects on the progress of society.

It is worth exploring this rather interesting property that knowledge can be digitized. How could Bell's idea of a telephone possibly be classified as knowledge when the definition that we use under new growth theory for knowledge is its ability to be digitized? Bell lived before digitization and computers had been invented. We can use this definition because something that can be digitized is something that can be reproduced cheaply and spread widely with little cost. Although the idea of the telephone was not spread (at least initially) digitally, it had those characteristics. The idea of the telephone could benefit a lot of people all at the same time, and the idea cost virtually nothing to share. The telephone itself or the telephone system all cost something and could only be used by a restricted number of users, but the *idea* could be spread easily and cheaply.

Before the internet and computers, such revolutionary ideas (technological change) were spread through word of mouth, through textbooks, experts and seminars, and printed word. Before computers, we certainly benefited from ideas, even though the spread of the idea was a bit slower and required some physical form. We all benefit from the idea of vaccines, maps and pasteurization. Each can take on a physical form and many, to be sure, made someone a profit in producing that physical form. But the idea itself benefited a lot of people, was spread cheaply and added to society's progress.

The fact that is can be digitized is just a convenient way to think about it. What distinguishes the idea of a vaccine from the actual vaccine I get in the doctor's office? The idea can be spread throughout the world. Many places are looking for ways of creating quick vaccines to stop the spread of a world flu epidemic. The idea of a vaccine was free to them (although the original idea was terribly expensive to create). Their own vaccine will also be expensive to create but be freely available to the world. But the actual vaccine I get from my doctor has a physical form that I need to pay for.

The fact that ideas are sometimes very expensive to create but are, thereafter, often cheap to be used widely creates a particular conundrum for countries. How do we reward the investment of time, energy and thought that went into a new idea such as a vaccine, but still reap benefits from its widespread usage? Currently we award patents or copyrights to the inventors. This allows them to "own" the product of their invention and its use for a period of time. Thus, the benefits that might otherwise be relatively cheap to reproduce are sold at a cost for a period of time in order to pay back the cost of investment in the idea itself.

But, in actual fact, the idea becomes public property almost immediately. Simply copyrighting something or getting a patent on it, one must describe it in detail; the idea is documented, but the products that stem from the idea, are protected for a period of time. In effect, the idea must be digitized (stored in some form of an application, registry or documentation) before it can be protected. If something could, potentially, be digitized (even if it never was, never will be or was not in its original form), then it has the property of being able to be spread for low or no cost and also has the property that many people can have it (the idea) without taking it away from anyone else. It is this characteristic that has thrown the economics profession into disarray.

The power of ideas

Romer's introduction of the value of ideas was built on the existing definition of economic growth—that one could add up the value of various inputs (land, labor, capital) and calculate how these inputs created economic growth. He simply added another element—ideas. The very fact that ideas were called technological change seemed to imply that its value would register the same way other production had registered in economic growth—through improved industrial production. The notion that these ideas emanated from people caused him to speculate that people's education was the primary means of producing more and better ideas—human capital investment.

Let's put aside the legalities in considering the impact of ideas. Patents and copyrights are being rethought and reformulated and, in fact, becoming less relevant for some forms of knowledge production. It is the special economic characteristics of ideas that are causing the world to reconsider how economic growth occurs and how it changes societies. This special characteristic leads to some pretty fundamental questions. Can knowledge truly be owned? Is knowledge value created outside of the industrial production process? How does a group of people benefit from knowledge? Which country owns or benefits from or, indeed, produces any piece of knowledge? Does knowledge come from education or does education come from knowledge? Who are the learners, who are the teachers and who are the creators? Are mistakes knowledge? Is culture knowledge? And, perhaps most important, under what conditions do people turn their creative thinking power into knowledge that has value for their society?

Climate change is a global problem, but it is also local. If affects poor farmers in particular because their only source of food is what they can grow. They do not have monied jobs where they can buy the food that others grow. As the climate warms up, the Sahara desert expands and people find that both their arable fields and their tree coverage recede. In Niger, one farmer decided not to cut the small saplings in his field anymore, but rather to nurture them and to plant around them. The result was better retention of water in the soil, cooler fields where crops were not so exposed to high temperatures all day and a higher water table because the tree roots carried water deep into the soil where it increased the water supply. This success spread and many farmers are now adding trees to their fields with equal success. The areas where this is practiced stand in contrast to neighboring areas where the desert continues to grow.

This is an example of how local knowledge created an idea. That idea was free to be used by anyone. Collectively, the knowledge not only improved the lives of the farmers who practiced tree growing, but improved the lives of the broader society that benefits from increased food supply and receding desert.

The knowledge was spread by word of mouth initially, but eventually was known to the larger world. The *New York Times* (Polgreen, 2007) article demonstrates that it jumped into the digital world and is now relatively available to anyone. It is new knowledge, it can benefit a lot of people since it is cheap to spread and use of the knowledge doesn't preclude anyone else from benefiting (unlike, say, a hoe might). And, it is not market-based nor is profit involved.

In this case, the benefits are an increase in productivity in the usual sense. The benefits mean that the farmers and their families eat better and, possibly, can sell some produce in the local market. It is not counted in GDP growth, but it certainly improved the lives of the people involved and those around them. It is an idea that fits well into the new theory of knowledge.

This knowledge is an outgrowth of the impact of a global force (global warming) on a local situation. It is a local adaptation that increases society well-being. One can imagine that it might have far-reaching consequences. As world populations grow, the price of food is increasing. For those at the margins will be most affected as they buy their daily food. Those in an area where production is increasing—by, for example, planting trees among the crops—will not face the full impact of increasing food demand. In fact, they might benefit because any excess food they grow might be sold in local markets. One of the global issues in the rising cost of food is that people who cannot eat enough have little to lose. But this destabilizes societies. So, these simple Niger farmers are making a small (and growing) contribution to their own well-being, those of their neighbors and to global stability. Admittedly, their small part of the world is not the center of the destabilizing effects of food costs. But, like many problems that are globally linked and locally manifested, it is the local solutions that help mitigate the global issue.

Nearly two million people each year are now dying of AIDS. About 33 million are living with AIDS. Why? We know how to prevent its spread. We know how to test for it and get people treated. The reason is that each society, each village, has a different set of contexts concerning the spread of HIV. Sociologists generally know the lifestyles, medical communities and social pressures of the West and have worked within these parameters to mitigate the spread. Sterile needles, social work among at-risk populations, high school education programs are all designed around specific populations and groups that need information, treatment or prevention assistance.

But what of a society far away from the medical researchers and sociologists of the West? What about a society where a man is partly measured by his ability to have more children or a society where women cannot always choose their partner? For many societies the threat of a seemingly distant death through an invisible disease (through exposure to HIV for example) cannot compare with the immediate rewards of having a relationship with a man who promises food and a home for one's children. Sometimes condoms are only occasionally available and HIV drugs are expensive or only sporadically available. Is one to forego relationships that bind families and social ties altogether? Outsiders to these societies do not have the local information to work within the parameters of these societies.

Such a situation existed in parts of South Africa. Although the AIDS medications were free within the country, the requirement that they be taken virtually at the very same time each day did not always suit the social customs. People might have a sick child to care for and did not get to the clinic this week. Or they decided they would take the medications when they came home from working in the fields, but their work took them all day and they did not take the medications until nightfall. In such instances, the virus finds no counter to its spread and growth; the necessary drugs are not in the patient's system, so the virus grows rapidly. By the time the drug is taken, not only has it grown very rapidly, but the strongest versions of the virus have survived the previous drugs and so the new growth is particularly virulent. The sick person has not only lost substantial ground in containing the disease, but his or her community is potentially exposed to a more virulent strain of the virus.

Facing this prospect, local villagers were employed as local health care workers by the South African health system. Their job was to go to the patient's house each day at the prescribed time and personally hand them the drug to take. This set of procedures solved many problems of supply, regularity of taking the drug and monitoring the drug usage. Thus, the local health care worker had a steady supply of the drug as part of his or her job and the patient took the drug consistently and within the right time period. It took local knowledge of a particular community to design this intervention but, once it was designed, it could be used in any community with similar practices. A globally linked problem (the spread of AIDs) required local innovations.

The current model for such communities is to send an expensive and highly trained anthropologist, social worker or sociologist into the area to try to find a local solution. Increasingly, these professionals can be found among the people in question. They speak the local language, grew up in a similar community and understand the practices. Regardless, the criteria are clear: understanding of modern medical practices, education in virus growth and spread, ability to manage the supply and transport of the drug, careful record-keeping and knowledge of local situations. If one person alone does not have this knowledge, then it takes several people comparing notes to put the information together.

In this example, the knowledge that highly benefited the individual, his or her society and, clearly, the larger world where HIV is a global problem, was not knowledge sold on a market. It did not get developed within a profit-making company. It is knowledge that improves hundreds, thousands and perhaps millions of lives and, by extension, reduces health-care expenditure locally and in New York and Singapore where the boyfriend of the village's university student lives, works or has traveled. It is actual economic value in all the definitions of economic value, but it is not produced, consumed or even distributed by industry. It was borne, spread and used within the civic and social sectors of many communities and countries.

Utilizing knowledge for development

In the Lotus Notes example, one of the primary values of the team was that it could apply its knowledge within a specific situation—that of a globally linked, information-intensive situation. If one is living in the actual situation, one's professional expertise can be aligned with one's life or situation and made relevant. The Lotus Notes team knew that people would want to collaborate globally without always having to meet physically. So, they designed a system that did not require much physical presence. They designed it and tested it within their own work environment. They minimized the need for their own team to meet, to have physical (paper) records, to have a secretary who scheduled things and coordinated calendars and resources. By using the very thing they were creating, they brought both their professional skills to the project, but also their understanding of a virtual office environment.

In the examples given above of growing trees in the Sahel at the edge of the Sahara desert or hiring community workers to distribute AIDS drugs, local knowledge is used in a specific situation for a specific group. In one case the knowledge was built locally, in another it was built using both global understandings (about the timing of taking anti-virus drugs) and local knowledge (structure of work life within the communities). In either case, the ability of a local solution to have global impacts depends upon linking the logic all the way from the local situations (farm field, busy village worker) to the technical implications to the global problem. If any one of these links is missing, valuable knowledge is not put to use beyond a local situation or never reaches the local community.

Today's current models of development require that the knowledge be made by a global expert. The AIDS expert already knows the extent of the global situation, understands its basic epidemiological characteristics, and understands how the timing of drug taking is critical. The challenge would be to learn how the local community works. This takes a lot of time; it often means putting the expert within the community, which might mean expensive housing or transportation costs (as was the case with me heading a multi-million dollar project in Zambia). It also means that the expert may understand one aspect of the local situation, but without understanding the larger social system comprehensively a seemingly good solution might fail.

The power of ideas clearly has enormous value. But it is these linkages that are expensive. The idea itself might be expensive, but to use it beyond the particular situation in which it was invented, those local—technical—global links must be built. As local communities begin to spawn their own educated young people, this linkage is a little easier to make. Bringing possible solutions into a community is one way to do this; this is the way that most development projects work. The solution is posited, the local community is involved in managing the solution and the project is implemented.

As the world gets increasingly linked through health, environment, economy, education, social structures and political stability, building the local-technical-global links will become increasingly important to mitigating the spread of global problems or expanding the spread of global possibilities. A new way to tackle these issues might be to expand the capacity of local communities to build their networks outwards. There are millions of local communities and local groups. If each one had a means of growing its network outwards to the larger world, then they become true partners—not just recipients—in building knowledge that is locally relevant, globally linked and, perhaps, globally important.

Although it has been known for years that local knowledge has global value, such knowledge has often been viewed in isolation. It is the knowledge about local herbs or medical treatments or even agricultural techniques that can be adapted within a global framework. Since intelligence is relatively evenly spread throughout the world, one can be sure there are some highly intelligent people in local communities and they, like intelligent people worldwide, are creative within their own environment. By capturing local knowledge, one is capturing the brainpower of thousands and millions of intelligent people who are using their brains to find local solutions. Sometimes those local solutions have global value.

It is important to get local knowledge into global circulation. A way to tap into the potential value of local knowledge is to work with communities to help them learn how to adapt to a situation that, without their active brain-power, may otherwise have marginalized them still further or even destroyed the village. The examples of tree growing in the Sahel and of AIDS medication distribution in South Africa are examples of stresses caused by globalization, impacting the viability of a local community, and the use of local knowledge and local *learning* to find a solution. In doing so, not only does the community gain an adaptive new method of survival, it also increases their ability to adapt to the next global impact. They have learned to integrate global situations into their local context and this learning can be applied to the next challenge. Further, the global community has learned how to mitigate a global problem through local knowledge and its researchers are also better equipped to deal with the next community or next global threat.

This type of knowledge is not the indigenous knowledge of age-old local remedies for arthritis (valuable as this knowledge may be). Rather, it is using the power of local intelligence, the wisdom of knowing local conditions and contexts and the *learning* ability of a community to change and adapt. It is a dynamic interface with a global world. By growing this dynamic global interface, we equip all communities to face global problems, to grow and to build their own strength and direct their own future. But, before that can even be considered, we'll have to go back and completely redefine what we understand to be education.

Reference

Polgreen, L. (2007, February 11). In Niger, trees and crops turn back the desert. *New York Times*. Retrieved from www.nytimes.com/2007/02/11/world/africa/11niger. html

8b New growth theory

The theory of knowledge economics started out innocently enough. Paul Romer is usually credited with introducing it in the early 1990s and it continues to evolve and mature as theorists work to define its many aspects and components. But, in fact, it has many aspects. Although it likely retains a core economic base, it now links to many areas and links to theories in many fields. As with many new theories that challenge established views, the theory had a shaky beginning (Kuhn, 1970). But its inherent strength in explaining the value created by the resource of knowledge has caused the theory to grow and expand (Warsh, 2007).

The theory

In 1988, Paul Romer addressed a conference of the World Bank and proposed a modification to the standard existing theory of economic growth. The existing theory included the contribution of land (natural resources, ports, etc.), labor and capital (anything for which an investment was required, such as a building or machinery). He suggested that the ability of a nation to grow its economy depended, in part, on its ability to generate new ideas. So, he added "ideas" to land, labor and capital as part of the development equation.

The notion that ideas lead the development of societies did not appear revolutionary at first. After all, most industrial products begin with an idea. What was unique in adding ideas (knowledge) was it had two particular characteristics —non-rivalry and decreasing returns to scale. Because it was cheaper to produce (replicate) each time one wanted another copy, it was substantially different than either physical goods or services.

This was only the beginning. As the theory evolved, people would begin to ask how knowledge was actually created, distributed and shared as a resource. The mathematics and systems theory of networks would begin to be applied. This new work would reveal that the value of new knowledge affects sectors beyond the private markets. Social networks changed governments, civic life, social structures and leisure and enjoyment. Societies began to notice that civil society participation, disaster management, social networks, gaming, entertainment and travel were all widely enhanced by the spread of knowledge, even when such knowledge does not make a profit or go through markets.

The theory began as a theory about economic growth and was immediately applied to the development of poor countries. Within a couple of years of Romer's initial articulation of the idea, he was invited to speak at a prestigious World Bank conference and talk about the concept's implications for development (Romer, 1993). This changed the thinking on how countries might pursue development because the old thinking was that all countries needed to go through a period of industrialization and gradually increase their human capital quality—raising the "value added" they could bring to industrial production. The new thinking is that countries may well be able to "leap forward" into a new development phase without first going through industrialization (Barron, 2006; Heeks, 2010). As the former World Bank Chief Economist puts it, "There are well understood limits to the pace with which countries can accumulate capital, but the limitations on the speed with which the gap in knowledge can be closed are less clear" (Stiglitz, 2011, p. 231). Today, this thinking is evolving into a new approach to development known as "development 2.0" (Heeks, 2010; Thompson, 2008).

Evolving theory

Although the theory began, as most new theories do, as a simple modification or addition to an existing theory, it quickly began to develop elements that strayed, substantially, from neoclassical economics. It became apparent fairly quickly that it was the *dynamics* of knowledge rather than the *accumulation* of knowledge that created momentum forward for communities and societies. Because already existing knowledge is "cheap" (increasingly able to be accessed), there is little value in mastering it. New knowledge (ideas) helps solve problems and creates new opportunities (albeit often built on existing knowledge). This involves learning (Lundvall & Johnson, 1994).

Of all the learning, the one most valued is the ability to solve complex problems or create opportunities from complex systems. Complex knowledge is constructed from many people—each with something to contribute. As network theory began to evolve into social network theory, researchers began to understand the power of how knowledge became ideas and how people became empowered to participate in the building and spreading of ideas. No longer was it possible to conceive of knowledge as something belonging to the individual (Downes, 2010; Lesser *et al.*, 2000). The theory began to move outside of the economics field and began to link with other fields such as networks, ICT, communication, education and sociology. The thread that held all these together was the notion that the world was increasingly linked. A complex system linked the world, technology was a part of this link and knowledge was becoming a fundamental source of value (Christakis & Fowler, 2009; Shirky, 2009; Weinberger, 2011; Wellman & Rainie, 2014).

The theory no longer fits within neoclassical economics. Mirowski's brilliant and comprehensive chapter did a good job of summarizing the early challenges to neoclassical theory. The various explanations of how knowledge worked within neoclassical economics could not proceed without threatening the entire neoclassical paradigm:

> Everyone seems to believe that knowledge is the key to economic success, and yet our most-developed schools of economic thought are mired in the most frightful muddles when it comes to modeling knowledge in an economic setting
>
> (Mirowski, 2009, p. 144)

The challenge to neoclassical economics was recognized early on and the theory made little progress at first. Most critics identified how the theory could not be tested using the existing mathematical models (Temple, 1999). In this vein, it developed much like quantum physics—an initial excitement, then downplayed because its basic tenets contradicted those of standard theory. Later it began to re-emerge when the theory itself explained so much of what was happening in the world (Warsh, 2007). It has since emerged from these dark days to gain slow legitimacy. A course on the theory is now offered at the World Bank ("Pathways to Growth," 2011).

Through this history, the actual term used for the theory has not stabilized. The original term used by Romer was "Endogenous Technological Change," but this title was not carried forward for very long. "The Growth Theory," is the term more widely adopted (Cortright, 2001; Temple, 1999). Commonly, "Knowledge Economy" (Chichilnisky, 1998; Peters *et al.*, 2013) and "knowledge economics" (Blakeley *et al.*, 2005; Mirowski, 2009) are sometimes used interchangeably although, technically, one is about how the economy works and one examines the characteristics of knowledge as a resource. More recently, the "Creative Economy" has been used because creative, new ideas are thought to drive the dynamics of the society (Howkins, 2002; UNCTAD, 2010).

References

Araya, D. and Peters, M. (eds). (2010). *Education in the creative economy: knowledge and learning in the age of innovation*. New York: Peter Lang International.

Barron, B. (2006). Interest and self-sustained learning as catalysts of development: A learning ecology perspective. *Human Development, 49*(4), 193–224.

Blakeley, N., Lewis, G. and Mills, D. (2005). *The economics of knowledge: What makes ideas special for economic growth?* (No. 05/05). Aukland, New Zealand. Retrieved from www.treasury.govt.nz/publications/research-policy/ppp/2005/05–05

Chichilnisky, G. (1998). The knowledge revolution. *The Journal of International Trade & Economic Development, 7*(1), 39–54.

Christakis, N. and Fowler, J. (2009). *Our social networks and how they shape our lives*. New York: Little, Brown.

Cortright, J. (2001). *New growth theory, technology and learning: A practitioner's guide* (No. 4). Washington, DC: US Economic Development Administration.

Downes, S. (2010). Learning networks and connective knowledge. In H. Yang and S. Yuen (eds), *Collective intelligence and e-learning 2.0: Implications of web-based communities and networking* (pp. 1–26). Hershey, PA: Information Science.

Gibson, D. and Heiton, M. (eds). (2005). *Learning and knowledge for the network society.* Lafayette, IN: Purdue University Press.

Heeks, R. (2010). Development 2.0: the IT-enabled transformation of international development. *Communications of the ACM, 53*(4), 22.

Howkins, J. (2002). *The creative economy: How people make money from ideas.* London: Penguin UK.

Kuhn, T. S. (1970). *The structure of scientific revolutions.* Chicago, IL: University of Chicago Press.

Lesser, E., Fontaine, M. and Slusher, J. (eds). (2000). *Knowledge and communities (Resources for the knowledge-based economy.* Woburn, MA: Butterworth Heinemann.

Lundvall, B.-Å. (ed.) (2010). *National systems of innovation: Toward a theory of innovation and interactive learning.* London: Anthem Press.

Lundvall, B.-Å. and Johnson, B. (1994). The learning economy. *Industry and Innovation, 1*(2), 23–42.

Mirowski, P. (2009). Why there is (as yet) no such thing as an economics of knowledge. In H. Kincaid and D. Ross, *The Oxford handbook of philosophy and economics* (pp. 99–156). Oxford: Oxford University Press.

Pathways to Growth. (2011). Retrieved from http://einstitute.worldbank.org/ei/course/pathways-growth

Peters, M., Besley, T. and Araya, D. (eds). (2013). *The new development paradigm: Education, knowledge economy and digital futures.* New York: Peter Lang International.

Romer, P. (1993). Two strategies for economic development: using ideas and producing ideas. In L. Summers and S. Shekhar (eds), *Proceedings of the World Bank annual conference on development economics 1992* (pp. 63–92). Washington, DC: World Bank. Retrieved from http://documents.worldbank.org/curated/en/1993/03/699081/proceedings-world-bank-annual-conference-development-economics-1992

Shirky, C. (2009). *Here comes everybody: The power of organizing without organizations.* Harmondsworth: Penguin Books.

Stiglitz, J. (2011). Rethinking development economics. *The World Bank Research Observer, 26*(2), 230–236.

Tapscott, D. and Williams, A. (2012). *Macrowikinomics: New solutions for a connected planet.* New York: Penguin Random House.

Temple, J. (1999). The new growth evidence. *Journal of Economic Literature, 37*(1), 112–156.

Thompson, M. (2008). ICT and development studies: Towards development 2.0. *Journal of International Development, 20*(6), 821–835.

UNCTAD. (2010). *Creative economy: A feasible development option, 2010.* New York: United Nations Conference on Trade and Development. Retrieved from http://unctad.org/SearchCenter/Pages/Results.aspx?k=creative%20economy

Warsh, D. (2007). *Knowledge and the wealth of nations: A story of economic discovery.* New York: W. W. Norton.

Weinberger, D. (2011). *Too big to know: Rethinking knowledge now that the facts aren't the facts, experts are everywhere, and the smartest person in the room is the room.* New York: Basic Books.

Wellman, B. and Rainie, L. (2014). *Networked: The new social operating system.* Cambridge, MA: MIT Press.

9a The social value of learning

We have a picture of education. It is a picture of a small boy, leaning over a desk, pencil in hand, studying a book and writing on a sheet of paper. We have a picture of children looking at a teacher who is pointing at a blackboard with a math problem. We have a picture of teenagers with enormous backpacks stuffed with textbooks, heading off to study their homework together. We can imagine schooling in inner-city neighborhoods where children need to be checked for weapons before entering the schools and discipline is a problem in classrooms. I've even been to schools in rural Uganda made out of mud and straw and the youngest children sat outside on benches under a big tree with a large blackboard propped up against a tree. I've seen children in West Bank refugee schools, all bundled up in layers and layers of clothing against the cold weather just outside the cement walls because there is no heat in the bare classrooms. But we can all imagine these as schools because they all have some basic elements of schooling. They all have children. The size of the classroom is about the size where a teacher can be heard. The children face forward to hear a teacher. They listen and write things down according to instruction. The teacher is imparting information and the children are trying to learn that information. In the best of worlds there is a classroom, but if there is not a classroom, there is a space that is similar to a classroom in size and organization. This is what education is. But it does not take too much to get us to extend our picture of education to other realms.

What of the mother, just having gotten her last child off to grade school, who is taking a class on pottery making? What of the new employee who is taking a class that teaches him how to manage basic operations within a glass factory? Is education also the online class that the mother decides to take to learn a new language? Is education also the online class that the employee takes to learn to handle customer complaints? This may not be formal schooling as it is usually defined, but certainly it is education.

What of the informal class the veterinarian offers to teach one how to handle a new puppy? What of the video that teaches one how to do yoga? If these were handled in a more formal, collective way, we might call them education. So, maybe they are education. So, too, then is the website you just accessed that told you about your new puppy or how to do some yoga. It is informal, maybe spontaneous, but you learned and there was a source of knowledge, so—in a broad sense—it is education.

Education as a collective activity

But what of collective learning? Is it education? I live in a city of 12 million people (Seoul). When I first arrived at my apartment complex I encountered a covered area where my garbage needed to be deposited, and in that area there are no fewer than ten containers for various types of garbage—glass, aluminum, other metal, food waste, paper, etc. Each, fortunately, was labeled in both English and Korean. I marveled at Korean efficiency and the expectation that each resident would do his or her part to ensure that garbage could be handled properly in a densely populated area. In all the years I've lived here, I have never seen a piece of garbage out of place. Even the garbage bins in the university require you to sort garbage into various types—bottles, cans and all others, for example.

What is amazing is not that people can sort their garbage—this is a kind of learning, but a simple one—what is amazing is that 12 million people do so regularly and consistently. It is a collective belief that sorting garbage benefits all, and requires each person's efforts. This would not be the case if citizens had a different belief—that garbage is not a problem. Nor is it a case of blindly following rules. These same people go through red lights regularly in front of my apartment. But, as people view compliance as in their collective interests, they willingly follow the rules. This is a kind of collective belief that comes from the fairly recent construction of collective knowledge. That is, most people have an understanding that garbage could be a problem and they are helping manage it through sorting their garbage. This collective knowledge is turned into action by the individuals and by the city that recycles these wastes. A kind of education or collective knowledge-building has taken place—an understanding, shared by many, that results in collective action.

Simple as this may sound, this form of collective knowledge-building has powerful consequences. We actually see this so often, that we forget the human capacity to learn collectively and take action. Tunisians rebel against their dictatorial government and Egyptians get an idea of how to do so themselves. We hear about an approaching hurricane, we go to the store and buy supplies and bring our outdoor furniture inside. Our workplace unplugs all the computers and closes its doors. The hardware store has anticipated this and stocked up with batteries and plywood.

Culture, in a sense, is collective knowledge. Christian culture believes in absolute rights and wrongs, generally, and each policy move by the government is debated as if there were, inherently, an absoluteness about it being good or bad. But, in much of the East, influenced by Buddhism, balance is the goal. People believe that policies must find the right balance—no one policy has all the answers, right or wrong. In Korean culture, gifts are frequently given to those higher up the social hierarchy then oneself—teachers, bosses, honored guests. But, in Western culture, gifts are more likely to be given to those lower in the social order—secretaries, the postman or the woman who does your hair. These are learned collective behaviors that reflect collective values.

A living, healthy culture adapts. Koreans have learned the value of recycling. No doubt, it was not too long ago when garbage was collected and dumped in a common place without the thought of recycling. We buy low-energy light bulbs not because they save us a lot of money (it is expensive to replace our cheap, older light bulbs) but because we feel that this minor expense contributes, in some small way, to a healthier environment. We complete the census form or vote, not because our individual lives are improved through this singular act, but because our collective lives are improved through our collective action.

So, how do cultures, communities and groups learn and adapt? Many anthropologists ask these questions and it is fascinating to read the individual stories. I remember studying the cultures of Micronesia. I read an entire book on how these Chuukese navigators learned to navigate their small sailing canoes through weeks of open ocean travel to find a particular island. They learned about the currents that were created as the ocean passed by particular collections of islands. These currents told them where they were in the open ocean. I read how they passed this information on to younger people. The islands were so small and fragile in Micronesia, they required a lifeline to other islands, and the development of the ability to navigate to these distant islands was necessary for the survival of the peoples.

But today's world is not so clean and clear. There are virtually no peoples who are unaffected by outside forces. Essentially, no group or community or culture lives alone. If nothing else, the global waves of disease, transportation, tourism and climate change reach them, even if their village is far from the nearest city. So, the question now is not how Micronesians learned to build a sustainable way of life, but, rather, how they survive given that their once relatively isolated way of life must now adapt to a connected world. The survival of their culture depends upon this adaptation, but the larger world also depends upon their successful inclusion. To think otherwise is to accept a growing body of marginalized, drugged and alcoholic population who cling to seemingly fundamentalist views of what they could have been if the world left them alone.

Understanding of how groups, communities and cultures learn and adapt is no longer the work of anthropologists studying the past, but of many professionals combining their knowledge to study the future. This need is joined by an allied need to study collective learning. Global problems and opportunities are complex systems; that is, they are composed of many parts, intricately linked, which change individually in such a way that the entire system adapts and changes. The internet is an obvious example of a complex system. Each person who uses the internet changes its nature because their linkages cause others to change their behavior. My use of Google—along with millions of others—causes it to change its nature which, in turn, changes my behavior and that of millions of others when we are on the internet.

All the global systems are complex systems—the world economy, transportation systems, terrorist networks, disease spread, Twitter, climate change and social movements. These global systems affect the well-being of everyone on the earth, yet their behavior is often unregulated and, indeed, not well known. We know that we can, indeed, affect such systems. The virus scanner on my computer keeps one complex global system out of my machine and keeps me typing away—the global system of computer viruses. We know that global economic systems can fail together—witness the recession of 2007—and also work positively together—witness the collective action to save Greece's economy.

Many of the most fundamental of human needs, threats, opportunities and possibilities are now bound up in global systems that can work together for collective good but also, like all complex systems, can collapse together and bring untold global destruction. System theorists, network researchers and complexity experts are studying the ways in which such systems change and respond. But the question that remains largely untouched is how collectives learn. We know how a system pushes individual elements to change, but we do not know how understandings cause collective action.

So, we go back to the original question asked in this chapter: What is education? We do not necessarily know what it is. We know that it is schooling. We believe it is something adults can do outside of schooling. We accept that it can sometimes be something done informally and, possibly, spontaneously. Now we need to begin to understand how collectives of people learn, adapt and change. What is collective learning? The answer not only provides a path to sustain diverse cultural differences from which the human race can build its strength but also tells us how to study complex issues.

The economics of learning

The odd characteristic of this kind of learning is that it exists largely outside of economic productivity. The usual understanding that economic growth is garnered through increased productivity does not stand here. Yet this kind of collective knowledge-building and collective learning vastly affects societal well-being. No one wants to earn hundreds of thousands of dollars through highly educated labor and lose one's life through the spread of a world flu epidemic or discover that rising sea levels are destroying the coastal city one grew up in or find that the banking system just collapsed due to unbridled global financial activity. Social well-being is increasingly defined by collective behavior outside the industrial sector than by individual investment in educated labor.

That people learn collectively is a given—it is the very definition of culture. It is also the reason why cultures can adapt to modern lifestyles and why we tolerate airport security screening, vote out bad politicians and get our children vaccinated. To a certain extent, such collective learning can be managed through a healthy, vibrant media and a lot of people who are educated enough to access that media and to talk with each other and build a kind of consensus. But this kind of learning through media is tenuous in some cases. First, it does not help us know how to bring marginalized populations into healthy, adaptive behavior that allows for their survival. After all, it is their very marginalization that renders this media flow ineffective. Second, it does not help us solve some complex problems to which there does not exist a media-ready solution. Once likely solutions are proposed, media can spread the possibilities. But the solutions must first be devised.

For example, many rural dwellers, part of the reason why they cannot sell their extra produce to markets is because they are the victims of middle men. This might well be the case in Pima's village. Even during a good year when extra rice is grown, they can only sell their extra rice to one buyer—the man who shows up at the end of the year with a truck to buy their rice. They must accept the price he offers them. They might know that the price is unfair, but they lack the transportation to get their rice to another buyer, so they have a choice in selling to this one buyer or not selling it at all. But give them a cell phone and they can call friends in the town and ask them to investigate the current reasonable market price for rice. This, then, gives them the power to negotiate, by phone, with many potential buyers. They can then join forces with other farmers in nearby towns to sell their rice at a good price and have buyers compete. The advantage they have here is not so much transportation, but knowledge. The knowledge is collective in nature—being able to pool knowledge from several sources (buyers) at once. As they learn to do this, they may learn to make deals ahead of time or learn to grow certain kinds of rice over other kinds to maximize their incomes at the end of the season. Why doesn't this basic impact of learning come into the development picture?

A major reason is that development is counted by measures of GDP rather than the dynamic of learning. Here's a stark example: I have made several trips to Malawi—one of the poorest African nations. As the economist on the team, I always try to read ahead about the economy of the country, its industry, its public financial condition and the lives of its people. So, before going to Malawi one year, I read up on the country: it was considered the second poorest country in the world that year and, to add to its troubles, was also experiencing a severe drought with a million Malawians likely to die as a result.

When I was in the country this situation was apparent. Riding along the north–south highway, past villages, I could see the condition of the people. They were in rags, walking slowly up and down the roadway, often lethargic. Fields were barren and grass huts in disrepair: these are the conditions of a people who are not well. They are struggling; even maintaining what they do has become a problem. The following year, I returned on another job and found a very different scene. That year, the rains had been plentiful and fields were green and abundant with crops. People had energy as they moved and some of the most tattered clothing had been replaced. Clearly, people were eating and had something extra to spend.

But my studies on the country revealed that the measure of well-being for the country had not changed at all. The standard measure—that of GDP (value of all goods and services produced in the country) divided by the population—had hardly moved at all. The reason is that GDP is a measure of all goods and services that go to market—that are bought and sold in a countable way.

It doesn't include the value of the food we grow in our gardens and then consume. It does not include the value of the labor of the woman who cooks food over the fire (or in the state-of-the-art kitchen) nor of the labor of the boy who tends the family's herd of cows. It only counts the dress you just made if you sold it to a store, which then sold it to a client and reported the sale to the government. If you made it and wore it yourself, it doesn't count. It only counts the oil change to your car if you had the local garage do the job, but doesn't count it if your teenage daughter does it herself (when only the cost of the oil is counted). In short, it does not count the labor of most households, whether incidental or sustaining.

This is clearly inaccurate, but it is more than inaccurate. The inaccuracy is actually destructive of development. If learning is a necessary function of a stable, progressive world, then pockets of poverty must be known and understood. To have people like Pima and her parents not part of a world that can participate in working together to fight global problems—such as warming, disease, famine, bad governance and terrorism—is a real cost. To not have them create clever solutions to join markets, invent ways to improve health care or reform their governments means the burden falls on all the rest of us: the world also cannot use their creativity. And, when the measure of social progress is GDP per capita and it simply cannot measure the difference between when Pima's family is starving or eating, then it cannot possibly be a measure of whether the world is progressing or not. It does not begin to measure the learning that is at the base of human progress and social well-being.

In countries where a lot of people live off the land, it is a mighty poor measure of national production and, in turn, a poor measure of national well-being. In fact, this generally accepted yardstick of how a country is faring could not measure the welfare of a million Malawians that faced death due to starvation. As far as the world's yardstick for well-being was concerned, one year looked very much the same as another year in Malawi—starving population or not.

No one would argue that the yardstick (GDP per capita) is a fair measure of well-being in such an instance. Rather, the argument might be made that it is the best overall, global measure we have of wealth production (value of all goods and service produced) and that wealth production, spread across the population (divided by the total population) was the best measure we have on an international scale. Equally, vast differences in wealth—for example, in modern India—do not register with this measure. If the educated class is living a stable, consumption-oriented life and the poorest still face starvation daily, the GDP per capita will register gains when those gains improve only the lives of those at the top—those who already were living in market economies.

Economists have known these problems with the data for a long time. In some sense it can be justified on technical grounds: GDP is simply a measure of all goods and services produced in the country *that go to market*. It is, to be fair, a good measure of this production, narrowly defined. It is the use of this value to measure well-being that is problematic. To be sure, it does measure changes in the value of formal production so that, as a country industrializes, for example, the measure rises. But it certainly misses the mark when there are lots of people living in an informal or non-monetary economy or in situations where the broad spread of people cannot benefit from these gains.

That aside, let's look at another problem with GDP per capita as a measure of national well-being. Let's look at me—the one typing on my laptop at 6:00 in the morning as the sun tries to get a start on the day in Seoul, South Korea. I was hired to teach in Korea's top university when the country was first making a move to internationalize their universities. The notion was that, by bringing in international professors, they would raise the caliber of training of their young professionals. Let's say that some lecture I give inspires one of my very bright students. He begins to envision his future. When he graduates, he builds a new enterprise that grows to global proportions and is soon gaining value throughout the world.

How is this counted in the country's wealth? To be sure, the employment of Koreans from this new knowledge enterprise is a gain to the country and their employment is counted. But what about the value of the idea that the student had? After all, it was the idea that created all the growth. It was the value of knowledge. It was, possibly, *my* knowledge that created the impetus for *his* knowledge that created the impetus for the knowledge company to make money from the knowledge of the global audience (as with the Google example). How do we count knowledge value? We would have to agree that if I had not given that lecture (or series of lectures, or mentored the student through his degree), the value would not have been created.

If I had given the lecture in the United States, would the same idea have resulted? If someone else had given a similar lecture, would the idea have germinated? If ideas create tremendous value (remember Lotus Notes, Amazon, Google, Einstein?), then how is that value captured? Let's first try to say that we could capture this value, then to which country do we attribute this value creation? The United States, where I am a citizen and was educated? Korea, because I work for it now and/or the student is a citizen? Possibly, we should spread some of this value to the 20 countries I've worked in or to Hawaii, which first inspired my desire to understand that nexus of culture, education and economics. Or, possibly, if the knowledge company is like Google, we have to attribute it proportionately to the users who supply the knowledge that makes it run. Since it is very difficult to understand where ideas come from and what makes one idea create value and another fail, we face even tougher problems in deciding who "owns" the value of knowledge. In this case, even if you could determine "ownership" and some of that belonged to me, you would have a difficult time deciding which country to award its productivity to.

But let's say you could determine ownership and could determine nationality (a very big assumption). How would you count it? Is the professor who regularly inspires creativity and innovation more valuable than the one everyone avoids taking classes from because the classes are boring? The answer has to be "yes." Korea will benefit more from inspiring, creativity-building professors than those who do not inspire and get students working well. But the only means we currently have of assessing their value is the amount we pay them. So, the value of different professors is not captured in their salaries. We might capture their former experience, research or even teaching skills, but we don't capture a central component of their ability to contribute to Korean innovation.

And so, global companies thrive on their knowledge production, but we can only capture the value of wages in GDP. In the Lotus Notes example, we can only count the brilliant output of the five engineers by counting their wages, but, we can also capture the value of the products they produced on the market—how many copies of Lotus Notes the parent company was able to produce. But, in Google's case, we cannot count the value—or millions of users worldwide—of a smart search engine that increases in value each time we use it (because, we learn from it and it learns from us). If we could, we would have to add up the value to each user worldwide and distribute it proportionally throughout the world. But we would also have to include in its costs the value of the learning it also receives from users.

And, where is the value of rehydration formulas captured? Or the value of trees planted in a field in an arid land? Or the value of Bell's idea of a phone? Or the value of Wikipedia? GDP per capita is failing us. It never did a good job of measuring the well-being of people who live largely outside the formal economy or the well-being of people who live in a highly inequitable land. Now, it cannot even do a good job of capturing value creation at the very top of the production ladder—within the knowledge industry. Nations zoom ahead or fall behind and we have no way to measure their relative gains or losses.

I started this section by asking what education is in a modern world and said that we would first have to revisit economics. The link can be most easily revealed through recent work by the OECD. It is a Paris-based organization that sets the numerical standards by which the world's wealthiest countries count their production and other national statistics. Countries actually become members of the OECD by applying and meeting particular standards. There are standards of how member countries' economies are structured, how they trade, and how much of their national income they must spend on foreign aid for poorer countries. As such, it is a powerful organization that is often looked to for pointing the way to new economic trends and to count these new trends effectively and reliably.

In 2009, the OECD had a major world conference on the measurement of national well-being (OECD, 2009). It built on work it had been conducting for the previous three years. The major papers that were presented or that served as background to the conference stated that the old measure of GDP per capita was no longer (maybe never was) an adequate measure of national well-being. It did not even measure national wealth. Since it had never been a good measure of either the poorest or most inequable of countries, one might assume that it was the failed challenge of adequately measuring the value of knowledge that finally brought about the OECD's impetus to change the measure of national well-being.

The problem of knowledge ownership, value and measurement is not likely to go away. The European Union, the OECD and numerous economists worldwide have been pursuing this goal for some time, only to conclude that no measure is truly adequate. There are valiant attempts to attribute a portion of production value in some industries to knowledge, but it is clear that the true value of knowledge is almost impossible to measure. To be sure, the value of handling systemic threats or opportunities (spread of flu, destruction of computer viruses, tracking the money of terrorist organizations, use of Twitter in revolutionary movements) exist, in substantial part, outside of the henceforth dubbed "productive sector" so the value of systemic changes—both good and bad—are not captured.

So, rather than try to fix the measure of productivity, the OECD took a different turn: it is trying to measure the quality of our lives directly. Rather than trying to measure the value of formal-sector production as an adequate approximation for how well we are doing, it is attempting to measure the quality of our lives. In so doing, things that were left out before are put back in. The proposed framework includes both the human system and the ecosystem. Since the human system's health is dependent upon the health of the ecosystem, both are included. It also includes measures of well-being for a wide spectrum of people—wealth (yes, the value of production still has its place), equality of income and measures of well-being that can exist outside the formal economy such as health, education, civic participation and the ability to link with a larger world.

No one at the OECD or elsewhere would claim that this multi-dimensional measure will be easy to produce and reliable and accurate enough worldwide to easily replace our old standard bearer—GDP per capita, but the attempt at such a major level brings home two clear realities. First, GDP per capita is such a poor measure that the expensive, complex and difficult task of replacing it must be undertaken—and the time is now. Second, the attempt itself might be the ultimate benefit as it will get a global conversation going on how to measure such things, how they are measured now and which measures are the most reliable. Perhaps a central core of measures will emerge as a temporary "stand-in" while the construction of simpler, more reliable measurements continues. Despite the challenges, the OECD and its member states, have decided that the status quo cannot stand.

So, if even the OECD admits that national well-being is not being captured by the productivity we have come to measure so well, if that replacement measure captures the outcomes of our new ideas that affect all sectors of our life, and if the framework used is one of systems, then how does this inform the goals of education? Perhaps equally important, how does it affect the very definition of education?

Education redefined

The formalization of schooling throughout the world grew out of a notion that individual and national wealth came from industrialization. Those industries needed educated people. They needed workers who had been socialized in schools to follow rules, carry out routines, read simple directions, reliably show up for work and on time and have mastery of some basic communication and numeracy skills. Industry also needed its engineers and scientists and designers. The growing economy grew demands for services of professionals such as dentists, architects and wedding planners. We needed skills and we needed people who fit into the environment of industry and professions.

But we now live in a changing world. We still have industries and the need to fill factories and management ranks with known skilled personnel remains, just as in the economy before it, land ownership had a certain linkage to wealth generation. But, increasingly, knowledge is a primary input. Sometimes knowledge is the only output. And our world is so complex and integrated, that a whole type of production is central but only beginning to be explored—complex systems. Our ability to make contributions encompasses all sectors. No one sector can be dubbed "the productive sector." We don't even really know what the productive sector is anymore. Often, some businesses are owned by their employees. Some non-profit organizations are huge global operations. So, "the private sector" is hardly a clear definition of anything, much less the "productive sector."

Further, the process of creating ideas that spur the high-growth industries and is needed to fuel our nascent global-systems workers, requires a whole new education. We actually don't want people who just follow rules or know only what they have been taught in schools. These people are much less likely to contribute to a creative process. We need people who do things that schools have tried to minimize for decades—rethink basic tenets, willingly try new things and make mistakes, move past what they were taught, seek information beyond the textbook, sometimes become the teacher and learn actively on the internet. Do we really want students who play on computers, tweet in classrooms, stray from the assigned readings when on the internet and redefine knowledge even when class is in session? Ask me. I wouldn't have it any other way. The old ways of teaching are boring and don't nurture imaginative thinkers. The new ways are fun, exciting, dynamic and build strength as we go.

Much of today's education looks very much like yesterday's. Although technology may provide cheaper or easier access to learning materials, the basic pedagogy of schooling remains largely unchanged. Teachers plan a daily lesson. They teach the lesson, which is allied with a section of the textbook. Students sit in their desk and absorb the lesson. When it is over, they turn to individualized work and later to homework. The homework may involve looking things up on the internet, but, in large part, it requires memorizing the subject material. A lot of life is that way. We need to learn the traffic rules if we want to drive a car. We have to learn vocabulary in order to progress from the speech of a two-year-old to an adult. We have to learn how to cook, choose the right light bulb, apply mascara and set up the television we just bought. Without basic skills, we would have none of this. Life is about mastery.

But, increasingly, life is also about other skills—networking, building new knowledge collectively and applying unique solutions or opportunities in a particular situation. We can get through school and learn these skills later, but it truly handicaps students to do so. If they have been rewarded for 12 years by scoring better on exams, by working individually and memorizing facts and practicing skills, then their learning patterns are well established before they need to use them as adults. Essentially, they now—in adulthood—have to learn a different way that they have not practiced.

Since many of these new skills are learning skills—that is, they are about how you construct knowledge not, generally, wholly new knowledge—the answer lies in teaching differently. It requires building teaching methods that use these networking, collective learning and application skills *within* the learning process. Students can be asked to work in groups to solve a particular complex problem —how to put out a fire without water, for example. This is curriculum built around solving problems. They can be asked to put together a resource web page on a particular theory or technique. They can be dividing into groups and build a wiki page, working together to form the outline and then content.

Increasingly, students can work at distances, but we are so used to thinking of education as a classroom activity that it is hard to imagine. Early attempts at distance learning generally mimicked the old style of teaching—one teacher, one class, one lesson at a time. Teachers delivered material and students learned it. Material might be delivered in the form of a video lecture or links to online material and students might react by using online chat but, in general, the formula remains the same. At the end of the "class," students are tested on the mastery of materials, receive grades, and teachers receive salaries.

But, using the power of collective learning and networks, we could imagine a different design. Teachers from around the region (or nation or the world) can collaborate on building particular curricula and exercises, or on rethinking how they can guide students in creative ways. Each collaborator can use his or her strength to build the new design and the team can assess the results and modify it together. One "lesson" or several can be put online and used for years across many schools. Students can log in to the material when they wish and work in groups to tackle complex problems posed by the teachers. For example, teachers might post their best lesson ideas into a module and sell them like apps for the iPhone. Those supervising the learning process for particular students might ask them to buy a particular app or to have the school system buy it.

Competition in designing the best lesson plan (app) would raise the quality of the learning material and keep it fresh. Or, imagine a school that decides, as a school, that they will tackle the problem of "greening" their community. Students and teachers work together to come up with ideas. As a "complex" problem, the solutions will involve knowledge of the history of the community, its social structure, the politics and geography of the community. Students will have to read the history and laws and know the legal possibilities. Then, individual projects can be undertaken to get people to ride bicycles or recycle or share rides to work. Science, math, reading, writing, social science, and research are all involved. They'll need to build their networks into the community and fit their group's plan into the overall plan for the town. In the process, they will use and hone many of the traditional pieces of knowledge and mastery, but they will also learn to learn collectively, build the appropriate networks and apply solutions to particular contexts.

We are beginning to know the basic outlines of this new learning. It is collaborative. Even many corporations are beginning to realize that collaboration with their competitors is a necessary survival skill. We know that all people involved must be learners—teachers, students and the community they work with. We know that the pace of new materials and new understandings and new knowledge creation is so fast that the ability to learn and absorb new information is itself a critical skill—not just what you learn but your ability to learn. And we know that this skill must be practiced throughout one's life— not just in a school and in a classroom.

We know that classrooms, while possibly here to stay, will change in nature. Learning will become networked throughout the world and learning will be done online, in a collective setting (like a classroom) and individually. Some of it will involve teachers, some of it will involve technology, but the entire spectrum of what is learned in any one subject cannot be defined by a lesson plan. It will also involve knowing where to find new information on the internet, building new information with others and building networks that lead you quickly to solutions in your specialized area.

We know that this kind of learning requires taking risks and making mistakes. The child who makes no mistakes is the one that is falling behind. New knowledge creation, especially in a collective environment, requires that people try things out and learn when they don't succeed. The mark of success is not that no mistakes were made, but rather that mistakes became rich learning material for building the next idea or opportunity.

We know all this because it is very efficient learning. It has become easily available given that we can build learning teams across distances and the material is accessible on everyone's electronic devices. We know this because it involves teaching, from an early age, how to learn, adapt and create in a fast-paced, ever-changing and dynamic world. We know this because these skills are the new "basic skills" for industry and for tackling global systemic issues. They are the skills that increase our ability to be creative in our own environment and raise the well-being of ourselves, our neighbors, our nation and the world. In my constant pursuit to understand education by understanding how it increases well-being, it passes my basic test for understanding the future of education—"follow the money."

Reference

OECD. (2009). *OECD world forum: Busan, Korea*. Retrieved from www.oecd.org/site/progresskorea/

9b Social economics of learning

The original thinking behind schooling and economics was that people became more productive when they became more educated. This increased productivity made them and their societies wealthier. But what happens when ideas are shared, when knowledge is a networked, evolving process that is linked throughout the world? What happens when it crosses sectoral, national and personal boundaries? What happens when it is more valuable when it is "open" rather than when it is privately owned? Knowledge economics—the study of knowledge as a resource—may well be the study of knowledge as a value-creating social process rather than a market good.

From industrial to social construction

A fundamental shift from human capital theory thinking to knowledge economics theory thinking is the way that ownership of knowledge is viewed. Human capital theory treats knowledge as something owned by the individual. Knowledge economics, on the other hand, recognizes that knowledge is publically shared and created. This was recognized at the early stages of the theory's development (Stiglitz, 1999).

> An equally misleading approach is to equate ideas with human capital and to treat them as conventional private goods. This misses the notion, correctly suggested by the public good analogy, that an idea can be used by many people at the same time.
>
> (Romer, 1993, p. 64)

> Because human capital and ideas are so closely related as inputs and outputs, it is tempting to aggregate them into a single type of good. After all, structures and equipment are different goods, and they both fit rather well in the category of physical capital. It is important, nevertheless, to distinguish ideas and human capital because they have different fundamental attributes as economic goods, with different implications for economic theory.
>
> (Romer, 1993, p. 71)

This does not mean, however, that investment in human capital (by individuals, families, communities or nations) no longer has returns. Rather, knowledge needs to be used creatively in order for a society to reap the maximum benefits from this resource. This substantially changes the way we think about education. Keith Sawyer outlines the older vision and new vision of learning:

> Knowledge is a collection of facts about the world and procedures for how to solve problems ... The goal of schooling is to get these facts and procedures into the student's head ... This traditional vision of schooling is known as instructionism. Instructionism prepared students for the industrialized economy.
>
> (Sawyer, 2006b, p. 1)

He goes on to explain the types of learning that will need to take place in an innovation economy, including the abilities to work creatively to build new ideas, to critically evaluate what is read, and to take responsibility for learning throughout their lifetime (Sawyer, 2006b, p. 2).

Sawyer (2006a) and Florida (2002) and others (Araya & Peters, 2010; UNCTAD, 2010) assert that the innovation economy is really about the rise of creativity. Yet, it is rarely linked to changes in education.

> The most pressing problems that face our world are large in scale and complex in nature, far out of the realm of any one person to resolve— poverty, pollution, hunger, disease, armed conflict. The creativity that matters in today's world is the creativity of teams and organizations with the capabilities to make a difference.
>
> (Sawyer, 2006a, p. 42)

Sawyer's leap, in a single paragraph—from the needs of industry for innovation to the social implications of a broad spectrum of people who are diverse and good learners—demonstrates a crucial link between education and innovation. The innovation process, albeit being spurred by industrial and national desires for growth, requires sets of skills that have broad applicability for social progress—often aimed at the reduction in use of scarce resources and in cooperative knowledge-building.

This cooperative knowledge sharing requires substantially different theoretical and mathematical approaches to the economics of knowledge than human capital affords. This kind of complex problem solving can only take place through a process of collaborative learning. This product of knowledge acquisition was not designed to be captured by human capital metrics. Rather, complex problem solving is a creative, collaborative, dynamic and ongoing process that not only involves a variety of professions and diverse thinkers, it requires networks and the dynamics of networks (Downes, 2010; Fowler & Christakis, 2010; Nicholls & Murdock, 2012; Norgaard, 2004).

Weak links, fragile networks and diversity

These intersections with knowledge—collective constructions, social learning and networks—represent the leading edge of knowledge economics theory. It is not really about traditional measures of economics at all since it is not centered around the creation of markets. But it is still about how humans create resources. Rather than producing goods and services that use scarce resources, it is about creating new ideas, which use an abundant, but unexpected, resource —creative thinking. The ideas come from unexpected places and sources.

To understand this, one must go back to the intersection of knowledge economics and network theory. Under the old theory of industrial economics, where industrial production was planned and rationalized, the allocation of scarce resources was thought to efficiently maximize profits and, therefore, increased production. But new ideas do not derive from a scarce resource. Knowledge-building is a vast, infinite resource, so there is no need to allocate it efficiently. Rather, it is important to ensure that new ideas are generated. Further, it is important that societies are able to adapt to the new environment that is created.

But the sources of the most diverse ideas are often at the outer reaches of the network—the weak links (Csermely, 2006). Mark Granovetter's landmark article showed that these outer links (weak links) were a more likely source of creative, new ideas. Such creative, new ideas helped networks adapt and survive (Granovetter, 1973).

Norberg points out that such weak links are considered "inefficient" in the older model of economics and may be overlooked. But this is not the case in a highly linked ecosystem such as a globally linked system of finance, ecology, political and social ties, communication and transportation or knowledge systems: "[T]here is growing recognition that diversity is the key requirement for long-term (sustainable) functioning of systems—biological and social" (Norberg *et al.*, 2013, p. 46).

The power law of networks shows how this works graphically. Figure 9.1 shows a power law distribution which is known to be the distribution of knowledge (Barabási & Frangos, 2002; Wellman & Rainie, 2014). Most people who contribute new ideas will have similar ideas because their education, upbringing and cultural background are similar. Hence, their distribution of ideas is clustered toward the left side of the distribution representing fairly similar ideas with lots of contributions. But some people will have rather unique ideas. They represent the right side of the distribution. Under the old human capital view of educational investment, one would want to invest in the people on the left side of the distribution because their ideas are more plentiful and easier to understand (because they are similar). Those on the right side of the distribution were expensive to educate because they required more effort.

But, in knowledge economics, these very people are the likely source of the most valuable ideas. Steve Jobs' way of thinking was almost unique in his industry, but his unique thinking moved an entire industry and changed how the world worked. Clay Shirky, author of *Here Comes Everybody*, articulates this idea and suggests that institutions tend to reward people on the left-hand side of the scale (see Figure 9.1) to the detriment of the often higher quality of ideas on the right. Getting the widest possible participation allows for the best ideas to come forward (Shirky, 2009). Within knowledge economic theory, equity has been shown—mathematically and theoretically—to be an advantage to societies.

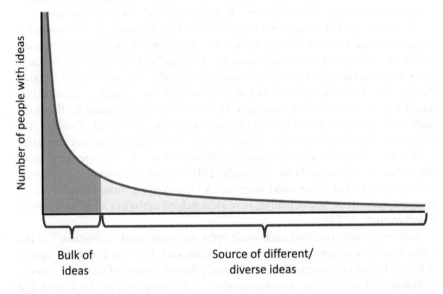

Figure 9.1 Distribution of ideas using power law
Source: Author

Nevertheless, diversity has its price. A healthy network is an ecosystem. A system that has too many unstable components can crumble because it either cannot adapt fast enough or it lacks the means to adapt. Too many weak links without the ability to adapt threatens the health of the network. Protecting the health and vitality of the weak links protects the entire system.

The field of security studies began to investigate this phenomenon by looking at weak countries. In 2000, Steven Miller editor of *International Security* surveyed 25 years of literature in the security studies field and suggested that the field should begin to focus on understanding how resources played a role in environment (and its link to scarcity of resources) and migration (and its impact on resource allocation) and other factors involving resource scarcity. The US Central Intelligence Agency used the same logic in establishing a State Failure Task Force to identify factors that lead to "failed states," which they viewed as global security threats (Esty *et al.*, 1995). Rice defined "weak states" as countries that "fail to meet the basic needs of many of their citizens—for food, clean water, health care or education" (Rice, 2006, p. 3).

Each of these authors began to view the poverty of particularly poor countries as a threat to the stability and security of wealthier countries because of their ties (links) to other countries. In a more recent but similar way, three major reports have now couched their global policy advice around the networked effects of global inequality. The UNCTAD (2013) *Trade and Development Report* says "there is now broad agreement that growth accompanied by high or rising inequality is unsustainable in the long run"(UNCTAD, 2013, p. 68). Their earlier report in 2012 subtitled "Policies for Inclusive and Balanced Growth" says specifically that at least part of the reason for the global financial crisis and political instability is the impact of inequality across borders—on a global scale (UNCTAD, 2012). The World Bank cites "A globally connected world" as a primary reason for the addition of a "second pillar" of "shared prosperity." As examples, it cites global linkage impacts of the global financial crisis, new social networking and the Arab Spring, increasing participation of people in government, and climate change as examples of global interdependence where inequality has spill-over effects (World Bank, 2013, p. 11).

Homer-Dixon (2006) links the idea of weak links or fragile states with network theory and a new, emerging theory of resilience. Folke (2006) is often credited with the first full articulation of the theory and others have extended it (Martin-Breen & Anderies, 2011).

> In resilient systems, dynamic interactions have the potential to create opportunities for new developments (windows of opportunity), for innovation and development . . . Sustainability is the capacity to create, test, and maintain adaptive capability . . . Development is the process of creating, testing, and maintaining opportunity . . . The motto is: learn to manage by change, rather than simply react to it and try to resist change. Uncertainty and surprise are part of the game and we have to learn to live with it.
>
> (Jansen *et al.*, 2007, p. 5)

Such systems are complex and cannot be governed, directed or built by individuals or individual behavior. A Los Alamos[1] project views resilient human systems as globally complex. The systems have interesting characteristics: they are functionality greater than the individual subsystems, robust, persistently in non-equilibrium, have the capability to find solutions in the presence of conflicting needs, and are scalable without loss of viability (Johnson, n.d.). Healthy systems have to have the capacity to experience a disturbance or change and still retain their basic function, structure and identity. Further, they must have the ability to self-organize and the ability to learn and adapt (Gunderson & Holling, 2002; Walker & Salt, 2006).

Note

1 Los Alamos is the location of the Los Alamos National Laboratory, which is funded by the US government to research issues that impact national security (Los Alamos National Laboratory, n.d.) A group of scientists are currently studying how humans

act collectively (Johnson *et al.*, 1998). A good summary of their work can be found on the website "The Symbiotic Intelligence Project: Self-Organizing Knowledge on Distributed Networks Driven by Human Interaction" (Johnson, n.d.)

References

Araya, D. and Peters, M. (eds). (2010). *Education in the creative economy: Knowledge and learning in the age of innovation*. New York: Peter Lang International.

Barabási, A.-L. and Frangos, J. (2002). *Linked: The new science of networks*. Cambridge, MA: Perseus.

Csermely, P. (2006). *Weak links: Stabilizers of complex systems from proteins to social networks*. Berlin: Springer.

Downes, S. (2010). Learning networks and connective knowledge. In H. Yang and S. Yuen (eds), *Collective intelligence and e-learning 2.0: Implications of web-based communities and networking*. Hershey, PA: Information Science.

Esty, D., Goldstone, J., Gurr, T. R., Surko, P. and Unger, A. (1995). *State failure task force report*. Working Paper, Science Applications International Corporation, McLean, VA. Retrieved from www.williamtsuma.com/sites/default/files/esty-d-c-et-al-1995-state-failure-task-force-report.pdf

Florida, R. (2002). *The rise of the creative class: and how it's transforming work, leisure, community and everyday life*. New York: Basic books.

Folke, C. (2006). Resilience: The emergence of a perspective for social–ecological systems analyses. *Global Environmental Change*, *16*(3), 253–267.

Fowler, J. H. and Christakis, N. A. (2010). Cooperative behavior cascades in human social networks. *Proceedings of the National Academy of Sciences*, *107*(12), 5334–5338.

Granovetter, M. S. (1973). The strength of weak ties. *American Journal of Sociology*, *78*(6), 1360–1380.

Gunderson, L. and Holling, C. S. (eds) (2002). *Panarchy: understanding transformations in human and natural systems*. Washington, DC: Island University Press.

Homer-Dixon, T. (2006). *The upside of down: catastrophe, creativity, and the renewal of civilization*. Toronto, Canada: Random House. Retrieved from http://proxy-net.snu.ac.kr/2b05b02/_Lib_Proxy_Url/books.google.co.kr/books/about/The_Upside_of_Down.html?id=rvk6tsE4UDcC

Jansen, S., Immink, I., Slob, A. and Brils, J. (2007). *Resilience and water management: a literature review* (No. P1027). Amsterdam: Aqua Terra Nederland. Retrieved from www.levenmetwater.nl/static/media/files/D1_2_Resilience_Literature-Review.pdf

Johnson, N. (n.d.). The symbiotic intelligence project: Self-organizing knowledge on distributed networks driven by human interaction. Retrieved from http://collective science.com/SymIntel.html

Johnson, N., Rasmussen, S., Cliff, J., Rocha, L., Smith, S. and Kantor, M. (1998). Symbiotic intelligence: Self-organizing knowledge on distributed networks, driven by human interaction. Presented at the Sixth International Conference on Artificial Life, University of California, Los Angeles, CA. Retrieved from www.informatics.indiana.edu/rocha/ps/alife6_lanl.pdf

Los Alamos National Laboratory. (n.d.). Los Alamos National Laboratory. Retrieved from www.lanl.gov/

Martin-Breen, P. and Anderies, J. M. (2011, September 18). *Resilience: A Literature Review*. The Bellagio Initiative; Background Paper. Retrieved from http://opendocs.ids.ac.uk/opendocs/bitstream/handle/123456789/3692/Bellagio-Rockefeller%20bp.pdf?sequence=1

Miller, S. (2000). International security at twenty-five. *International Security, 26*(1), 5–39.

Nicholls, A. and Murdock, A. (2012). *Social innovation: Blurring boundaries to reconfigure markets.* London: Palgrave Macmillan.

Norberg, J., Wilson, Walker, B. and Ostrom, E. (2013). Diversity and resilience of socio-ecological systems. In J. Norberg and G. Cumming (eds), *Complexity theory for a sustainable future* (pp. 47–79). New York: Columbia University Press.

Norgaard, R. B. (2004). Learning and knowing collectively. *Ecological Economics, 49*(2), 231–241.

Rice, S. (2006). Global poverty, weak states and insecurity. Presented at the The Brookings Blum Roundtable: Session I; Poverty, Insecurity and Conflict, Washington, DC: Brookings Blum Roundtable. Retrieved from www.brookings.edu/~/media/research/files/papers/2006/8/globaleconomics%20rice/08globaleconomics_rice.pdf

Romer, P. (1993). Two strategies for economic development: using ideas and producing ideas. In L. Summers and S. Shekhar (eds), *Proceedings of the World Bank annual conference on development economics 1992* (pp. 63–92). Washington, DC: World Bank. Retrieved from http://documents.worldbank.org/curated/en/1993/03/699081/proceedings-world-bank-annual-conference-development-economics-1992

Sawyer, K. (2006a). Educating for innovation. *Thinking Skills and Creativity, 1*(1), 41–48.

——. (2006b). The New Science of Learning. In K. Sawyer (ed.), *Cambridge handbook of the learning sciences* (pp. 1–16). New York: Cambridge University Press.

Shirky, C. (2009). *Here comes everybody: The power of organizing without organizations.* Penguin Books.

Stiglitz, J. (1999, January). *Public policy for a knowledge economy.* World Bank, Department for Trade and Industry. Retrieved from http://yil6.inet-tr.org.tr/BT-BE/knowledge-economy.pdf

UNCTAD. (2010). *Creative Economy: A Feasible Development Option, 2010.* New York: United Nations Conference on Trade and Development. Retrieved from http://unctad.org/SearchCenter/Pages/Results.aspx?k=creative%20economy

——. (2012). *UNCTAD trade and development report, 2012: Policies for inclusive and balanced growth.* New York: United Nations Conference on Trade and Development. Retrieved from http://unctad.org/en/PublicationsLibrary/tdr2012_en.pdf

——. (2013). *Trade and Development Report 2013: Adjusting to the changing dynamics of the world economy.* New York: United National Conference on Trade and Development. Retrieved from http://unctad.org/en/pages/PublicationWebflyer.aspx?publicationid=171

Walker, B. and Salt, D. (2006). *Resilience thinking: Sustaining ecosystems and people in a changing world.* Washington, DC: Island Press.

Wellman, B. and Rainie, L. (2014). *Networked: The new social operating system.* Cambridge, MA: MIT Press.

World Bank (2013). *World Bank group strategy.* Washington, DC. Retrieved from www-wds.worldbank.org/external/default/WDSContentServer/WDSP/IB/2013/10/09/000456286_20131009170003/Rendered/PDF/816970WP0REPLA00Box379842B00PUBLIC0.pdf

10a Learning together

As a new professor, I worked with a senior professor who had a background in educational administration and had, thus, taken a class in the financing of education. Universities were about to go through a major upheaval in which the notion that a government would largely finance the operation of a university was receding. Now, many state universities were being asked to generate their own funds. So, the question was: Where would the additional money come from?

He had the idea that we could have larger classes. Indeed, years later in another state-run university, we began to make classes larger and larger. But the question was: What is efficient? If the goal was simply to hear a professor lecture, I had a better idea. Stand at the lecture hall door on the first day of class and hand everyone a CD (well, at that time it would have been a bunch of video tapes) with your entire lecture series pre-recorded. Turn off the heat in the classroom and stop building classrooms. If all we were to deliver were lectures, then there was no reason to appear at all, nor to build classrooms, nor to have students show up. But, of course, this raised the question of what our goals were.

If a higher education class was about more than simply hearing what a professor had to say, then maybe this notion of taped lectures would not work. If students needed to think through the ideas or needed to ask questions during the lecture, then maybe the learning that needed to take place would not happen in a taped lecture. Of course, if it was simply a matter of answering questions, that could be done through a chat space on the internet. It motivated me to ask two important questions. First, it was clear that education could not be efficient if it does not accomplish its goals. So, what is the goal that education is trying to reach? Second, if education is about delivering material (like video lectures or textbooks or online classes) then is there a reason why anyone would ever hire me?

Why the question about me as a professor? At the time I was new and could not, for example, write this book. I just did not have the experience or exposure. So, why hire an "ok" professor at a pretty high annual salary, when one could simply purchase the videotapes of the "best" professor in the world (these days, simply stream video of lectures off the internet) in my field and deliver them pretty cheap. After all, take my salary and divide it by the number of students

I taught a year and you would get a pretty high cost of delivery per student per year. Although the cost of videos of the best professor in the world might be relatively expensive, it would, no doubt, be cheaper than hiring me.

There is a reason why this does not make sense and it has to do with the goals of education. This is what this book is about. Even if we could have defined the goals well in 1986 (when I was first a professor at the University of Zimbabwe), they would have changed by now, otherwise, this book is pretty useless. What is clear is that education is an integral part of improving individual and collective well-being. So the ultimate goal of education is to improve our lives in some manner. How a graduate class of 15 students fits into this picture is up for debate, at least in small part. But, for example, if a face-to-face lecture is less effective in delivering content than online delivery bolstered by lively debates online, then low-cost delivery is more efficient than the higher-cost personal interaction.

But, do lectures in any form get us to our educational goals? There cannot be any question that there is a lot of material "you've just got to know." You need to know how to add things up and how to read. You need to know how to follow a recipe. Maybe you need or want to know what is in this book or why a computer virus was designed to destroy the nuclear production of Iran. But what you need to know is only part of the picture. As discussed earlier, you also need to know how to build new knowledge; how to collaborate with others; how to use and build networks to gain access to the knowledge you need; and you need to know how to apply what you know to specific situations.

Maybe we always needed to know these things. But in a linked, dynamic system of global finance, disease, climates, social networks, news, education, communication, government instability and media, the world changes systemically. A change in one part of the world spreads quickly to another and then changes the nature of the network. That changing network (take climate for example) then changes the global system (global climate), which affects everyone. In a globally linked world, the pace of change is fast and getting faster. So, learning some basic material, while necessary, is not nearly enough to equip you with the tools you need to function well—to raise your well-being. Without networks, collaboration and group knowledge you will find your education keeps you in one place while the rest of the world moves on. What was a good life yesterday turns into a marginalized life later on. The reason why we need to apply our learning to specific situations is also about systems. Systems respond to changes in the individual units. If you want to improve the global climate, get the Vietnamese to follow the Korean lead in recycling. It is within these individual units that change happens. Each unit has both global characteristics and local characteristics. We know the global, but applying it to the local situation is where the change begins to affect both the local and the globe.

So, comfortable as it may be to define education as "the basics" that can be "delivered" and can be measured by individualized "tests," it is, in fact, an out-dated definition of education. It does us no good to know how to read if we cannot work together to design or test or use a recycling system. We read, but our world deteriorates around us. We may know how to add up the costs of the items we buy in the grocery store, but it does us no good if the wheat crop was wiped out in Russia due to climate change, which raised the price of grains, which worked its way through the food chain and caused our grocery bill to go up 10 percent. We may know basic hygiene but if our neighbor takes a vacation to Indonesia and brings back a bad strain of flu, throwing out the two-day-old chicken in our refrigerator won't keep us healthy. We live in a globally linked world and our learning needs to be networked as well. We need to build knowledge collectively.

From education to learning

So, let's say that we build a new company. We build a knowledge company. We design better word-processing software. We already know that our product does not have a physical form; that the knowledge we embedded is given away once our product goes to market; and that we built new knowledge even as we built our new product. But what keeps us competitive? If our competitors know everything we know once our product is released, then our revenue stream from the product lasts only until our competitors can build on our product and get an even better product to market.

Our competitive advantage is that we have a diverse team that works well together, that built new knowledge together, that can now be put to work in building the next iteration. They have learned to create together. They know each other's personalities, strengths, problems and who can solve which issues. They've developed a vocabulary that everyone agrees to and they have honed their communication networks. In short, they have learned to learn. And they have learned to learn collectively. Our competitive advantage is that we are the best learning team around. We have a learning advantage.

Learning is more powerful than knowledge. Some knowledge—such as a knowledge product in the form of word-processing software—has a shelf-life. That is, it becomes less useful as time goes by. But learning builds itself. The more you practice, the better you get. The more complex and integrated your learning networks, the harder it is for someone to get your learning level mastered. Learning to learn is a skill that just gets better with use. It is a resource that grows. Learning to learn as a team is complex, hard to duplicate and hard to keep up. A learning team is a tremendous resource for industry, governments, educational institutions, civic action and your neighborhood.

This is not to say that having facts, procedures and skills in your brain is unimportant. To be sure, knowing specific information and being able to invent and experiment with these skills or procedures or information is critically important. Google may well be a complex system requiring teams that are highly skilled in learning collectively, but it is also true that each team member brought with them a set of knowledge, skills and procedures that was required by the team. They also brought with them culture, gender, lifestyle, parenting, travel, hobbies and social networks that constitute what they know and how they approach their problems. Imagine me, for example, on such a team. If the team became stuck or had problems, I might well ask myself how a particular culture would solve such a problem because I have a life of traveling and exposure to reference in my head. I am also female and American, which predisposes me to approach issues in a certain way. Nevertheless, I also have coursework in anthropology, education and economics that taught me analytic methods, ways of viewing the world and procedures that are helpful. Our school-learned knowledge combines with our life knowledge to form a unique set of knowledge we can bring to a group.

But perhaps one of the best pieces of knowledge I could bring to a group is my understanding of how knowledge is constructed collectively. I could suggest certain processes and procedures that might work for the group. When I think someone is going off track I would understand that a group needs to let each person explore their ideas and let the group process bring the idea into something workable. I know a good group process will do this and also strengthen the groups' ability to build knowledge next time. It builds a good process that all can participate in. So my knowledge of group learning may be equally or more important to the group than some particular fact I learned in school.

So, borrowing from the influence Korea had on me, we need to find a good balance (not an inherent right or wrong) between mastery (of facts, skills, procedures) and learning skills (collaboration, networking, application in particular environments). The best way to do this is to teach material that must be mastered in a learning context that uses collaboration, networking and applications in a specific context. Think of it this way. Instead of me giving my students a lecture on how important collaboration, networking and applied context is (delivering the knowledge in the old way), I ask them to use their nascent mastery to build new ideas or solve problems or apply it in a specific context. They master new material but the learning environment uses collaboration, networks and applications.

Here's a problem I face right now. Only one existing text I know of covers the materials I'm putting into this book (Peters, Besley & Araya, 2013). In fact, searching a huge educational database for work that simply mentions the new knowledge economics (using the names and catchphrases used for these emerging theories) delivers 14 documents out of 1.5 million articles and documents on education. That's why I'm writing the book.

Now, this book might be fun to read because I've chosen to write it like a story with lots of examples. I took out most of the jargon in the narrative chapters. As a result of the publisher's review I was asked to add these theory chapters.

But, another way to have added academic content would have been to supplement the content in order to use this as a text. So, the question is, how do I help the professor who wants to use this book as a text.

One way is to supplement the book with a website that is either open to the public or requires you to buy the book and get a password to access the website.

But this is a lot of work and I'd have to keep it fresh. Another way to solve this problem is to teach the course for my own students using this book. Then ask them, as an assignment, to build the online lessons for the course. In order to build a lesson, they would have to truly understand the material and find other articles, videos and websites that are good sources of the theories. Then they would have to work together to design good exercises and find appropriate graphs and tables to illustrate the points. They might have to go into the many global databases to either design an exercise or mount data that showed the trends.

Now, I can also design my course to give a lecture on the material and have my students read supplementary material and do a paper at the end of the semester. This is pretty traditional and follows the old notion of education as "mastery." But, if I follow the new way, perhaps they would learn the material more thoroughly. But they need to build networks of information (website, videos, articles), learn collaboratively (suggesting good ideas for exercises and building networks together) and then apply their knowledge of a particular problem (audience of future students taking a course in education who need to master the material well). Mastery of material "you've just got to know" can be taught in an environment that builds these new skills.

We are, no doubt, at the very beginning of rethinking education. My idea of a new way to teach this material and keep it fresh and updated still works within an old framework. It assumes there is a "class," there is one professor, there is a finite set of material to master and knowledge comes from the expert (myself). We actually know that none of these characteristics is inherent in good learning. Although we can be fairly sure there will always be a body of material you need to master, it is also true that its very nature continues to change.

I loved statistics. In one of my advanced (statistics) classes, the professor started on the left-hand side of the front board in each class period and worked his way around the boards on all four walls by the end of the class. Since class started at 7:00 at night and ended at 10:00, most students had worked themselves into a stupor about half an hour into the class. But I loved it, even though my head hurt by the end of class. I looked at the syllabus of my Korean colleague who teaches statistics here at Seoul National University. In my opinion, she is brilliant. Surprisingly, students were not being asked to master the complex formulas, much less the infinitely complex derivations. I thought, "Wow. Don't tell me they aren't learning statistics anymore." But my colleague is so brilliant and dedicated to her job I thought I should find out her reasoning.

Although she ensures they are exposed to the formulas and that they understand what the math is accomplishing, equally importantly she has them run data through the software and makes sure they can properly interpret the results. I don't know how many students I've had over the years that bring me lots of data in printouts and just don't have a clue what they are looking at. It is frustrating—they learned how to use the software, but they don't know how to evaluate the results. In today's world, where computers run our statistics, you need exposure to the underlying formulas in statistics because those formulas imbed the logic. But, once you understand that, the next most important thing is to properly interpret the findings.

Statistics mastery has changed (at least for those who will only apply it, not for people who specialize in its complex manipulation). I doubt that the statistical classes in economics are taught this way. But what is important to master about statistics has changed. I can remember, for example, that a linear regression is built around a matrix of correlations. This helps me remember what is going on when I see results. But I have not seen the formula for linear regression since I had to derive it long ago in advanced econometrics.

When I first taught a class on how to use a spreadsheet to help build models of educational expansions and costs in poor countries, I had to begin the class with walking the students through the basics of the software. I could not assume they had this mastery before the class. I'll teach this again this semester and I'll simply tell students that if they don't know the software, they ought to go through the online tutorials and get the mastery outside of class. Knowing how to use certain types of software on the computer has become a topic that needs mastery.

Curriculum theorists have long studied how the new ideas are frequently introduced in classrooms for the elite schools whereas the old "memorize" and "discipline" rules are used for poorer students. So, I can see an argument here that it may be well and good to introduce these techniques into classrooms where we can hand children the latest technology, but old-fashioned black-boards and textbooks need to go to classrooms in rural Nepal for Pima. A quick calculation would show that a teacher, teaching the same curriculum over and over again, year after year, in poor conditions with little support, is an ineffective and inefficient way of delivering education—technology is getting cheap. But who says that classrooms are the right way to deliver education anyway? Getting basic skills to rural kids is likely to be a relatively easy challenge in two to three years with technology and software. But getting them into groups that think, create and interact is the learning challenge we need to tackle. We need to break out of the classroom/teacher/textbook mode of thinking that children are simply sponges for absorbing facts and skills. How do we use innate curiosity and networks to get students active, participating and creating? That is the question at hand.

So, even what we think are "the basics" that need to be mastered change when we rethink education to be about dynamic learning. Further, everything we learn changes as we go along. The software for educational planning gets more sophisticated, but it does not encompass the paradigm shifts of global learning networks. To incorporate such a paradigm shift would require rethinking whole education sector structures. Rather, projections make predictions based on past performance and project a few years ahead. Yet, the whole educational system is evolving and transforming— the projections will be obsolete in a couple of years. Many things we master need updating all our lives. Adults need to learn new things as well as younger students. I'll send my students to the web to learn the spreadsheet software—there is no reason to teach that in a classroom environment. We can collaborate using software that accommodates different time schedules for the participants. We can build lessons collaboratively and share knowledge.

So, whereas we still think of education as classes, teachers, lesson plans, tests and learning materials (albeit these days textbooks are extended to the net), in fact these boundaries are not inherent in learning. What is inherent in human learning (and much animal learning) is that it is a collective exercise whereby what one person knows gets shared. Also, groups build knowledge, which changes group behavior and environments. Networks, collaboration and applications in a specific environment along with mastery are inherent characteristics of knowledge—not school buildings, fixed-age groups, locations or "experts" who differentiate themselves from learners. So, whereever education is going, it will be networked. Everyone will be, at times, a learner and an expert; the new global learning network system will involve collaboration and it will build new knowledge along with mastery.

Highly innovative industries—such as bio-medical engineering or technology —already imbed these learning practices. Most texts and professional books on these fields now have at least one chapter on learning. I brought my class 20 books off my bookshelf from the technology field and read their chapter headings. I told them that I could only find one book in education that talked about this innovation economy/learning link other than to mention that innovation would be important. But industry cannot wait for the sanctioned theory of knowledge economics or for educators to reinvent education. Industry depends upon continuous learning, collaboration, networking and innovation applied to particular circumstances. So they are writing about it absent an important understanding of pedagogy. Education will catch up, but what educators know about culture, learning and learning contexts is not being integrated into the new science of networked learning, for the most part.

New learning sciences

Educational psychologists are beginning to explore this new area. The importance of innovation is beginning to get the attention of educational psychologists: something called the "new learning sciences." The new approach to learning and teaching is a substantial departure from the older models. We used to think of a good learning environment as somewhere students were quietly studying or were participating in organized classroom learning with the teacher as the primary source of knowledge. Some educators have called this method the "banking" approach to schooling: you wanted to make as many deposits in the bank (pieces of knowledge mastered) as you could during school time. But, more recently, attention has turned to a different view.

Students are actively engaged in constructing their knowledge—they are not just recipients. For example, this semester, I am teaching a class on educational planning. But, instead of having students read about how to do planning and giving them lectures, I have assigned them to groups that will examine particular countries. I'll begin each week by telling them the next piece of the country plan they are to build and asking them how they might build it. Step one, for example, is to get some basic demographic information about the country; step two is to get information on the educational system; step three is to find out what the educational challenges are, etc. What information will they need? What sources might they access. What logic will best demonstrate this? Using the old method of teaching, I would simply tell them how to do it and judge them on their ability to produce a good plan. In this case, they are asked first to "construct" the logic, to understand the concept well enough to build a piece of logic. Later, they will present each piece to each other and critique it. Which pieces of evidence were the most insightful? Which country appears to have the best prospects? Then, they will be able to go back and improve their own group work on the basis of what they learned from each other.

You might think this works well for graduate students but not for young children. Actually, young children do an incredible job of constructing knowledge. Many teachers start the year by asking the students to build a set of rules for classroom behavior. They talk about what is a good environment in which to learn and which behaviors bother them. They then use this knowledge to build a set of classroom rules. The role of the teacher is to guide the knowledge-building, the "construction" but not to present answers or final material. This kind of teaching, thus, is known as "constructivism."

There are several goals of this kind of instruction and several underlying assumptions. First, it is assumed that changing and learning are primary skills that everyone has to learn in order to live a good life. So learning how to learn and being comfortable with change is taught early and continuously. Students are encouraged to be curious, to look for things that intrigue them and explore further, and to make meaning out of what they learn. They should ask why things are the way they are, not just accept facts.

Students need to be resilient. Making a mistake is no longer a problem. Rather, one has to be able to experiment and correct mistakes. As in the example of my class, students will construct the logic of the next step in a country plan. They will be asked to build a piece of logic even as they search for the right information and data. They will then show each other what they have done and learn from other groups. When we've identified which pieces helped us the most in understanding a country, groups can go back and build on the knowledge they learned from other groups. There is no assumption that each group will be perfect at the first attempt. Rather, there is a continual process of learning, analyzing, searching and rebuilding.

Students are taught to think strategically. This is aligned with the notion that knowledge must be applicable to a particular situation. They must also learn to work with others. Putting several minds together to construct knowledge often builds better solutions than one person working independently. Educational psychologists are beginning to explore how this new approach can best be used in a classroom.

But, in some sense, we are all bound by our former beliefs and practices. When we reach out to change, we generally change from where we were—making things better. It is enormously difficult to invent something that is wholly new—never seen before. Amazon started out as a "traditional" bookseller that used the online environment to give you access to any book—and rather quickly. It did not imagine that it could attract people to the site to "see which books were around" in a given topic, to expose you to other books that people bought on a similar topic, to customer reviews, electronic versions, special lists of books you might like based upon your buying patterns. All this came later when they realized they had information stored that might boost sales. They became a knowledge site, not by initial design but by evolution.

Thus, it is true that the new learning sciences are making substantial headway in redefining how we learn and teach. But the approach still assumes (rightly so since it is their reality) that children are in a classroom, a teacher is in charge, that the classroom is a physical space and there is predefined subject matter to be learned. During the decade when young people were just beginning to have good computers linked to the internet, I was an avid observer of their learning behavior away from the classroom. So many young people had computers that were connected to game consoles, the internet and lots of software. These young people were teaching themselves how to use computers far beyond anything their teachers had any awareness of.

I used to ask them what they were doing. They would show me the latest "cool" things they had found—a new video game, something interesting they had discovered online or a group conversation in which they had built something innovative. Many found employment in fixing other people's computers or in building websites. They entered a world of their own making when they sat in front of their computers. They were building new knowledge just as fast as their minds would go.

In this learning environment, there were few constraints. Their curiosity and enjoyment (not too far from learning and growing—ask any two-year-old) was their guide. They spent hours experimenting and trying things out on their own, then shared what they were learning with each other. At times they met collectively to build things together or explore new ideas. They were each other's teachers; they learned from the internet and books and instructions. They built new knowledge without a classroom or an assigned teacher or an assigned subject lesson plan. They learned incredibly fast. And while they learned, they also became good at collaboration, curiosity, applications, new concepts, skills, facts and rules.

Of course, we all need to master subject matter that might not be as much fun as computer technology was to these young people. But, observing their behavior and learning practices, we can begin to understand what learning looks like when it is free of the physical environment we often associate with schooling—a teacher, a classroom, a school building, a set of texts. In fact, if we can free our minds of this definition of learning, restricted to schooling, we begin to realize that it is already all around us. We engage it in every day and technology makes it all the more easy.

Let's take an example of someone who has mastered a very high level of knowledge. Let's say we are looking at the best biochemist in the world who is inventing the migraine drug I now take when I have a headache. That well-trained person may have some ideas of an approach to migraines—to constrict the extra flow of blood to the head. She may have some ideas of chemicals that will do this job and, as a skilled person in the field, she will know how to test her hunches. She assembles a team of researchers, puts together a lab and starts building the experiments. Eventually, she has a good result, which becomes a drug sold on the market.

This scientist may be able to construct this knowledge largely by herself, although her dependence on the published findings of others is a clear link to other knowledge. But most scientists in the majority of fields cannot do this kind of relatively isolated research. Even the migraine researcher would be handicapped if she had to conduct research in total isolation from the input and the knowledge exchange of others. She has no possibility of learning from the conversations or collaboration of others. She might be the best in the world, but others might be the best in something similar from which she could learn. Working largely in isolation might keep her employed because she is the best, but her ability to stay at the top is severely limited because the natural flow of ideas, concepts, successes and failures in her field are not flowing to her as readily as a counterpart who is well networked.

Increasingly, as knowledge becomes more complex, more multi-faceted and more dynamic, it takes many people to find the best solution. Each has specialized knowledge that might be closely related but is, nonetheless somewhat different. It takes two elements to stay at the top—specialized, highly competent knowledge in a field (or fields) and the ability to combine that knowledge with that of others. A specialist can hardly work alone anymore and have a chance to stay ahead of the next best person who is good at working with a team. Indeed, competitive industries are now studying the necessity of collaboration *even with their competitors*. Collaboration is a powerful learning tool to which there are few alternatives.

Sony and Samsung used to sue each other regularly—once a year in fact, on the 23rd of December. In 2004, they stopped their annual ritual of suing each other and, instead, agreed to share patents. This is not because they suddenly became best buddies or because of some corporate merger. Indeed, the history of the two companies' distrust likely stems as far back as the distrust of the countries from which them emanate. Rather, the co-operation was pure business strategy. In order to compete in an increasingly competitive global environment, at least some collaboration would be necessary. Thus, their collaboration involved sharing selective patents while deliberately keeping other patents at a distance in order to maintain a distinction between the two companies. This collaboration/competition mixture demonstrates that, in today's interconnected world, some degree of linkage is becoming unavoidable.

We have already seen, though, that the benefits of knowledge accrue to ourselves and our societies not wholly through industrial production; much of industrial production was built on what we could call "vertical knowledge," that is, knowledge which is highly specialized and somewhat isolated from other knowledge. A person who previously designed vehicles or researched a new drug had a lot of vertical knowledge—specialized knowledge within their field. But the knowledge that increases global stability is the knowledge that tackles the challenges of a linked world and is not necessarily defined by industrial production.

None of us—even the biochemist in my story—can work well within a research environment if a flight is cancelled or delayed because of a terrorist threat. The flood or hurricanes that threaten her house or the house of her mother or the village in Indonesia (which must be rebuilt in order not to cause a pocket of political instability) will distract her or siphon off some funds she could have used for research. The migration laws that restrict the flow of people causes her to not have access to the best lab workers; the restriction on the internet in a destabilized country means that a lab report will be delayed or cancelled. The linkages that bind a highly integrated world create the possibilities of learning in new ways and of new collaborations. But, an interlinked world is not inherently stable. Only learning stabilizes a network.

The kind of knowledge that is required when a global system is composed of many working pieces and is integrated and dynamic is as much *horizontal* as it is vertical. I can write this because I have backgrounds in education and anthropology and economics. I have worked in 20 countries and lived in five major regions of the world. I have brilliant students who ask important questions. I have colleagues I can talk with and I am constantly networked around the world. I can put together many pieces in a way that most others cannot. I doubt that anyone in the world thinks I'm the best economist, best educator or best anthropologist, but I am a good networker and I love the challenge of bringing these disparate perspectives together.

So, as we move forward, we not only have to rethink what the best learning environment looks like, we also have to make room for at least one other type of learning that vastly affects the well-being of societies—horizontal thinkers who collectively tackle complex issues. They may well have their own special-izations and may have progressed very far up the ladder of vertical education, but they can apply their work collaboratively. They view the world as an inte-grated system and they can apply their knowledge to specific circumstances. We already have such people and no one would argue that the World Health Organization (WHO) or the people studying the causes of national political instability do not have a critical job. We must now recognize that their work is not ancillary to the "private sector," and societal well-being. Their work funda-mentally requires the approach of the new learning sciences.

Finally, it is worth exploring how this kind of learning is acquired. Try as we might, we still don't know very well how to test for collaborative, complex, dynamic knowledge. How do we test someone's ability to make mistakes and learn from them? We are mired in an educational culture of testing for facts, skills and rules. Every few years, countries compete to see if their children score higher than other countries on these facts and skills. This testing of vertical learning is not a bad thing; some of the vertical learning (mastery in isolation of others) must be done. But, by emphasizing the results of tests that measure vertical learning, we lock ourselves into an increasingly outdated curriculum. When high school students complete for college entrance based wholly on their vertical mastery, schools will necessarily focus their curriculum and pedagogy on this mastery and the type of traditional learning environments that optimize this type of learning.

In a sense, it is rather like the problem of GDP (discussed more thoroughly in Chapter 11b). It no longer measures enough of what we care about to be effective. The faith we place in it as a foundational contribution to social well-being is outdated and holding the world back. Because well-being is not so uni-dimensional anymore, our well-being is based upon our ability to adapt— to learn. Our testing systems are holding us back. It is not that vertical is unimportant (any more than production is unimportant), but it is just one dimension of a multi-dimensional outcome. What do we want education to do? Where does it fit in our society? How do we best prepare students for a fulfilling life, and societies for resilience, robustness and progress?

Much of the work I mention in this book is the work of Nobel Prize winners: human capital theory; the theory that businesses tend to co-locate so that they take advantage of collaborative environments—and now the new theory of social well-being, which has been substantially rethought since. But it is not so far from Pima's world. She may appear to be isolated in her small village and grass hut, but her world is very much like that of the kids competing to get into the best colleges or the parents sacrificing years of income to see their children educated. Everyone wants a life that is stable, comfortable and has dignity and social standing. Everyone wants to be able to make a contribution to society that is recognized. Everyone wants to have children that have a fulfilling life without a lot of worries. Everyone wants to know that their life, beyond what they produce, has dignity and stability. Everyone wants an identity within one's community. Each community, each society, each household and each country has norms and it is within these norms that we make these judgments. But we all want the same things within these norms. Pima's world is no different than my own. When I visit Pima's mother I see, very much, myself. I can imagine myself making the same decisions and wrestling with the same choices. And Pima's abilities are no different than my son's. It is only that her opportunities are different; and those opportunities are not because of her intelligence or her race, her will, her country, but only because of which parents she was born to.

10b New learning structures

Education that prepared people to work in industry was organized around formal institutional environments. These environments were hierarchically organized and had top-down organizational structures. But networked learning environments are self-organizing and require little management hierarchy for people to find, build, organize and share information, new knowledge and creativity. They have a networked structure rather than a hierarchical structure. Participants are simultaneously learners and teachers. Will schools migrate from institutions to virtual or informal communities? Will learning be defined by the dynamics of creativity rather than grades, marks, scores and assignments? The structures are not yet obvious, but the theories and concepts are beginning to take shape.

From mastery to creativity

The understanding of learning in knowledge economics is well articulated by new learning sciences (Sawyer, 2006). The new learning sciences began in the 1970s based on research emerging from psychology, computer science, philosophy, sociology and other anthropology. As they closely studied children's learning, researchers discovered that teaching students through rigid rules of instruction and mastery was not an effective way of teaching (Papert, 1993; Sawyer, 2006). It leaves students with no ability to build new ideas.

The OECD assessed these older educational practices as one of Korea's primary weaknesses in achieving an innovation economy: "High school curricula place too much emphasis on preparation for the national university entrance exam and rely heavily on rote learning. This leaves little room for creative thinking and the emergence of an exploratory spirit." (OECD, 2009, p. 14).

Learning researchers began to investigate how creativity, experimentation, problem solving and collective knowledge-building could be brought into the classroom. What has evolved is an approach that encompasses the notion that a lifetime of learning and exploration needs to replace the notion of a set period of time in formal education (Chatti et al., 2007; Field, 2006; Jarvela et al., 2007). Sawyer, referencing emerging view of learning and innovation, says that:

> Knowledge is not just a static mental structure inside the learner's head; instead, knowing is a process that involves the person, the tools and other

people in the environment, and the activities in which that knowledge is being applied ... [This] moves beyond a transmission and acquisition conception of learning; in addition to acquiring content, what happens during the learning is that patterns of participation in collaborative activity change over time.

(Sawyer, 2006, p. 5)

In other words, the process of collaborative innovation leads to changes in *participation* and *collaborative activity* over time. This shift implies many changes in the formal learning environment. Teachers need not take the role of the expert. In fact, technology's entry into the classroom provides substantial evidence that content is more efficiently delivered individually to students. Class time can be then used to help students with specific questions and problems (Kronholz, 2012; Zappe *et al.*, 2009).

Table 10.1 Comparison of teaching vs. learning

Teaching as efficiency	Learning as adaptation
Teachers provide answers	New ideas are constantly evolving through a dynamic learning process; answers evolve. Teachers provide learning resources, guide inquiry and participate as advanced learning participant
Students follow directions	Participants develop approaches and reassess them continuously
Optimal curricula are designed and set up in advance	Questions in a particular context are posed as a beginning point
New curriculum is developed infrequently; implementing change is a huge undertaking	Learning to learn is a primary goal; competencies are geared toward building learning skills and evolve and change as individuals and teams grow in skills
Feedback is typically one-way (from teacher to students) and corrective ("You are not doing it right")	Collective-adaptive system builds feedback such that approaches that work in context are reinforced and given more attention and more energy for design
Problem solving is rarely required; judgment is not expected; students ask teachers when they're unsure	Problem solving is primary goal. Solutions are judged in context of problem. Learning group references each other and larger network for feedback. Teachers and experts are coaches and provide guidance
Fear (of the teacher or of grades) is often part of the schooling experience and generally does not appreciably harm the quality of learning	Self-regulating process provides variety of incentives for participation. Pay-off for experimentation is rewarded with better solutions

Source: Author

Table 10.1 compares the paradigm of classroom-based instruction with the emerging paradigm of learning as networks. The teaching paradigm on the left-hand side is teacher centered with teachers as experts transmitting the knowledge, correcting students when they have not mastered the knowledge and measuring their progress. On the right-hand side, all participants are in the process of learning, including the person who might be guiding the process. Learning is focused on solving problems within a context. The networked environment means that everyone learns and "teaches" (creates and consumes knowledge), which has its own rewards for participation.

Although one person might have more expertise in a particular aspect of the problem, that person simply guides the process of looking for information and organizing information but the guide is also learning from the process, diverse ideas and outcomes. Participants work collectively to solve a problem within a context and learn skills, facts and information on the way to finding increasingly sophisticated solutions to the problem.

How schools will evolve remains to be seen. Certainly the notion of a school as a physical location is already being rethought. Severance *et al.* (2008) describe such an environment as a *Virtual Learning Environment* and suggest that teachers and students will use a mash-up of existing tools available on the internet to learn, build and create.

Collective creativity and technology

When technology was first used as a tool in a learning environment, it simply delivered the same learning in a new way. Some thought this new way was more efficient, while others thought technology was a hindrance to learning (Attwell & Hughes, 2010; Ferdousi, 2009; Mumtaz, 2000). Allen and Long's article talks about how the simple way that technology was first viewed—as a more "efficient" way of delivering tradition learning—was a naïve view, given the way that networks interact with learning software (Allen & Long, 2009). Because knowledge is distributed through social networks, the way people construct knowledge changes:

> . . . it means creating new kinds of educational systems that do not adopt the affordances of the Internet for knowledge work and repackage them. Instead, these new systems need to be gateways or interfaces between the educational environment and the complex, rich world of knowledge already to be found and created online . . . If early ideas about networks and learning emphasized the transmission of "the university" to remote places . . . then future developments will need to explore the distribution of students through their knowledge across the Internet . . . [A]ttention must be paid to expanding the network of productive interactions beyond the students' peers, to include judicious interactions between students and the real knowledge networks in which they are learning to be a part.
> (Allen & Long, 2009)

People do not appear to collaborate purely for self-gain. Research indicates that, even when economic structures are in place to reward participation, people will often forego the economic reward in order to share information, expertise, knowledge and ideas (Golle *et al.*, 2001; Raban, 2008). The web provides a particularly good environment for sharing, building and collecting information. Information can be built rapidly and adapted to a new environment quickly. Unlike books, lectures or even expertise, the web can change its environment and knowledge quickly. This is because of a combination of two elements—its collective nature and its resultant adaptive nature.

This quality is called collective-adaptive (European Commission, 2009; Ilon & Altmann, 2012). The knowledge of any given individual is often less than the knowledge of a collective of people who share information. As this information is collected and shared, the information changes—information adapts. When we post a blog or a new article goes up on the web on a news event, the nature of the story changes. The world learns. A new understanding emerges. The knowledge adapts and we move on to add yet another piece of information and adapt the story further.

This is highly linked to crowdsourcing. People can *combine* their knowledge to build an entirely new set of knowledge (Malone *et al.*, 2009). This kind of possibility evolved informally at first but is now being harnessed in a formal way. A good example is the University of Washington using the power of the online gaming community (and later, untrained people with good visualization skills and a bit of time to spare) to visualize how a protein structure might be folded into its smallest (most efficient) structural form. People did not have to know anything about proteins—only to have intuition about how a complex structure presented to them visually might be folded down into a more compact form. Their work resulted in an HIV protein structure being compacted in a matter of weeks—something top researchers had been trying to do for years (*UW|360*, 2011). The value of this crowdsourcing effort to the scientific community has resulted in a formalization of the effort for other protein structures and, reportedly, is fun for at-home players and produces results useful for scientists.[1]

Frequently, such abilities as crowdsourcing and collective–adaptive techniques are used in communities of practice. Such communities are formed, often informally, by people who have a common set of interests, goals, ideas or contexts and wish to share knowledge, ideas, solution or a learning environment (Lesser *et al.*, 2000; Wenger, 2000). Such communities often have the advantages of social networks in that they are emergent and self-sustaining. Norgaard shows how such communities can combine diverse knowledge to solve complex problems (Norgaard, 2004). These communities will look substantially different than the teacher-led, hierarchical environments where students were asked to master knowledge (Jin *et al.*, 2010). Sawyer (2007) sees these possibilities as a new kind of "group genius" that can be brought into the classroom.

Even as it is collective, such creative learning skills require the incorporation of diverse thinking because, if everyone thinks alike, no new thoughts can be incorporated (Granovetter, 1973). Sawyer maintains that the old ways of instruction—developed for an industrial economy in the early twentieth century—require that students learn free of the context in which they live and will work. Learning to be creative requires that learning be linked to context, social interaction and personal reflection (Sawyer, 2006, p. 4).

This type of learning has been studied by psychologists and is called situative learning (Greeno, 1998; Lave & Wenger, 1991). This shifts the focus of learning context and analysis from the individual to cultural, social, political or community systems. This draws from social learning theory because the assumption is that people learn in the context of other people (Bandura, 1977; Davidson-Hunt, 2006).

Note

1   To say nothing of the challenge it presents to human capital theory, which posits that you are paid what you are worth to society. The online gamers are paid nothing, but produced results worth millions of dollars. The biologists, on the other hand, are paid large salaries but couldn't produce the highly valuable results. In truth, it was a collaboration over a complex problem that produced the results. The biologists conceptualized the problem and now know what to do with the results, the computer scientists conceptualized an online game that would attract gamers, and the gamers contributed their collective intelligence.

References

Allen, M. and Long, J. (2009). Learning as knowledge networking: conceptual foundations for revised uses of the internet in higher education. In *Proceedings of the world congress on engineering and computer science, 2009* (pp. 652–657). San Francisco, CA. Retrieved from www.iaeng.org/publication/WCECS2009/

Attwell, G. and Hughes, J. (2010). Pedagogic approaches to using technology for learning: literature review. Lifelong Learning, UK. Retrieved from http://dera.ioe.ac.uk/id/eprint/2021

Bandura, A. (1977). *Social learning theory* (Vol. viii). Oxford: Prentice Hall.

Chatti, M. A., Jarke, M. and Frosch-Wilke, D. (2007). The future of e-learning: a shift to knowledge networking and social software. *International Journal of Knowledge and Learning*, 3(4), 404–420.

Davidson-Hunt, I. J. (2006). Adaptive learning networks: developing resource management knowledge through social learning forums. *Human Ecology*, 34(4), 593–614.

European Commission. (2009). *Collective Adaptive Systems*. Brussels: European Commission. Retrieved from ftp://ftp.cordis.europa.eu/pub/fp7/ict/docs/fet-proactive/shapefetip-wp2011-12-02_en.pdf

Ferdousi, B. (2009). *A study of factors that affect instructors' intention to use e-learning systems in two-year colleges*. Dissertation, Nova Southeastern University. Retrieved from http://dllibrary.spu.ac.th:8080/dspace/bitstream/123456789/2541/1/Bilquis%20J.Ferdousi.pdf

Field, J. (2006). *Lifelong learning and the new educational order*. Stoke on Trent, UK: Trentham Books.

Golle, P., Leyton-Brown, K., Mironov, I. and Lillibridge, M. (2001). Incentives for sharing in peer-to-peer networks. In G. Schneider (ed.), *Electronic commerce* (pp. 75–87). Berlin: Springer.

Granovetter, M. S. (1973). The strength of weak ties. *American Journal of Sociology*, *78*(6), 1360–1380.

Greeno, J. G. (1998). The situativity of knowing, learning, and research. *American Psychologist*, *53*(1), 5–26.

Ilon, L. and Altmann, J. (2012). Using collective adaptive networks to solve education problems in poor countries. In *Society for design and process science*. Berlin: Omnibooks Online. Retrieved from http://sdps.omnibooksonline.com/2012/index.html

Jarvela, S., Naykki, P., Laru, J. and Luokkanen, T. (2007). Structuring and regulating collaborative learning in higher education with wireless networks and mobile tools. *Educational Technology & Society*, *10*(4), 71–79.

Jin, L., Wen, Z. and Gough, N. (2010). Social virtual worlds for technology-enhanced learning on an augmented learning platform. *Learning Media and Technology*, *35*(2), 139–153.

Kronholz, J. (2012). Can Khan move the bell curve to the right? *Education Next*, *12*(2). Retrieved from http://educationnext.org/can-khan-move-the-bell-curve-to-the-right/

Lave, J. and Wenger, E. (1991). *Situated learning: Legitimate peripheral participation*. Cambridge: Cambridge University Press.

Lesser, E., Fontaine, M. and Slusher, J. (eds). (2000). *Knowledge and communities*. Woburn, MA: Butterworth Heinemann.

Malone, T., Laubacher, R. and Dellasrocas, C. (2009, February 1). *Harnessing crowds: Mapping the genome of collective intelligence*. Working Paper, Alfred P. Sloan School of Management, MIT. Retrieved from http://hdl.handle.net/1721.1/66259

Mumtaz, S. (2000). Factors affecting teachers' use of information and communications technology: a review of the literature. *Journal of Information Techology for Teacher Education*, *9*(3), 319–342.

Norgaard, R. B. (2004). Learning and knowing collectively. *Ecological Economics*, *49*(2), 231–241.

OECD. (2009). *OECD reviews of innovation policy: Korea*. Paris: OECD.

Papert, S. (1993). *The children's machine: Rethinking school in the age of the computer*. New York: Basic Books.

Raban, D. R. (2008). The incentive structure in an online information market. *Journal of the American Society for Information Science and Technology*, *59*(14), 2284–2295.

Sawyer, K. (2006). The new science of learning. In K. Sawyer (ed.), *Cambridge handbook of the learning sciences* (pp. 1–16). New York: Cambridge University Press.

——. (2007). *Group genius: The creative power of collaboration*. New York: Basic Books.

Severance, C., Hardin, J. and Whyte, A. (2008). The coming functionality mash-up in personal learning environments. *Interactive Learning Environments*, *16*(1), 47–62.

UW|360 (November 2011). Foldit. University of Washington, Seattle: UWTV. Retrieved from www.youtube.com/watch?v=9tI3GioaH8Q

Wenger, E. (2000). Communities of practice and social learning systems. *Organization*, *7*(2), 225–246.

Zappe, S., Liecht, R., Messner, J. and Litzinger, T. (2009). "Flipping" the classroom to explore active learning in a large undergraduate course. In *Proceedings, American Society for Engineering Education Annual Conference & Exposition*.

11a Social well-being

Surely there must be as many definitions of social well-being as there are people on the earth. Each of us wants just a slightly different mix. I value the freedom to travel without many constraints; you value safety and don't mind the constraints. Abdullah wants his children to have access to good education; Alejandra wants to pay fewer taxes. No one can define social well-being in specific terms that have worldwide acceptance. But surely we could agree to some generalities: absence of poverty, the freedom to make important choices, the ability to plan ahead without large instabilities throwing our lives into chaos. We think that basic health is necessary but might disagree where to draw the line on public expenditure. We would all like to know the latest news, to shop where there are foods we like and to be able to celebrate the weddings and births of those close to us.

Counting poverty

It would be easy if we could find one measure that could capture all these possibilities, all these options, all these potential definitions and boil it all down to something concrete we could quantify. If we had such a measure, we would know if we were making progress and if, based upon the measures of others, we might be able to do better. For decades, perhaps longer, that measure was money. Money, it was assumed, could capture our ability to buy things, to travel, to learn, to participate, to stabilize our lives. Simply, if we had more money, we had more things, then, we assumed we had more possibilities, stability and freedoms. So, it stood to reason a society that had more money had a higher social well-being than one that had less money. We could hope that this wealth would be reasonably equitably spread, but the first goal might be to ensure that there was a lot of money to spread around.

It turns out that this particular measure does not do a very good job of capturing social well-being—at least not in today's world. And, even if it did, money itself is hard to measure. For example, if a paper mill opens upstream from your riverside house, you will notice that the river becomes polluted and is not as pleasant as it once was. The value of your house goes down, the quality of the water deteriorates making the town's water supply more expensive to maintain and the tranquil country road you once lived on is now filled with noisy trucks. Although the paper mill is generating money (some of which is given to the society in taxes and wages), it is doing so at a price; and that price is not subtracted from profits. Of course, with today's pollution laws, this may no longer be the case in some countries.

Nevertheless, it is an important idea. Not all costs are truly accounted for. There is a price for inequality as well. People left at the margins of society are less likely to be contributors to its common goals such as laws, conventions, common expenditure, civic participation or volunteering. Their lives are less stable, and in order to stabilize their lives the society must support them in some way—housing, food or other services. In this way, the society also stabilizes itself. Furthermore, the lower levels of education of the poor mean they have fewer opportunities to contribute knowledge, creative ideas and insights—the resources that run a knowledge-based economy.

The problem of properly capturing wealth, has been covered in Chapters 5a and 5b. But the ability to understand social well-being is a somewhat different puzzle. Are people with little money genuinely worse off than those who have more money? Let me transport you back to my days in Micronesia, which was then a very remote, only marginally developed set of islands. There were no paved runways; there was one flight a day on the main island of Chuuk—it headed east or west on alternate days. There were no traffic lights. There was electricity on only one of the hundreds of inhabited islands. There was virtually no indoor plumbing. My family gathered rainwater on the roof for us to make tea and brush our teeth in the morning.

My husband was from an even more remote island. To get there, one had to board a small ship that traveled to his island about once every six weeks. If one was lucky, one could book an actual bed in a room with six or so other beds. Most people just went to the deck and laid out woven mats, which they shared with their family, chickens and goods they were transporting. It took about five days to reach his island—Oneop.

I clearly remember my first trip to Oneop. We had been on the ship for days until finally I was told we were near the island. Someone had come alongside the ship on a small outboard motorboat and I was hauled over the side into the waiting arms of strange men who caught me and planted me on the boat. From there, we motored out into the open ocean for an hour or two—no islands visible. I had to have faith that someone knew where we were going and had a sense of direction—a good sense of direction.

Finally we arrived at a small dock where, it appeared, the entire island was lined up to meet us. I was introduced to person after person and told I was related to this one or that one. They wore colorful dresses and loose-fitting pants and shirts. The children hid behind their parent's legs but stared at me endlessly. For the next several days I was able to wander this small island (about

15 minutes walk from end to end) and see the ocean, houses, small fields, children and daily life. People, it appeared, had a good life. There was plenty of food. There was enough formal income from relatives (like me) living elsewhere that people could afford cloth, rubber flip-flops, tea and fishing line. The culture had developed a way to preserve some foods so people did not worry about having enough to eat. There was a lot of native medical treatment, so if you broke a bone or burned yourself, someone knew a way to treat you.

No doubt, if people had a chance to have a refrigerator, they would have one—the occasional cold coconut juice would have been welcome. Women faced the possibility of complications from childbirth and there were no antibiotics around. But, as a general way of living, people could eat, make decisions about their lives, count on stability from one day to the next, were not bothered by a heavy-handed government and could learn basic skills in the village school. Yet, if one could measure the wealth or money on that island, it would have looked abysmal. I am sure that it was less than one dollar a day per person—the standard measure of absolute poverty.

I am reminded of the many posters of African children showing poor living conditions and asking for donations. Usually, the children chosen have good skin, proportional arms and bellies, a toothy grin and glossy eyes full of wonder. For anyone who has seen widespread poverty, this is surely not the picture of destitution. Such children are listless, have distended bellies and skinny arms and their eyes stare at you without focus. The children of Micronesia tended to be naked until about puberty, but lack of clothing was not a sign of poverty; nor is it fair to view all black-skinned Africans as poor. Poverty is something else.

Poverty is, indeed, lack of food and water, shelter and security. But it is also lack of stability—not knowing if your life will be secure the next day or the next year. Freedom from oppression. It is being able to avoid polio in a world where polio is a distant threat for most people. But, beyond these basic needs and freedoms, it is the opportunity to use one's intelligence, culture, creativity, relationships and social structures to seek and build opportunities for oneself. This is why education is often considered a basic human right—not that an education necessarily feeds you in and of itself, but it opens many other doors— it expands the possibilities.

People who see that their lives have possibilities, that they can create new ideas, explore opportunities and build new things are not the ones who are protesting on the street against their governments, or the ones who are making bombs to destroy the lives of others, or the ones looking for a creative way to rob the neighborhood store or attack you on the subway to take your money. People who have lives of possibilities are happy, busy, engaged. They are also building new possibilities for those around them, showing others what might be and finding opportunities where none existed before. They are building their societies. This is a good definition of social well-being.

Poverty as lack of opportunities

If, as the World Bank (and others) used to point out that "the poor's most abundant asset [is their] labor." (World Bank, 1990, p. 3), then this is true only because their opportunities to create non-linear resources is constrained. The lingering belief that poverty is properly defined by the accumulation and production of physical resources is partly to blame here. Anyone who has witnessed a population on the edge of starvation will attest to the very real fact that people who lack food, water or shelter are at the edge of existence. In these conditions, their daily—even hourly—pursuit is to ensure that there is enough food to eat to maintain life. One's time, energy and thinking power will turn to nothing else. This is why schools in many parts of the world provide food for children in school: a child who is hungry cannot concentrate on the lessons at hand.

Just one rung up the ladder are people whose life is threatened by instability. Those caught in political or military instability can think of nothing more than to get themselves to safe ground. Living with the threat of annihilation means that one's time, energy and thinking power will be put to finding a safer existence. People in any of these circumstance need immediate relief because, not only is their daily existence in peril, their ability to use their resources to improve their situation has been stifled.

Once one can get beyond the struggle to survive on a daily basis, however, there is is the inevitable human desire to improve one's life. Humans are enormously creative in this pursuit. The pursuit is often focused on the *possibilities* as much as it is on daily needs. Someone invented the telephone as much out of curiosity as out of necessity. Twitter founder Biz Stone described developing Twitter as a "fun project" among a group of friends with no idea that it would help start revolutions (Gross, 2011). But equally as creative was the woman in rural India who methodically researched and developed a better feed for cows made out of local resources that were not otherwise being used (Shroff-Mehta, 2002). After years of work and development, her knowledge spread and she was able to make a small business selling the feed. She had no education or training in research, just a desire to make her own life better and enough spare time, energy and thinking power to devote to the development of a new idea.

Although people everywhere, given even the smallest opportunity, will try to invent some means of improving their lives, not all have much opportunity to do so even if they live beyond the bare margins of life. In 1960, North Korea was viewed as having surpassed it neighbor, South Korea, in development. The country had increasing industrial capacity and its people had stable lives with opportunities to work productively. Just 40 years later, one can hardly imagine that North Koreans ever surpassed their South Korean neighbors. Today South Korea is the highest scoring country on international achievement tests. It is the 15th largest economy in the world, although its population accounts for less than 1 percent of the world's people.

Hundreds of books have analyzed how South Korea grew from one of the least developed countries in the world to one of the most developed. Its political, social, educational, economic, spiritual, cultural and structural changes worked to reinforce this growth. But what binds all this analysis together is that the South Korean people have been freed, increasingly, to create, explore and invent in their own context. In so doing, their world—once confined to scratching out a living from the land—has gradually expanded to minor industries, more education, better opportunities and increasing links to the rest of the world.

Each of these changes increased their opportunities. In a sense, it freed their creativity and they used these opportunities to build a world of their making. Much can be said of the Confucian work ethic, the long hours of high-pressure study and the coordination between government and industry. But each leads to a central conclusion: each step along the way, South Koreans have been able to broaden their horizons and make use of increasing opportunities. While their North Korean neighbors now largely sit in non-electrified villages without so much as a telephone (much less a cell phone), South Koreans are the most linked people in the world.

Amartya Sen, an Indian who migrated to the United States originally to pursue a doctorate, looked at the problems of poverty and its attendant theories in economics and ultimately rejected those theories. He had seen poverty and, like me, knew that the poor did not lack in intelligence, creativity and drive. Given even the barest of opportunities, the poor would exploit to the fullest any opportunity given to them. Ultimately, he was elected President of the American Economic Association and also won a Nobel Prize for his work. His theory was that, while the poorest of the poor focused daily on mere survival, given any opportunities to improve their situation, they would do so. His theory was it was lack of opportunities that constrained development—not necessarily lack of physical resources. His theory has revolutionized the field of development economics and is now widely known as the "Capability Approach." It is so named because he claimed that it was the capability of the poor (to use what opportunities that existed) that leads the poor out of poverty.

Thinking this way, the focus is not necessarily on market production—how much the poor can produce and contribute to a market. Rather, it is on reducing their barriers to create and build. In this sense, the "solutions" do not come "down to them" but rather are adapted or invented "by them." Their increasing abilities gradually link them locally and globally. The rural Indian woman who learned how to make better cattle feed out of available agricultural waste could, in fact, go further if her opportunities were greater—if she had the capability. If she had links to a banking sector or an agricultural network, she could franchise her feed and educate herself enough to continue to improve on the feed. Her ability to improve her life, the life of her family and of her community (and her nation and the world) is constrained only by the barriers to opportunities.

The theory is revolutionary in that it places the central heart of development at local levels rather than at global levels. Rather than thinking of development as a linear path from the market economies to the poor, it assumes a system's logic—the cycle of opportunities is as strong as its linkage building. The old thinking assumed that poverty was alleviated by bringing resources in from outside and linking markets such that formal-sector employment added to one's buying power. Development assistance monies were aimed at increasing the resource base whether that resource was infrastructure (dams, roads, airports), natural resource exploitation (farms, mines) or labor (education). The new thinking is that we all exist in a linked, systemic world where resources, opportunities and ingenuity are created from a shared world system. Adding nodes (people, villages, countries) increases our resources, opportunities and ingenuity and when those nodes are strengthened, the entire world benefits.

In this view, strengthening the margins does not always imply sending resources down the network although in unstable and dire poverty situations, this may be the only starting point. Rather, strengthening these nodes is much like South Korea's development–remove the barriers to local development and let the people build a world that makes sense to their culture, their way of life and their chosen means of linking to the world.

Examples of success abound, but let's look at one good example. Eleni Gabre-Madhin, an Ethiopian woman, has broadened opportunities for Ethiopians and increased income, not by giving away resources but by removing market barriers. A PhD from Cornell, she asked the question, "How could one part of my country have starved in the mid-1980s when another part had excess production?" She learned that the ability of local farmers to sell and transport their produce was constrained. They could only sell excess produce when some-one came to their village, offered them a price and transported the produce. The farmers knew that the prices they were offered were unfair—just enough to ensure they would produce the next year.

She began by creating a trading market for coffee, where local villages are linked in to a central core. Local farmers can go to the village headquarters and offer their coffee beans for sale; buyers bid for the farmer's coffee beans, based on market prices and their transport access to the village. The farmer can sell his/her coffee beans instantly. The coffee is stored for pick-up and the buyer, in turn, can instantly sell the beans on the national or global market. Prices are globally competitive and local farmers have access to prices set by global demand. Local farmers have a reliable outlet for their coffee beans, which gives them a much higher price. Although Ms. Gabre-Madhin began with coffee, the idea has been extended to other farm products so that excess produce in one part of the country can easily be shifted to another part of the country or another nation.

What changed the lives of these poor rural farmers was an idea—it was not a resource transfer from the wealthy to the poor. The idea removed the barriers to trade that constrained local capabilities. As a result, farmers are producing more, accumulating more capital and changing their agricultural practices to upgrade the quality and quantity of their produce. More money circulates locally to improve local schooling, health care, housing and food. It is notable that this idea included creating links all the way from the local village to the global market, so a critical part of its success was not just increasing local resources, but linking those villages to a world that had additional capabilities. The capability of local Ethiopian villages to grow produce, to get a fair price, to have it transported quickly and to link it to the entire world, increases the capability of the entire world.

The ability of these Ethiopian coffee farmers to create income from a mere idea is a stark reminder that the resources of the poor go far beyond their labor. No doubt, the farmers are still working hard, but they are working for more money, increasing their own opportunities, increasing education and learning themselves. They will learn, grow, work and pass on information to the extent that this new capability will increase their income. Their constraint was not physical resources; the constraint was knowledge and networks. Viewing the poor as intelligent, willing and capable of learning, vigorous, creative and possessing sustainable social networks that work on their behalf turns the development equation around. How can the world benefit from their intelligence, creativity and energy?

Is Pima's education too focused—as it traditionally was in an industrial world—on memorizing "the basics" so she can join the labor at the local factory? Perhaps this is one option for her. But if we think of her potential capability, we will also help create a world of ideas, opportunities and possibilities for her. We will teach her about the networks from which she can get new ideas. We will help her build her own networks to neighboring villages and her nation. We will help her understand that she can grow based on the foundation of her village, her culture and the ways of life around her. Pima will do what Eleni Gabre-Madhin did: she will look around her at local ways, local constraints and local opportunities and create a new way of doing things.

Pima's educational success depends fundamentally upon her education's ability structure to introduce not just skills and mastery, but also networks, collaboration and applications to specific situations. Remember, these are skills that made Lotus Notes so valuable to IBM. It is what Eleni Gabre-Madhin did; it is the education of the future. It fits within Amartya Sen's ideas of capability and a view of the world as a networked system. Strengthen Pima and you strengthen the world.

Education and social well-being

Picture Pima's school. Although I did not see her particular school, I have seen many poor schools. Many are literally grass shacks that are unstable in a storm and drip in the rain. I have seen schools where the writing instruments were sticks used to draw in the mud. I have seen schools consisting only of benches under trees. I have seen "modern" schools without windows, where children huddle together in the cold while even colder air seeps into the classrooms. I have seen blackboards that are so worn that the contrast with the chalk is barely visible. Many, many schools do not have texts for the children or only a notebook of a few pages, which must last them the entire term—no room for mistakes. I have a bottle filled with 42 pencils I collected in rural Malawi. I traded new pencils for the pencils they were using. I can easily hold all 42 pencils in the palm of my hand. Many are so short I find it incredible to believe that anyone could write with them.

How could a school so poor, so under-resourced, so desolate, possibly do anything more than teach the basics—if that. And yet, sitting in those classrooms are children equally as smart, as motivated and as curious as were the world's greatest leaders, scientists, economists, civic organizers and entrepreneurs. If you ever sat in a classroom and were bored because the lesson was moving too slowly, imagine being taught in such a school without even the ability to write down an idea or practice your math problems. These children are not short of drive, curiosity, thinking power or ideas. They are short of the opportunities, links and possibilities that children in much better schools face. Just as a South Korean child has a good chance of an excellent education and a place of productivity that satisfies his family and his nation, so, equally, would Pima if she faced the same set of circumstances. If it is only about the location where one is born, how is it possible that we have been under-educating the poor for generations?

We do so because our education for the poor follows the old industrial thinking of development: we assume that the possibilities for the poor lie primarily in moving them up through the ranks of the educated, who can then, step by step to join the modern or wealthier world. The goal is to move them—one step at a time. Move away from their lives as poor people and toward the lifestyle of those who have more resources, more money. With basic math, one can be part of a market and buy and sell. With algebra, one can take a job as a clerk in the local government office. With calculus, one can move far away and possibly go to college and get a specialist's degree. The source of "development" is far away from the village and has little to do with the village itself.

If we move our thinking to a world system of learning, then the village is a critical element of learning. It can be the path toward social well-being. In some sense, grounding in a particular culture, physical environment and values is the *only* starting place for education. If a network consists of nodes that are linked to a larger system, then each village is a possible node if it has linkages to the larger system. Education is one of these links. One has a unique role to play in the system. Social progress means that the unique characteristics of the particular environment become part of a world system and the linkages are the strength. Rather than thinking of education as moving a person away from the village, rather, the village (or town or city or culture or nation) is *the very source* of the strengths that create social well-being.

This is not to say that a village child, once educated, will necessarily choose to live within the village, although they might. Rather, it is to say that the child's education is only as strong as the child's initial grounding within the village. And, rather than thinking of a child "moving further and further away" from a village as a sign of progress, rather the link to the village strengthens the child. The village benefits and so does the child as she becomes increasingly educated.

How does this work? Let's go back to the example of the Ethiopian coffee growers. Their incomes are rising substantially, not because village people left the village for jobs elsewhere and abandoned the village, but because the village got linked to the larger system. The unique characteristics of the villages of Ethiopia provide the potential for this increased social well-being. Had the same system been put into, say, the hills of Ireland, it would not have worked; it was designed for the specific needs and opportunities of a unique group of people living in a unique area. If the idea grows and is exported, it will have to be changed to accommodate very different circumstances.

In this instance, the creative person behind the idea had received her PhD elsewhere and understood the characteristics of a global market as well as the characteristics of the local communities and their needs and possibilities. But this is the point: without her grounding in the culture, understanding of local circumstances and ability to work within those particular circumstances, neither she nor the villages she has affected would have had the same opportunities. Without her grounding in Ethiopian culture, her understanding of the history, internal workings and possibilities, she could not have created this business; her Cornell classmates from Iowa or Bangkok are unlikely to have built the same business.

The success of this business actually moved Eleni Gabre-Madhin closer to her cultural roots. She had lived most of her life in the United States, but she had to move back to Ethiopia and become reacquainted with local conditions and circumstances in order to make her business successful. It was her very knowledge of the country, its challenges and its potential that created her success. Her thinking encompassed a world system of human food, trade, communication and knowledge; the link she created between local villages and global systems (in this case global markets) strengthened not only herself, but the local villages and the world. Education for development was not a path away from the village, but was based on the elements of village life and a knowledge of the larger world system. Once again, we can identify the educational elements: (1) mastery of skills and knowledge; (2) ability to use and create networks; (3) ability to build knowledge in a collaborative framework; and (4) ability to apply the first three within a particular framework.

Eleni Gabre-Madhin's ability to increase social well-being derived, in part, from her unique understanding of Ethiopia and her existing networks within the country. None of her Cornell classmates had this knowledge and those networks. Pima will have a similar set of unique characteristics as she is educated. She won't have to have a PhD to link her village to a new way of distributing medicines to local villages; she won't need a PhD to use existing social networks to spread the word about new opportunities. Just as the rural woman in India used her local knowledge to improve the output of milk from local cows, the foundation is the understanding of local circumstances and opportunities. If the rural woman had more education, she could possibly have started an industry that helped farmers all over India; her constraint was lack of knowledge of the larger world.

If you wanted to design a new, competitive passenger plane, would you choose the entire team from Ohio or a team of individuals with equal skill levels from around the world? If you choose the team from around the world you receive not only in their skills, but you also get a diversity of ways of understanding the world, of putting together logic and also of people who can image the diverse passengers, mechanics and pilots who will use the planes worldwide. Diversity of cultures and ideas helps the entire world and increases the creativity and innovation. But to reduce poverty, it is not so much who you can "pull out of the neighborhood" but whether their special knowledge and skills can build links to and from the neighborhood. This applies to poor neighborhoods in Los Angeles and villages in rural Nepal.

These scenarios, nevertheless, overlook one other element of education in development. We need no longer think of education as one child, studying by lamplight, mastering a subject area and passing a test. The impact of education can be applied to an entire village or neighborhood. Provide an opportunity and the village will rise to the occasion. Bore a well in a rural area and it increases their agricultural productivity. But begin with having the village analyze its local situation, look into alternative agricultural techniques, decide to adapt them and seek assistance to bore a well and one has moved the village in a number of ways. They have done the research to know how agriculture is done elsewhere; they have used their local understanding and projected the possibility of moving collectively to a new system; they have made a decision that a bore hole might be a starting point; they have begun to understand the local NGOs and their resources; they have applied for and been given the well. In a sense, they have raised their knowledge, understood the application of knowledge from elsewhere to their unique situation and utilized this new network to locate the resources.

They have, (1) mastered new knowledge (research into new farming techniques); (2) worked collaboratively; (3) built networks; and (4) applied broader knowledge and networks in a particular situation. Just as a child builds her world as she uses these new abilities, so does the community build its world. When they hear of a new strain of seeds, they are likely to utilize these same networks, research skills and local knowledge to investigate and adopt it. This form of education—thinking of *collective knowledge*, understanding that in a linked, world system of learning a village is not something at the bottom of the education ladder, but a potentially important link to a system and builds social well-being at a collective level. Further, it answers one of the lingering conundrums of development projects—how to make them sustainable. The knowledge gained by the community is the center of sustainability because it does not disappear when the donor funded project members get on the plane home.

References

Eleni Zaude Gabre-Madhin, Founder of Ethiopia Commodity Exchange. (2009, July 22). Retrieved from www.pbs.org/wnet/wideangle/episodes/the-market-maker/intro duction/5000/

Gross, T. (2011, February 16). *Twitter's biz stone on starting a revolution: Fresh air.* WHYY, Philadelphia, PA: npr.org. Retrieved from www.npr.org/2011/02/16/133775340/twitters-biz-stone-on-starting-a-revolution

Shroff-Mehta, P. (2002). *Mapping local knowledges in Indian rural development* (PhD Dissertation). State University of New York at Buffalo, Buffalo, NY.

World Bank. (1990). *World Development Report 1990: Poverty.* Washington, DC: World Bank. Retrieved from http://go.worldbank.org/XWTCZ81300

11b Changing views on social welfare economics

If ideas benefit society in ways that don't always show up in markets (industry), then industrial progress is not the right way to measure a society's progress—at best it is an undercount of what benefits the society. The current measure that focuses purely on industrial output could actually work against the interests of society. Wars and natural disasters, after all, increase national output because they require the production of new goods and services, but they do not add to the overall well-being of society. New apps that help us mitigate the human and market costs of disasters or forego wars might not register in markets, but have substantial value within society. The value and problems that cross borders (such as Twitter or refugees) also are difficult to capture if value is only measured in national terms. These problems are increasingly recognized and the race is on to find new measures of social welfare.

Education and society welfare

This shift in thinking is fairly new. Since the 1940s, neoclassical economists have been in general agreement about what constitutes optimal social well-being (social welfare or welfare economics). Mishan, writing in 1960, reviews the history of social welfare and maintains that the fundamental theory of welfare economics has remained largely unchanged (Mishan, 1960). Most authors trace the modern version of the theory to Samuelson (1947). Neoclassical social welfare theory says that a society's happiness (well-being or welfare) is the sum of each person's optimal use of their resources (time, money, energy). By extension, increasing resources to individuals within a society increases the happiness of the society; even if only one individual gets more resources, the total sum for the society is raised. One way of raising the society's overall resources is to increase industrial productivity. In so doing, both the resource base of the society grows and so does the resource base of at least some of the individuals within the society (Feldman & Serrano, 2006; Fitzpatrick, 2001).

There are many problems with this view of social welfare in today's world —especially given the characteristics of knowledge. The conditions required to meet the optimal conditions for society were explicitly and mathematically based on an assumption of increasing returns to scale (Mishan, 1960)—whereas knowledge has the opposite characteristic (Romer, 1990). But, even if this technical/mathematical condition was not a problem, it fails to take into account the social conditions of the population, which may not be reflected by their income. Suppose there are two subsistence farmers—one lives in a place where she can grow abundant crops to feed her family and another lives in a place that has gradually become desert. Yet the current measures of GDP count both as having the same level of welfare.[1] Further, it also fails to take into account the fact that the world is highly interlinked: the use of resources in one society affects the well-being of all other societies.

Much of the value created in the world is no longer accounted for by market metrics. For example, Google's search engine is important to the knowledge productivity of many nations. This book was substantially enhanced by the use of Google and Google Scholar and many other free online tools; office works and scholars worldwide use it daily to improve productivity, yet they pay nothing for this service so it has "no" market value in terms of GDP. Even if they did, the use and creation of knowledge through Google is no longer separable by countries. There is increasing evidence that it is the very links *between* nations that most determines new value (The Royal Society, 2011).

Many attempts are being made to completely rethink how value can be measured in this emerging world and most involve global system measures

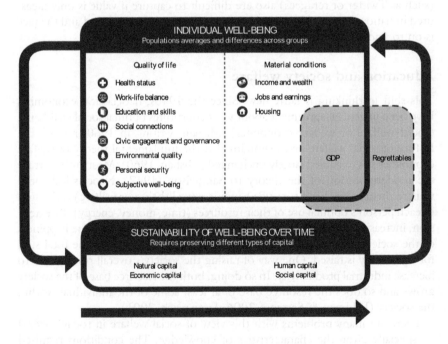

Figure 11.1 The OECD well-being conceptual framework

Source: OECD (2013, p. 21)

rather than national linear measures. The OECD has produced an alternative framework that gives weight to both material goods and non-material goods (OECD, 2013). The goal of the system is sustainability rather than growth (Figure 11.1). The OECD has taken a first stab at a new metric based on this framework. It is called the "Better life index" (OECD, n.d.).

Capabilities, equity and social well-being

For many, it seems incongruent that social well-being could have nothing to do with poverty but, within neoclassical economics, this is the fact. The thinking is that if each person acts on their own behalf to maximize their happiness vis-à-vis their resources, then there can be no redistribution of resources by the society that improves social well-being (Arrow, 1963; Sugden, 1993). Because people are free to make their own choices about what to purchase relative to their own preferences, who is to say (the government, your neighbor or even a well-meaning charity organization) that one person is better off with something that another person has (Friedman & Friedman, 1980). What if I have a lot of oranges to eat and you take some away to give to someone who is hungry, but they are allergic to oranges? They would never have made the purchase and I'm not happy with my oranges being taken away, so society is not left better off. In this view, economic theory is neutral to the unequal spread of resources.

But Amartya Sen challenged this view (Sen, 1993). In his view, a poor person doesn't so much want oranges (or a house, or clothing or food), as they want the *capability* to get such things. Thus, maximizing any society's overall well-being is not really about redistributing *resources* so much as it is about ensuring that people have the capability to use their own skills, intelligence, time and energy to pursue the things they care about. Distribution of capabilities improves the well-being of the society because it creates the possibility for people to improve their own lives. In so doing, this improves the overall well-being of the society. They have the choice of whether to buy more oranges or not.

Knowledge economics is compatible with this view. It begins with a new definition of efficiency. In an industrial society, people who had been similarly trained and educated produced similar ideas—this was efficient: they thought alike, communicated easily with each other and got through schooling in a similarly "easy" manner. In this environment, scarce schooling resources and industrial resources could be efficiently allocated (allocative efficiency). But knowledge is not a scarce resource; rather, new ideas require a different kind of scarce resource—fresh, creative thinking. Network theory shows that people who lie outside one's usual reference group are more likely to be the source of different ideas (Granovetter, 1973; Norberg *et al.*, 2013). Thus, spreading knowledge-creating capabilities broadly among the population may well reap positive social returns.

This is known as adaptive efficiency (Arthur, 1996; Ma & Jalil, 2008; North, 1995). Adaptive efficiency is the new efficiency in a knowledge-based economy.

Arthur speculates that Bill Gates may have been particularly good at this kind of efficiency. "Bill Gates is not so much a wizard of technology as a wizard of precognition, of discerning the shape of the next game" (Arthur, 1996, p. 5).

Note

1　In fact, if neither of them take any of their produce to market, neither contributes to GDP, so their welfare contribution to GDP is zero whether they manage to eat and thrive or whether they starve.

References

Arrow, K. (1963). *Social choice and individual values.* New York: Wiley.

Arthur, B. (1996). Increasing returns and the new world of business. *Harvard Business Review, 74,* 100–109.

Feldman, A. M. and Serrano, R. (2006). *Welfare economics and social choice theory.* New York: Springer Science & Business Media.

Fitzpatrick, T. (2001). *Welfare theory: An introduction.* New York: Palgrave.

Friedman, M. and Friedman, R. (1980). *Free to choose.* London: Secker & Warbur.

Granovetter, M. S. (1973). The strength of weak ties. *American Journal of Sociology, 78*(6), 1360–1380.

Ma, Y. and Jalil, A. (2008). Financial development, economic growth and adaptive efficiency: A comparison between China and Pakistan. *China & World Economy, 16*(6), 97–111.

Mishan, E. J. (1960). A survey of welfare economics, 1939–59. *The Economic Journal, 70*(278), 197–265.

Norberg, J., Wilson, Walker, B. and Ostrom, E. (2013). Diversity and resilience of socio-ecological systems. In J. Norberg and G. Cumming (eds), *Complexity theory for a sustainable future.* New York: Columbia University Press.

North, D. C. (1995). Economic theory in a dynamic economic world. *Business Economics, 30*(1), 7–12.

OECD. (2013). *How's life?* Paris: OECD. Retrieved from www.oecd-ilibrary.org/ ;jsessionid=3pnn04dlf3xm8.x-oecd-live-02content/book/9789264201392-en

———. (n.d.). OECD better life index. Retrieved from www.oecdbetterlifeindex.org/

Romer, P. (1990). Endogenous technological change. *Journal of Political Economy, 98*(5), 71–102.

Royal Society [The]. (2011). *Knowledge, networks and nations: Global scientific collaboration in the 21st century.* London: The Royal Society. Retrieved from http:// royalsociety.org

Samuelson, P. A. (1947). *Foundations of economic analysis.* Monograph, Harvard University Press. Retrieved from http://trid.trb.org/view.aspx?id=630481

Sen, A. (1993). Markets and freedom: Achievements and limitations of the market mechanism in promoting individual freedoms. *Oxford Economic Papers, 45*(4), 519–541.

Sugden, R. (1993). Welfare, resources, and capabilities: A review of inequality reexamined by Amartya Sen. *Journal of Economic Literature, 31*(4), 1947–1962.

12 Mis-education

Viewing education as a globally linked learning network is fairly new; its antecedents are fairly new. The collapse of the Soviet economy created a competitive global market where raw materials, cheap labor and small manufacturing had a global price. Global competition increasingly focused on knowledge inputs. The growth of a global system of communication meant that information could grow rapidly in many places at once. The speed of knowledge formation meant that "mastery" of facts and skills could no longer define a good education. Rather, the dynamics of learning, relearning and learning to learn were as essential as simple mastery. Innovation began to define industrial output and the ability to collaborate, build on diverse knowledge sets and apply innovations to particular circumstances grew in importance. Finally, the intensity of financial, transportation, digital and cultural links grew globally such that both threats and opportunities had to be assessed using an understanding of systems. Systems could both build social well-being using fewer resources but also transmit threats quickly such as disease, terrorism, social movements and climate change. The value of understanding these systems began to rival industrial output as a determinant of global social well-being. A new learning network uses these global ties but also has structures that can help solve the problems that emerge from the complex, interlinked systems.

Before the world was so densely interconnected, we could assume that this new way of understanding the role, structure, purposes and methods of education would begin with research at, say, the world's top universities and slowly trickle down to other universities, high schools and primary schools. It would also spread out like waves from the central universities to less central universities and eventually, through trickling down and spreading out, it would reach Pima. Her little neighborhood school would eventually have a teacher, who had been taught by a more educated teacher, who had been exposed to the new learning systems that would reorient Pima's education. With any luck, in 20 or so years, Pima's small village school would see a change in the way that education is delivered.

But systems do not tend to work in this old way—top down and center to periphery. In fact, innovations frequently happen at the edges and spread inward toward nodes that spread them around. There is no real "top" here, but if there were, it would be the "top" of the old structure—government leaders, professors, intellectual elites and CEOs. In fact, they are likely to be caught by surprise. Twitter was not started there; neither was Microsoft. Tunisia's popular revolution wasn't started in any center of power but rather by a street vendor who set himself on fire in protest. Very technical innovations may require a mixture of the old knowledge-building framework (top funding, research centers, government assistance) but the innovation of systems begins at the margins.

The notion that knowledge is centered in a particular area and held by the most educated is, likely, one of the primary constraints to Pima's education. The very notion that the center or the top has answers that can be spread down and around until they reach Pima is a constraint in itself. We have seen how Pima's education is part of a larger system of learning and how her village is a critical part of a world system of knowledge, learning, collaboration and innovation. What we have to deal with now is the very real possibility that it is the education of the *educated* that is holding back the benefits we can garner from integrating Pima and her village into this world system.

If we define education as a "goal" of mastery, then it makes sense that the "educated" can educate the uneducated. If we define education as a system of learning that links the world and is, potentially, a positive link that strengthens the best possibilities of the system, we need to examine the very education that the most educated have received. Is it possible that our adherence to old development models, aging notions of mastery and outdated definitions of development are, themselves, constraints to Pima's successful education?

Charity for the poor

There is a poster on the wall of a building at my university. It shows a Korean helping a young African child wash her face. The poster exhorts us to help the poor. It makes me cringe each time I see it. How many mothers in poor countries have I seen go without food for the day, work far beyond their limit or sacrifice badly needed cooking pots to ensure that their sons and daughters can go to school? I've seen the daily rituals of poor households where extra care is taken to make sure that clothes are spotless, children are clean in every crevice and school work is carefully packed away so that all arrive at school in perfect condition.

I never fail to be amazed when I'm in a classroom of truly poor children— especially those that have to go to school during cool or even cold weather. Although their sweaters may have holes, although their clothes may have all the signs of being handed down from older siblings and still do not fit, each child was sent to school scrupulously clean. I know that, in some cases, the water in which the clothes have been washed and children have been bathed is not very clean—rather muddy looking. And I wonder what effort it took to ensure that the clothes are so clean. How do the rickshaw drivers come to work each day with a spotless shirt when even drinking water is in short supply?

I can reassure everyone that, given even half a chance of staying clean and showing that their children deserve respect, all parents ensure that their children are clean. No one needs to come from a distant land to show a mother how to wash her child's face. Indeed, the child probably knows all by herself how to do so because she's been told repeatedly to "wash behind those ears" or "don't come to breakfast with a dirty face."

So, how did we get so far from reality to have a poster of a Korean washing an African girl's face? Even someone who has never been in the field—as I have—could imagine that an outsider washing the face of an African child does not fit reality. Only 50 years ago Koreans were among the poorest people in the world, yet their clothing was spotless and probably was when they attended school. Surely they would know that their grandparents were exhorted to wash their faces—no foreign aid workers needed to show them how. So, if the poster is supposed to show us what good charity could do in Africa, why would it show a poor child's face being washed by an aid worker?

We live in a world of non-reality. A story comes to mind of when I was first in Zimbabwe during the late 1980s when the country was doing rather well. I came to teach at the University of Zimbabwe and was put in faculty housing—a small townhouse not far from the University. It was quite simply furnished, but the furnishings were adequate. I walked around the neighborhood quite a bit when I first arrived and was amazed to find that each house was surrounded by a tall cement fence. Basically, one could not see into the yard of any of the houses. This was the old "white" neighborhood—now largely occupied by black Zimbabweans but originally built as a white neighborhood.

Some weeks later, I gave my maid a ride back to her housing complex far out of town. Generally, she had to walk to a bus stop, take a bus into town, transfer there to a bus to her neighborhood—it took her an hour to get home. But what amazed me was that her neighborhood was not on the main road—as all neighborhoods are usually located, at least in the beginning—rather, one had to turn off the main road and follow a dirt road for about a mile or so to enter her area. The area was crammed full of small houses that had very small yards; people lived packed in beside each other when there was all this land between the community and the road that was vacant.

I put the picture together: I realized that the white community had been "walling themselves" away from the danger (perceived or real . . . I couldn't tell) of people who did not "belong" to their neighborhood. And blacks had been placed far out of town and then far off the main road. No one wanted an easy reminder of the poverty that existed literally on their doorstep or in their own houses during the day. I remember thinking, "this is a country of walls." I asked myself what price these people had paid for walling themselves off. What would you have to teach your child in order to make the world seem ok in such a situation? I remembered telling my young son, when passing a beggar on the streets of New York, to pay no attention: "We can't help him." I actually knew what it took to live in such a situation, for I faced it in my own country. You had to teach your children to "not see" the reality around them.

They had to be taught that reality was a particular place (where they were allowed "to see") rather than the world that surrounds them.

But this "walling off" does not change reality. There really are poor people in our midst; they really do have lives we could understand and we sacrifice our own children's knowledge in order to keep this view of reality. We teach them "not to look" or "not to pay attention" because it is the only way we know to view reality. We see a poster of a Korean helping a four-year-old African wash her face and think it shows what charity can do—instead of asking how far we have come from seeing reality.

You have seen the same commercials on television. You have seen the pictures of some man or woman holding a small child in their arms and the child looks into the camera. The man is telling you to send your money to help the poor child. A practiced eye will immediately see that the child is well-nourished: their little arms and legs are proportional to their height and stomach. The glazed look of a child devoid of calories, devoid of energy and devoid of curiosity is not present in the TV child. The TV child's clothing still has bright colors so we know it has not been washed thousands of times and left to dry in the sun. It may be a bit large, but it does the job. Let us assume that most of the world cannot assess the relative poverty of the child. Nevertheless, the message is clear—give money so that a poor child can go to school and eat.

Indeed, a poor child who cannot eat or cannot go to school needs the means to do so. But what parents the world over want is the ability to work, to have a stable life and to provide for their children—not a handout, but the dignity of work. Given even the slimmest of possibilities, they will use their intelligence, creativity, labor and love to create new opportunities and guide their child. Parents all over the world are the same. We don't want to be in a position that someone from the outside "gives us" food and clothing. We want to live a life of dignity where we can provide for ourselves through our labor. We want a place of dignity within a community where we take care of our own children.

Whether you choose to give to the charity on television or on the poster of washing faces is not the point. The point is that a picture is being painted of poverty in poor countries that provides us with a comfortable "view" of their world. We have only to give them some money and they will be able to have clean faces and the children will be able to eat. This is the view of poverty from the metaphorical "view from the main road looking a mile away to the poor neighborhood." We don't need to get too close. We don't need to see the stark realities at close range. We don't have to admit that these very people are in our houses cleaning our floors or begging for money on the street corners of New York City. We can keep our distance and we can keep our comfortable myth about poverty—just send money.

What if we had to admit that the world is increasingly connected? What if we needed to see that "their" world is indeed "our" world? What if we saw the poster and knew instantly that it could not be reality because all parents wash their children's faces (assuming they have the means to do so)? What if we asked ourselves if the child on television showed any signs of poverty other than not being white?

Here we are offered a comfortable (perhaps charitable) way of viewing the situation. "They" (the poor) need our compassion. If we can transfer some of the wealth in "our world" to "their world" they will live a better life. We will be generous and help them by giving money (foreign aid, our presence) to them.

Here is the reality. Gross inequities destabilize everyone's world. When so many people have lots of opportunities, information, education and possibilities and some have virtually none, the lives of all are somehow restricted. Although everyone needs charity in dire circumstances, in the long run, increasing their possibilities, freeing them to use their intelligence and creativity not only improves their lives, but it makes a richer, fully and vastly more stable world for us all.

The poster ought to show people selling vegetables at a local market, working together on a village project or accessing health care that is supplemented by local herbs or techniques. It ought to remind us that poor people are highly motivated to be creative and productive if their possibilities are expanded. We ought to be asking how we can be part of the networks that free them to decide where their energies should go, how to build their village and how to contribute to their community. We ought to ask what freedoms allow the mothers of children like Pima to choose that their girls go to school, and which restrictions of opportunity keep the Pimas of this world at home. What frees people to build their lives and use opportunities is the same the world over—stability, education, health, and a glimpse at the possibilities. It is a network extending from the world of the poor to the world of the wealthy. Keeping our distance and staring across the divide hurts us all—certainly the poor. Understanding that their world is not separate, but only another piece of a global network, forces us to view them as we view ourselves: people who strive for opportunities, creativity, humanity and dignity.

It does not feel safe to shift views; it feels safe to view the poor as living in their own, largely separate world. That way, we only have to ask how to "transfer" resources from our world to theirs. Any such transfer will be viewed as a charitable act and framed as "the right thing to do." But once we accept that their world is much like ours, at its most fundamental level, we realize that it is our actions, our attitudes and our worldview that is part of the poverty problem. We can't donate our way out of this illusion. Now, we must examine our actions, our attitudes and our views. Suddenly, we are thrown into a world that is connected and for which we have responsibilities. Charity is a simple act and is immediately rewarding. On the other hand, remaining constantly aware of our actions, attitudes and views is a lifelong commitment that, in truth, never leaves us.

But we don't need to feel so burdened. All of life is a process of change, awareness and self-examination. Reading this book is a true act of making a difference, for the book no longer allows the reader to hide. As you talk to your friends, rethink the latest news of poverty, assess the political speech you just heard or decide how to spend your free time, you make simple actions that move us all toward a more harmonious world. Not one of us can change the world single-handedly. But our awareness, our simple everyday actions and our worldview changes how we interact, how we greet each other, how we view the colleague who has childcare problems. We can count each of these simple actions as a contribution.

How can a simple awareness, simple actions and simple worldviews, possibly change the way that the world's poor connect with the world's educated and powerful? How can it re-stabilize a world that is increasingly out of balance? Let's examine the world of expertise and see how attitudes, actions and worldviews profoundly shape our world.

The myth of expertise

It is 1993. I am being called repeatedly by a major consulting firm that does education work all over the world. They are asking me in various ways to go to South Africa to help plan a higher education system for the new government. It is the year before democracy radically changed the power structure of the country. I do not want to go. I have told myself I will not travel to South Africa until the money I'll spend there goes to a government I can believe in. Yet, I am told that I will work with the African National Congress—the likely future government. I am told that the higher education system will need reforming to allow blacks to attain higher education. I am told that my political views are welcome and other economists may not bring in such views. I agree to go.

But the question I had to ask myself was why an outsider like me would be telling the South Africans how to redesign their higher education system. This was a country with a lot of good academics of all races (albeit fewer blacks than whites). This was a country where lives had been lost in a battle to win the right to self-determination. Was it really a good idea to send me, admittedly a kind of world expert on the topic, to tell them how to redesign their system? I was with an all-US team. Would we, could we, have the answers?

Here is a scenario. A team arrives in some country—say Vietnam. Let's say the job is for the team to design a project for secondary education. The team has been assembled from a set of global professionals who are chosen for their expertise and field experience. Sitting on the "other side of the table" are a group of Vietnamese who work for the Ministry of Education and have some background in planning secondary education. In this scenario, the "experts" are the international team and the "informants" are the local (Vietnamese) team. The experts can analyze the situation, ask questions, look at trends, do estimates and put together a plan. The locals are there to assist, to give the experts the necessary local information and, perhaps, to guide them in understanding the parameters around which the policy must work. It is, distinctly, an "expert"/ "locals" model of development.

Now imagine another scenario. The same international team arrives, but this time the local team is also regarded as "experts." The local team may or may not have the same number of degrees, but their understanding of local circumstances, policies and culture give them a necessary "expertise." The two teams share their various types of expertise, trading observations, ideas, concerns and possibilities. The goal is to find a plan that works in the eyes of both sets of experts. This is distinctly a "local/global expert" model of development.

In some sense, the two teams may be almost identical. Often the international experts are accompanied by local expertise. But, in the first model, the assumption is that the expertise lies with the international team (which has higher degrees and/or more international experience). The power lies with them to make the decisions. Local knowledge, per se, is simply another piece of the puzzle they are trying to put together. Just as they have previous reports and statistics on the country, they also have local interpreters and informants.

In the other instance, the local team is considered to be "experts." They not only have advanced degrees, they also know the local context—presumably from the village to the ministries. The two teams have different areas of expertise and the right plan is thought to evolve by combining all the information from the two teams.

It is clear that there is a substantial difference in power between these two scenarios. When an international group assembles a team of international experts, the assumption is that they have the expertise to make the decisions regarding the project. Indeed, it is written in their terms of reference that they have the expertise and their job is to produce a plan. But, when the local team is considered to have equal expertise, then the international team works with them to find a solution that works for all. If there is a disagreement, it cannot be solved by deferring to the "expert." Rather, it must be further analyzed to see what a possible solution might be.

More than just a power relationship, there is an underlying philosophy of development in each scenario. In the first scenario, the assumption is that there is a "right" solution and the "right" solution can best be determined by experts. In the second scenario, it is assumed that the best approach is found by blending various types of knowledge; there is no inherent "right" solution, rather, there is a "best approach" that works for that context, that circumstance and that period of time. The first assumes the old linear view of development—move everyone up the ladder of development toward the top. The second assumes a systems view of development—both global and local circumstances are relevant and dynamic.

Which is right? Let's go to a particular situation I observed in Zambia. Agricultural experts from a major international cotton company had done research that found local farms could produce two to three times the amount of cotton per acre than they were currently. The inputs were exactly the same —same fertilizer, same seeds, same amount of labor—but the timing of planting, fertilizing and labor intensity was different (not more or less) with their methods. So the company went about training local farmers. The farmers divided their fields into two halves, planting one half in the old way and the other half in the new way. At the end of the year, the farmer could see that the half planted and tended in the new way yielded much more cotton. He received more money for his cotton from this half of his field.

However, the international company told me that the following year the farmer would, invariably, return to the old methods. When they explained this to me they shrugged their shoulders; they could not understand why the trained farmers would go back to their old ways—it seemed irrational and the problem seemed unsolvable. Now, I'm no expert on Zambian rural villages, but my understanding is that such villages survive on a system whereby the collective is as strong as the individual. So, a farmer would isolate himself by being on a rhythm of planting and labor that was out of sync with his community. Further, costs of schooling, funerals and celebrations are borne—at least in part—on the basis of who has extra cash. So a farmer who has more cash relative to other villagers is likely to be asked to contribute more until his cash reserves begin to equal the other members of the village.

Let's assume, for the moment, that my observations are correct: the notion that the agricultural specialist is the "expert" actually hurt the company and did not further development objectives. No one, essentially, benefits. The cotton company was left with the impression that even the best expertise and demonstrations were, inexplicably, not followed. But if a local farmer or community leader was also considered an expert and was asked to combine his knowledge with that of the agricultural expert, a solution might have been found. Train the entire village at one time, then they are all on the same schedule and the income for the entire village is raised.

These examples in the way that "expertise" is perceived demonstrate a fundamental difference in approach to solving issues. In one instance "expertise" is assumed to be a "scientific" solution. In the other instance, local history, social structures, practices and economics are also necessary to find an optimal solution. In this second instance, both local and global teams are experts. Anyone who has worked in a number of projects has a story or many stories that lament how global experts misread local conditions and recommended inappropriate remedies. The lack of local knowledge has meant that the project fails or is not as successful or sustainable as it could be. The explanation of why this local knowledge was not explicitly sought and partnered is the underlying assumption that expertise is global in nature—it understands the larger scientific, global and macro components—and local culture is something to be overcome rather than viewed as a critical input.

If this is the case, what is missing? How have the global experts been mis-educated to follow the "expertise" model rather than the "systems" model? Is it possible that this mis-education could be a fundamental part of foreign aid failure—indeed, of the failure of development in general?

Can the poor educate the wealthy?

Our pervading notion that the answers lie with the lifestyles, institutions and values of wealthier countries handicaps our ability to work within an integrated world system. It also harms the very long-term goals underpinning the reasons why citizens in wealthy countries agree to be taxed for foreign aid purposes. It leaves the wealthy—usually educated—population centers of the world with two handicaps. First, it assumes the answers can be found and revealed by experts on foreign aid and education who derive their expertise from their formal education, degrees and experience. Second, it leave the general public with the impression that foreign aid and collaboration are "gifts" to the poor, which can be increased in times of plenty and reduced when budgets are tight.

In both cases, it leads to large inefficiencies in the ways that monies are spent and it reduces the gains that could be accomplished. A classic case, in my mind, is a survey that is done again and again in poor countries concerning the education of girls.[1] Parents are often asked why they removed their girls from school. The multiple choice answers provided to the parents are always connected with the distance to school, the labor the girl provides at home, concerns about her sexual vulnerabilities, etc. The questions revolve around the "costs" (social, personal, household) of educating girls. I have not yet seen a questionnaire about why parents continued the education of their boys but discontinued the education of their girls. But, if they were to get to know the cultures, families and social structures of these communities, they would realize that boys are more likely to be employed when they become adults. These standard surveys have led to endless projects designed to remove the barriers to girls' education (which are very much the same as the costs to boys' education) rather than focusing on the rewards (benefits) of girls' education, which are substantially lower for the family than that of boys.[2] Girls do not have the same employment opportunities as boys after schooling.[3]

The wrong question "Why don't parents send their girls to school?" is asked over and over again because researchers assume that not sending one's girls to school is an irrational act. If the parents' behavior is irrational, then it is reasonable to ask the question. But, if one were to assume that parents, living within a long-standing culture and responding to outside forces, are rational, reasonable and thoughtful people, then one would have to ask the question in a different way. One would ask questions that sought to understand the logic of the parents—that sought their understanding and their knowledge of local context. In this scenario, it is the researchers who need to be educated. They cannot assume irrational behavior of parents; rather they have to assume that the lens (cultural, social, political, etc.) through which they look is not correct for that cultural situation.

If a research project begins with the assumption that rational actions would pattern those of the educated researcher (coming from, generally, a wealthier culture), then the question at hand is what is wrong with the culture under study. This wrong must be "fixed." But if the assumption is made that there is culturally consistent, culturally rational behavior being observed, then the question should be "What does the community know/perceive that I (as the researcher) do not?" This is not to say that all behavior in all contexts is, in fact, broadly rational. All cultures (including those of the educated researchers) are slow to adapt to changes. After all, cultures have survived because culture is a basis upon which to adapt; thus, this base changes slowly, choosing carefully which changes are necessary.

Nevertheless, whether the actions are rational in a "broad worldview" or not is not the question at hand; rather, the question is why perfectly intelligent, perfectly functional, contributing, thoughtful adults see their behavior as rational. Once this is known, changes can occur that, with any luck, will help both sets of cultures adapt to each other. If girls don't continue in school because formal-sector jobs are not generally available to them once they graduate, then the focus ought to be on the gender bias of the workforce.[4]

Let us revisit the example of the cotton farmers. By assuming that the farmers were irrational in not following the more productive cotton farming methods, the cotton company is using a lot of resources trying to educate farmers and also the company is losing its productive potential. If researchers were to assume the cotton farmers were rational within their cultural framework, the cotton company might have learned that the education of a collective (village) would have produced better results. In the case of the girls going to school, the incentives of the outside world needed some reconfiguring; in the case of the cotton farmers, the training methods of the cotton company needed some reconfiguring. One cannot know what the proper approach is unless there is an assumption of rational behavior.

This begins with an assumption that poor communities have as much knowledge to contribute as do expert researchers. In fact, both bring their expertise to the table. The outside experts sit at the table with local experts and assume that they "do not know" the context and must learn it. So, the initial step is to seek the education of the communities and individuals. The outside consultants need to humbly request the community members' time and energy to provide them with the necessary information. The reason I say "humbly" here is that, in fact, the wealthier, resourced researchers are asking for a precious resource from those who, in fact, have little to give. It takes time to educate us! It may take more than one community meeting and a strategy on the part of the community on how they will expose researchers to their context.

But, invariably, communities throughout the world want to help each other and there is a sense of goodwill. Likely, outside researchers will be allowed time with community members. But, once outsider researchers understand the context, they will again need to turn to the community for collaboration on a solution. Imagine if the agricultural specialist from the cotton company had understood the context and then asked the community how a successful training program might be structured. After 30 years of experience, I can tell you that the community will immediately start a discussion among themselves; they will propose an approach. The final design might be a hybrid of the outside expertise and inside expertise (community) but it will likely succeed.

The example of Pima used in this book comes from a real-life example of a project in which I participated in Nepal. I really did visit a small grass hut in rural Nepal and speak with a woman and ask her why she sent her young daughter to school. I was with a team, equipped with clipboards and a questionnaire. Because I was the economist on the team, I was not part of the questionnaire group so I wandered around the village, just observing the life and people, and watching what they did and how they operated. Quietly, I watched their daily activities and tried to understand the rhythm of their lives. I noticed, at midday, the women returned from the rice paddies and went into the huts, unwinding their saris and lying on the mud floors with the top halves of their bodies naked; I assumed this was to transfer the searing heat of the day from their bodies to the mud floors. I observed the dreadful poverty—as poor a village as I had ever been in aside from refugee camps.

I found a place at the entrance near one hut and was resting with some villagers when my energetic teammates found me. They told me they were going to walk across the rice paddies to the next village to interview people there. I pointed out that the women had come off the rice paddies because it was too hot to be in the sun. But the team thought they could make it, so I told them to go ahead. They soon returned and joined me to rest until the sun had died down for the afternoon. Again, I wondered when we would learn to let the villagers teach us; learn that local people are the experts of their own environment. Is it such a difficult lesson?

So, the most important lesson the poor have to teach us is that their actions appear quite rational and sustainable within their context. If their worldview is somehow wrong (usually only the case when outside forces are changing their context), then it is *their* worldview that must be changed. This is very much the case when educating people about the threat of HIV and AIDS. If, on the other hand, the outside worldview does not fit their context, then the proper response is to change the approach to fit the cultural framework. The lesson is that our formal education only allows us to see a large worldview; we are bound by our own cultural precepts. The cultural precepts of others must be learned from them—their expertise.

If our view of expertise is wrong—our notion that "expertise" is wholly derived from formal-sector education—then how is it we are so mis-educated? In part, it derives from the industrial era where any engineer operated much like any other engineer. Expertise was derived from the classroom and exported, via a degree, to the workplace. But today's complex global linkages and innovation-driven value mean that education is continuous throughout our lives. A degree is a starting point for continuous education—not an end point. We are never fully educated—never an expert in any complex problem.

There is another misconception educated people are taught: that international development occurs in stages. Thus, any person or any nation with lower levels of formal education has nothing to contribute to the knowledge of the educated world.

A more systemic view of education means that we are all connected in a vast world of information, data, learning, understanding, creation and innovation. All points in this network have both unique characteristics, some connection to a world system, and some value to bring. The links can be tenuous or strong but the links and the flow of learning along these links is critical. How do communities get stronger through these links? Sometimes it is through their unique characteristics. Sometimes it is through adapting to the larger system. But, until the unique characteristics and the possibilities of the links are both known, the right approach cannot be identified.

Until our own worldview can change, we will continue to design the education of the poor in inefficient and unsustainable ways. If we ask naïve questions such as "Why don't they want an education?" and the assumption may be untrue, then neither do we design our projects and research correctly nor do we spend our funds properly. When we ask, instead, "Why are they not seeking education as we would in this situation?" we remain open to their knowledge. It is possible that they are blinded by older values that don't adapt to a modern world and are therefore at risk of losing their culture. Do they see formal education, perhaps, as a threat to their way of life? Do our approaches need to take into consideration local customs, values, precepts and lifestyles?

This assumes we've even asked the right question in the first place. Perhaps communities need to be more involved long before the questions are formed. Perhaps traditional methods of farming or medicine are more effective, more sustainable or more feasible in a particular circumstance. Perhaps the problem is that the outside world thinks there is a problem when, in fact, there is no problem.

Another assumption we make is that development can and should lead to the same lifestyle as, say, Middle America or northern Europe. Yet our own evidence suggests that this may not be a good goal. Modern, educated people are making choices to have fewer possessions, live simpler lives and build personal and communal satisfaction around creativity, exploration and social networks. Perhaps pursuit of wealth may not lead to maximum happiness. Indeed, a popular new magazine with world circulation is called *Real Simple* and fills its pages with articles on how to live a simpler, less materially based lifestyle. "Simple" is "in;" it suits a more flexible lifestyle where jobs and locations may change many times during a lifetime. It also suits a lifestyle where increasing amounts of productivity and pleasure are derived virtually. I used to have to buy a new computer each year to keep up with the rapid changes in technology but now a well-chosen computer will last me three years or more. Technology marches on, but my needs are met with the—now simple—uses of technology.

The notion that a modern lifestyle and its concomitant high levels of consumption is a reasonable goal of a society is mistaken. It is not ecologically sustainable. In this instance, it is the wealthy and the educated who need to adapt the most to a world system. The notion that a single adult or childless couple needs 3,000 square feet of living space is ridiculous in any nation. Neither does it make sense for all adults to own and drive a car. We also don't need to transport our strawberries from South America in November or use gallons of fresh water to take a 30-minute shower. This lifestyle simply cannot be attained by all, nor is it desirable. But it might be attainable and desirable to have internet access for most adults and to have an internet that is structured to share and exchange information freely. Those pleasures and chances at productivity are likely attainable and desirable.

Our mis-education means that we lack a worldview of education as a global system that is dynamic, diverse and, optimally, accessible. Our donations to world charities, to foreign aid and to the expertise that drives development is poorly used, sometimes ineffective and often not sustainable. We do not recognize our own shortcomings in education. Sometimes our existing worldview is comfortable because, like all cultures in the world, it is easier to see our world through "traditional" views rather than to adapt and change. Nevertheless, it restricts the potential for development and causes the world to not make the necessary adjustments to our ecology, productivity, creativity and threats. One of our first duties as world citizens it to pursue this new knowledge and find reasonable outlets to act upon it.

Notes

1　Interestingly, in development work, a girl is often referred to as a "girl-child," indicating that there could be girls who are not children (i.e. an adult woman can be a "girl"). Conversely, a boy is never referred to as a "boy-child." Boys are always children; adult males are always men. So, gender bias is also inherent even in the language of development.

2　The social benefits for schooling of girls however, are substantially higher than that of boys. See for example Schultz (1993).

3　This leads me to wonder why the question is never asked. If it were asked, would it have to lead to a policy intervention asking government to equalize the hiring of women? Would foreign aid agencies be willing to push governments for such policies—a different kind of "structural adjustment"?

4　The notion that it is perfectly rational to retain girls at home flies in the face of cultures that have adapted to a modern world by educating girls. Also, many poor countries have high female participation rates in the workforce. There is nothing inherently "right" about keeping girls at home. It can be a cultural choice, and this choice assumes that both sexes benefit by choosing various lifestyles.

Reference

Schultz, T. P. (1993). Returns to women's education. Women's education in developing countries: Barriers, benefits, and policies. In E. King & Hill (eds), *Women's education in developing countries: Barriers, benefits, and policies* (pp. 51–99). Baltimore, MD: Johns Hopkins Press.

13 Education in a new age

Here is a problem that many communities face: the streets are filled with cars; the morning commute is getting longer; public transportation is not used by most commuters. Residents are not enjoying their neighborhoods much—it is just a place to sleep for them. They want more exercise but find few options for doing so. A solution is to rethink commuter towns and neighborhoods using "green" options. How can neighborhoods be made more appealing so walking through them is enjoyable? How can transportation be rethought? How can walking and biking become part of the daily routine?

Schools are put in such communities with none of this context in mind. Schools have a singular purpose—to teach the children particular goals, how to function in a world when they become adults. Walled off from the city in every way, they exist in physically, psychologically, virtually and socially isolated spaces for the time they are in school. Indeed, the current thinking is the more isolated the school environment is from the world outside its walls, the safer it is. Integration is for later life—life after school. Schooling is preparation. But the reality is that the walls are harder and harder to maintain; cell phones have become virtual tunnels to the outside world, even if computer connections are monitored. Social interfaces tunnel in through this virtual interface. The outside world and the "school" world are merging.

Now, imagine a different scenario—one where integration is the explicit goal. The high school has a theme: the theme is "green communities." The high school is working with the town to find different approaches to make their community more "green." Every part of the curriculum is linked to this theme. Rather than simply asking, "How can we link the curriculum into the theme?" teachers are asking, "What do they need to know to be able to assist in helping with this problem?" They will need to find the people who make the decisions; understand the planning that has gone before; build networks to the community and leaders; find out how other cities have approached the issue; survey people and analyze results; write up the analysis and disseminate the findings. In short, they will need to read and investigate knowledge; they will need to build and use networks; they will need to form groups and work within groups and across groups and they will need to know about their community so that solutions work in their particular context. They will be putting into practice the very skills that a modern "knowledge builder" needs—knowledge, networks, collaboration, application to specific environments.

In this context, teachers can make lists of various knowledge, skills, practices and group work that need to be undertaken and then approach it as a large, complex problem. How can all this best be delivered? Maybe there is an online program to teach the survey and analysis skills needed for the surveying, but no computer program yet provides the kind of collaborative space they'll need to talk through the issues very well. Clearly basic math, civics, statistics, history, writing, reading, research, science and sociology information will be needed so—somewhere in the plan—these basics need to be embedded.

The difference between one scenario and the other is that one begins with classrooms, lesson plans, teachers and time schedules and asks how to fit the problem into the existing, largely physical, constraints. The other scenario starts with a problem, asks how students might best be prepared to answer it and then organizes physical, virtual and conversational space around the learning. In one plan, the question is how to fill class time. Class time is defined by physical inputs—teachers, classrooms, time schedules and texts. In the other, the question is how to best learn. Teachers, classrooms, time schedules and texts are some of many resources that can be used flexibly.

Learning—not schooling

Education in a learning economy begins with the basic question, "How do people best learn?" Physical resources are not the initial parameters, rather they are part of a package of resources that can be brought to bear. As real-life problems are tackled in real-life situations, students learn facts, skills, procedures and techniques. They learn to reference each other and other groups to get more information. They build networks—both face-to-face and virtual. They work in groups and across groups. They innovate when necessary and learn the rules and routines when that is necessary. This question pervades when we are talking about children in grade 3 and when we are talking about adults who have knowledge-building jobs and when we are talking about retired grandparents. The question begins with what needs to be learned and how people learn best.

In this view, formal schooling is only one of the many resources that form a lifetime of learning and a lifestyle of learning. Schools work from real problems because such problems are the best way to learn. Real problems are solved through lots of knowledge and investigation, specialized knowledge group, collaborative groups and applications to particular circumstances. The mark of success is the ability to use these various tools to solve problems.

These methods are hindered by today's tests. In order to get to the next level of schooling or to get into a good university or in order for a country to be competitive, test scores must be high. The tests generally used today measure only one dimension of learning—individual mastery. These tests usually measure how much one individual has mastered particular knowledge—say algebra or biology or English. It does not measure how quickly a person can investigate a problem or how well she might work with others or how generalized knowledge can be applied to a particular situation. Yet, these are just the skills that prepare them for a fulfilling life in a globally connected world of learning. Societies worldwide are facing this dilemma: test scores have served us well until recently, but now tests are driving a curriculum that is increasingly outdated. Until the tests change, the approach to teaching and curriculum is unlikely to change.

This same problem was faced in another realm. The easy measure of societal well-being of GDP per capita provided a good benchmark for the success and relative well-being of a society. It was a singular measure that seemed to capture many dimensions of life. But the underlying concept that productivity could be adequately measured and used as a singular indication of social well-being was problematic in a knowledge-driven world. The measure had to be rethought despite the fact that alternatives were missing, complex and difficult to measure. Likely, the same will need to be done with today's school tests. Learning is a process that is multi-dimensional. Like GDP per capita—which was a singular measure of productive outcomes—test scores as a singular measure of academic outcomes will need to be rethought. Instead, we will need to ask a more complex question: "Where does education lead us and how can we measure that contribution of education to our quality of life?"

What we know is that humans are driven to learn. As a mother, I observed that I could interrupt my two-year-old when he was eating or watching television and he would not protest too much. But if I interrupted him in the middle of something he was trying to figure out, he would fight with me to continue. He wanted to keep focusing until he understood—how to break through a sheet of ice or stack some blocks or make a simple Lego animal. As adults, we are attracted to puzzles and games—striving for a goal. We know that when a class can engage our minds, time flies by. We seek new knowledge in our curiosity for news, understanding of home repairs, new cooking techniques and, indeed, reading this book. Learning is a lifetime pursuit and even the eldest are trying to understand the emerging world around them.

Learning is part of everyday life. It is satisfying. It helps us operate better in our world and do everyday things. It improves conversation and helps us understand the events around us. It helps us make better choices and be better parents, sons and daughters, employees and employers. We are better citizens, neighbors and world participants. We seek self-growth whether we are studying Zen Buddhism or psychology or physiology. We also love to work together. We are a very social species: we love to talk and share stories and readily explain new ideas, events and techniques with each other. We like to invent group activities, try new ideas and build things together. We arrange collective events and share our human experiences. Learning is a very human activity.

Much as we might enjoy it and pursue it at every turn, come the industrial age, it had to be integrated into our lives in a less natural way. The skills needed by industry required high levels of mastery—math, reading, following a set of steps, reporting mistakes. We needed people with high levels of training such as engineers, teachers, nurses and managers. We were unlikely to acquire these skills in everyday life or through apprenticeships. This kind of learning required a fairly intense effort and required taking people away from normal activities and putting them in an environment where they could concentrate. The source of information was a teacher and textbooks, so people were organized in settings where it was reasonable to be exposed to a master teacher. As microphones and projectors became more abundant, adult classrooms sometimes became larger because more people could listen to a single lecturer.

These circumstances were relatively efficient in delivering a set of knowledge. If you needed to learn the chemistry tables, a lecture would do the job. If you needed to master the tables, a textbook would be a good supplement. Teachers taught the concepts, texts gave you the facts. But the human impulse to learn collectively, to pursue interests based on the world around oneself, to explore self-growth were quelled because the environment was artificial—removed from real life. It was a necessary compromise to imbue a set of knowledge.

Today's environment makes this less compelling. Technology provides a means of delivery that is certainly as efficient as a large lecture hall or a textbook. The rationale of organizing classrooms separate from a real-world environment in configurations that focus on a teacher is no longer compelling. Indeed, children all over the world are learning to read and do math long before they attend school because they are exposed to interesting computer programs. People of all ages turn to the internet and computer programs to learn facts, put together logic, understand world events, learn languages, study statistics, read the latest findings in their field and learn new home repair techniques. Delivery of material (knowledge) is being made easier, more palatable and, indeed, more efficient, through technology.

But this is only the beginning of the learning revolution. Our desire to grow, share and create is enhanced with technology. Because knowledge delivery is so much easier, because it can be done when and where we desire at our own pace, our learning time is somewhat freed to do what humans do best—build new ideas collectively. We do so by pooling our knowledge and sharing our ideas. We do this whether we are trying to figure out how to grow a new crop, how to preserve the tree growth around us or how to get our community to use public transportation. We begin with conversations. We can get together in a community hall, in a coffee shop or in a classroom. We seek solutions to the problem. We build a network of people who are interested and extend that network to experts, others who might be involved and similar communities.

Our networks provide us with different perspectives, new ideas and various information. From networks we garner the possibilities. We can combine ideas to build a new way and apply it to a particular circumstance. We can solve the problem or find an exciting new possibility. This is not to say that we no longer have to memorize chemistry tables—we do. Our engineers still need to know how to find the tensile strength of a steel bar. But knowing bare facts such as tensile strength—while important—is vastly more valuable in the context of complex, interlinked problems, such as how to make cities more liveable and creative. Surely, to solve that complex problem, somewhere in that equation someone has to know the tensile strength of something. To solve such problems we need not sit in classrooms of boring lectures or even memorize the contents of textbooks. Rather, we need to begin with a problem, within a context, and then work toward a solution. In so doing, we not only learn the individual pieces of information and skills, we learn how to learn, to discover, to create, to collaborate, to network and how to work in a team of diverse thinkers.

Our diverse learning minds—whether we learn through lectures, reading, videos, experimenting, talking, drawing or building—can be used. I learn a lot through listening. I listen to the radio for my news. In lectures, I can usually remember almost the exact logic or words used. I barely take notes because visual learning is not my strong suit. Neither am I particularly kinesthetic. If I hear directions given to the nearest restaurant, even if it is many sets of steps, I'll probably remember it because I'm mentally drawing a map. But a good friend of mine needs a small map drawn—even a rough map: she is visual. We all learn differently and now our different learning styles can be accommodated.

Because of the variety of ways of getting the raw knowledge, we can focus our learning energies on the types of environments that build collaboration. In my college classrooms—still designed to hold a set number of students for a set period weekly—I have still managed to become a learning organizer. Students get their facts before entering my classroom; in the classroom we share what we've learned. We analyze the results and we talk about the meanings. We pool our understandings to find the best approaches then we think through the next steps and build ideas for moving ahead. I am the learning director but rarely the knowledge source.

Still my classes are organized, around singular topics, one teacher, uni-dimensional subjects, inflexible time periods and inflexible classroom space. Is this the best structure to accomplish what we want the students to know how to do at the end of their schooling period. The best way might involve some delivery of materials—perhaps by exposing students to a variety of online materials, texts, mentors, various media. It might involve meeting in groups over the entire time to solve a problem in a particular country and share ideas, approaches and experiences. It might involve some learning-while-doing. There might be some work done in classrooms, some work done in groups and—clearly—some supervision by professors. But the freedom to mix knowledge delivery, teamwork, experimentation, exploration, collaboration, innovation and to use networks would improve the learning situation.

Three stories

In many poor countries, year after year, up to 98 percent of their annual recurrent educational budget goes to teacher's salaries. I have seen many of these teachers at work in unenviable conditions. Despite taking many pictures of the classrooms crammed full of children, I could never capture the stifling heat, penetrating cold, lack of resources or poor infrastructure. One year I took pictures of the blackboards; many were propped up on rickety frames or were crumbling or had been used to the point where chalk no longer contrasted against a worn-out background. In one school I visited in rural Uganda, the classroom had been built from mud and sticks; there were no writing materials, so students used sticks in the mud to display their work for the teacher. The younger brothers and sisters of these students—too small to go to school, yet needing to be attended to while their parents did the agricultural work—sat under a tree and "pretended" to be at school, mimicking teaching each other their ABC.

In systems so underfunded and so impoverished, one can well imagine that the systems keeping track of teachers can be antiquated at times. I remember being asked to help revamp a scholarship system at the University of Zambia for university scholarship recipients who were supposed to repay their scholarships after completion of their studies. But the antiquated computer program could only hold two years of records, so it was clear that no one was ever held to account to pay back their scholarships.

In schools worldwide, it is generally the parents who are the watchdogs on a daily basis. If things go awry, the parents can protest that their children are not getting a good education. But, if the parents are illiterate, not only do they not know if their children are being properly educated, they also do not know what the real function of a school is. Further, they are likely much less powerful people within the community than the teachers or headmasters, so if the system is broken, they are in no position to know about it or protest. If a teacher dies and a relative is collecting his paycheck for years in the future, who is to report this abuse? If a teacher takes another job and splits the paycheck with the headmaster but does not appear for work, who will know?

There are many costs of schooling in poor areas that are hidden because the system controls can be easily manipulated.[1] Before I address a possible role for technology, here are the three stories.

Story one: Khan Academy

Salman Khan started Khan Academy, which is an online resource where one can find videos that teach various subjects from algebra to biology to art history. Anyone can apply to upload a video on a topic and anyone can watch a video and learn a topic. Mr Khan started his academy by accident. He was helping his niece with her math lessons when he lived in a different city from her. They communicated using the telephone and an online whiteboard. Sometimes it wasn't convenient to talk with her at the time she was available, so he would record his lesson by video for her watch later, by loading the videos onto YouTube. Later, she told him that she preferred to watch the videos rather than to speak with him directly because it allowed her to repeat certain things and go at her own pace. Also, he began to realize that others were watching his videos. Over time, his videos became quite popular so he expanded his efforts and started Khan Academy.

Story two: *Grameen Bank computer program*

Grameen Bank started as an idea from a professor of economics in Bangladesh. Realizing that his economics classes had little to do with the economics of the poor people in the village just outside his classroom, he asked his students to study the economic situation of these villages. Using his students' findings, he started a bank that lent small amounts of money to these poor people to help them get out of poverty and by financing small enterprises. His business expanded to millions of dollars of revenue a year—still loaning to the poorest people. Later, he experimented by putting computers in remote villages and found that even illiterate young people would start using the machines and were soon learning from them. The computers became a source of learning and communication for villagers, people who no one thought could make use of sophisticated telecommunications equipment.

Story three: *Thunderbird software*

Most software is developed by a company that later sells it for a profit—like Microsoft Word or Acrobat Professional. The money we pay for the software pays for the cost of development. However, some software is actually developed by volunteers and is provided to anyone who wants to use it. Why? Because these volunteers have a little spare time and they believe in a good cause and if many of them combine their spare time they can start with a very basic piece of software and gradually improve it. Each person works on an improvement when he/she has a little time and, gradually, the software just gets better and better. Eventually, it is as good as that of the commercial competitors and the volunteers get the satisfaction of knowing that their product helped compete against a big commercial interest. One such software is Thunderbird (an email client software), which competes against Outlook and recently won me over. It was finally good enough that I switched—and then switched my best friend in order to solve a problem she had with her email. There are a lot of computer programs designed like this and they are called open-source software—designed by "open" sources of people.

The economics of schooling

Now, on to the economics of poor schools—or, possibly any schools for that matter. It makes no sense for teachers to be employed, year after year, to be teaching the same thing to student after student, when one really good teacher can be employed, recorded on video, using the best pedagogy, where each student can replay at his/her own pace—once or hundreds of times—in any language he or she may be most proficient. The video needs to be recorded just once. Just once. One time. We don't have to hand each student a $3,000 computer each year and employ a trained technician for each village; these days, many options are cheap and getting cheaper, like tablets that cost $100. Technology is getting smart, cheap and interactive. I am currently working in Zambia, which has just had fiber-optic cable laid. Suddenly, the people I work with are carrying smartphones, receiving email on their phones and carrying around tablets that are connected to the internet. In fact, as I write the last edits of this book in January 2015, I am at a school that has wifi throughout the campus—simply unheard of even a year ago. Soon, even people in remote villages will have their uncle's hand-me-down smartphone, which will be video enabled; competition among cellular service providers will reduce the cost of streaming video. But learning videos don't need to be delivered in real-time; USBs cost $5 and can hold a year's worth of curriculum.

Do we still need schools? Of course we do. But teachers can organize children according to who has learned the material and who is lagging behind, so that some can tutor others. Then class time can be used to mentor, discuss and do the homework. The classes organized around a worn-out blackboard with 50 children in sweltering classrooms can give way to children learning in informal situations at their own pace, and coming to school for extra help, mentoring and discussions. Lessons are online; extra help and discussions are done collectively in a more conducive environment. Classrooms can be organized to be less crowded. Far fewer teachers will be needed because the lessons that needed to be repeated, year after year, in inefficient, poorly resourced classrooms are now individually delivered at the pace of each student. This is the lesson of the Khan Academy.

The Grameen Computer experiment tells us that even undereducated people are creative. Give them a resource and they will find a creative way to use it. They don't need highly skilled computer programmers to show them how to make use of a computer. Poor people will take whatever resources are at hand and make use of them—even, as the Grameen experiment shows, if that resource is in another language (as it was when Grameen first tried this). So, technology should not be viewed as a resource just for the classrooms of the wealthiest schools. There is no reason to believe there is a "natural progression" from a teacher with a blackboard to a high-tech classroom. Poor children, given a smartphone, will make the learning leaps that wealthy children will make. Creativity, learning and experimentation are universal human traits and the poor will use their mental energies to exercise these human traits every bit as much as the children of the wealthy—perhaps more so, since they are highly motivated to see their way out of poverty.

The lesson of the Thunderbird software is the lesson of open-source software. There is no reason why curriculum and lessons need to be fixed in time or space, or sanctioned by committees or individuals. It is possible that nations or school districts or schools feel the need to specify subjects or levels of mastery for given degrees, but whether one learns this through a video, a book, a friend or a class should not be a concern. Nor should it be a concern whether a teacher builds a lesson solely on his own or through collective efforts with other teachers. Nor is there a reason why a group of teachers, along with their advanced students, couldn't collectively build lessons on a topic. And, why not open it up to the world, to build a lesson on, say, global learning networks using techniques like open-source software? A core committee can vet each new piece and make a decision as to whether it fits and each person can decide what new piece would add to the overall quality. When one part of a lesson or syllabus gets outdated, it can be revamped.

There is an economics that could be linked to this—much like apps for smartphones—that would make this sustainable. But the point is, with collaborative software, there is no reason why each teacher needs to operate in isolation anymore. Rather, building lessons and curriculum collaboratively, and using local or global networks to keep them up to date and fresh, makes a lot of sense. And this fresh content can be made available to wealthy schools and poor schools at the same time. Open-source logic makes it possible, cheap and, with the addition of some knowledge-based incentives, it could be sustainable.

Education was once the province of the elite; it had to be taught one-on-one and only the most privileged could access it. The printing press made an education more widely available but the very fact that it was illegal to teach a slave to read and write was evidence that an education was a link to independence and power. The industrial revolution required that education be made widely available but this education was limited to following a set of rules and directions. Mass education meant schools had to be within walking distance (or at least driving distance). Classrooms were built to be within the hearing space of a single teacher as learning sources were restricted to teachers and books. These were the economics of yesterday's learning.

Today's economics of learning mean that we are not restricted by physical limitation. People learn best in their own time, in their own time in a place where they are comfortable. Sometimes people prefer to learn in groups, sometimes alone. Some learn best from a video or from a book or friend or tutor. Some knowledge doesn't change—like what a derivative is in calculus. But, it is interesting to note that the pedagogy by which one learns material like derivatives might well change with learning networks.[2] Other types of knowledge, like the subject matter of this book, needs updating almost as soon as it is in print. So some knowledge can be used year after year while others might be updated constantly by a network of people throughout the world. There is no reason why an isolated teacher or professor needs to be reinventing a lesson in a classroom each semester. There is no economics that makes sense for a teacher to be in front of a class of 50 students in an unheated classroom with a poor-quality blackboard, when each child could be learning from a video that taught similar children successfully for the last five years.

Equally, there is no reason why the learning available through the internet—whether it is the Khan Academy, the YouTube videos, Wikipedia, the *New York Times* or someone's blog—should be available to the private school student in Cairo and not the poor student in rural India. Each can learn, invent, create, grow and prosper with new ideas. Each can link to people, build networks and try new things and finds new opportunities. Pima's community can be linked to the world in imaginative ways that don't necessarily put an iPad in her hand. Although her community is currently isolated, it does not have to be; it is isolated—in part—because of the assumption we make that knowledge is a one-way flow, from the top to the bottom. Teachers and textbooks bring knowledge in, but no knowledge out. But if we think of the community as a part of a world of knowledge creators, innovators and participants, then we have to change our ways of thinking. We then realize that the region, country and world is losing a valuable resource when they are not linked to their neighboring community, or their town, and to others that share resources, problems, ideas and concerns. They cannot transmit what they know, what they understand, what they are learning and what is working for them and what is not working. And, when ideas are brought to them, we gain nothing from their experience. Knowledge is a dead-end in Pima's community unless we regard her community as a "flow" rather than a dead-end for knowledge dumping.

Pima's school ought to be an active community center that is part of a regional community learning network that is linked to the higher education center, research centers, social networks, other communities, other schools and networks of learners, mentors, teachers and older and younger students. Without thinking of the community as a learning network, we are back to the old thinking of knowledge as a dead-end stop rather than a lively dynamic. Poorly resourced communities have the same possibilities of learning through dynamic networks as any other communities; their internet connections may have to be configured differently, but it still links them to the rest of the world.

Learning is inherently a social activity. Learning the basic building blocks of reading, math, communication and science is really the easy part. Let the Khan Academy and others do that. Schools—whether they be virtual or community based—will still be in demand as collective spaces where people and ideas come together to share and build new ideas. How our current educational institutions morph into these new institutions is not clear. What is clear is that they have little choice but to do so.

Notes

1   This is not to say that there are no inefficiencies in wealthy schools. But the focus of this section is how technology can play an unexpected role in reducing costs in poor community schools.

2   As Khan Academy has shown us (Thompson, 2011), no longer do you necessarily need a teacher. Many people now learn languages without a classroom, using a variety of inventive and even entertaining software.

Reference

Thompson, C. (2011, July 15). How Khan Academy is changing the rules of education. *Wired Digital*. Retrieved from http://resources.rosettastone.com/CDN/us/pdfs/K-12/Wired_KhanAcademy.pdf

14 The cost of not educating

Imagine a land that has lots of natural resources—water, trees, iron ore, coal, land for farming, natural gas. Now imagine that someone decides that the north-east quarter of that land will not be used at all: it will not be inhabited, it will not be protected, it will not be used for farming or tapped for natural gas. Everyone will have to live on the rest of the land, live off the food the rest of the land can produce and exploit only the natural resources from three-quarters of that land. The usable land will have to be used much more efficiently so as not to be exhausted; environmental protections will have to be higher; people will have to be more careful in their farming, mining and recreational activities. The society will not be as well off and will have to work harder to find a sustainable way to live.

This is the situation for understanding the cost of not educating some of the people. Whether we are talking about boroughs of New York City, sections of Amsterdam, regions of Nigeria, cities in India or whole countries in Central America, the *rest of us* carry the cost of not educating the *least of us*. If we think of the *least* as walled off from the most educated, then it is the most educated who are fooling themselves, who carry the burden, who carry the weight, who face a world that is less sustainable, more burdensome, more exhausting, less easy to protect. To be sure, in the short run, it is easier to believe that the burden lies solely on the poor—to see them as separate and downtrodden. It is easier because we don't have to take up the burden of understanding the world as integrated and the burden of re-educating ourselves.

In a world that is linked through dynamic, real-time learning and financial flows, your understanding, dialogue and interaction does influence the global institutions that affect these global systems, such as Google, Facebook, Twitter, the IMF, National Public Radio, the G20, the BBC, Al Jazeera and the Federal Reserve. As you join and participate in learning and financial systems, express your ideas, choose what to learn, vote and choose where your resources and energy goes, your influence builds momentum as does that of others. Effectively, one of the most important things you can do to make a change is to educate yourself. This chapter is designed to show you how important that self-education is.

The economics of inequality

How is it that the burden of inequality is not well understood? The predominant theory of economics has a somewhat different view of inequality. To be fair, that theory—known as neoclassical economics—fits reasonably well when national economies were somewhat isolated and built around industrial growth. In this view of economics, a country maximized its growth potential. So, if the north-east part of a country wasn't the best or easiest place to put manufacturing, then neglecting it might make sense; just put all the manufacturing elsewhere. Maximize manufacturing wherever you can; get the most production going. Once you maximized production, the country had the maximum income it could have. Equality was not a factor at all—maximizing income was the goal. Spreading income around was the politician's job. If the north-east corner of the country needed some income, then the wealth could be spread around later to the poor people who lived there. If they needed to eat or have housing, then the wealth created by the other three-quarters of the country could be used to house and feed the poor people in the unproductive part of the country. Under this theory, poverty was not a concern for economists or for productivity.

In terms of learning and education, education was simply an input to the productive process. Since the goal was maximizing production, education was designed around the production process. What different kinds of manpower were needed to maximize the production process? How many engineers, factory workers, bankers, fast food workers, street cleaners, tax collectors, accountants, pharmacists etc.? Since no one could actually plan such a complex system of supply and demand, a general high school education was designed. After that, students chose their profession based on their own abilities, matched with the demand of the workplace and its salaries. If there was a high demand for nurses, salaries rose and more students chose the profession. In poor areas where students could not afford to go to higher education and where higher education institutions could not attract good professors, few could get a good education and most did not try or failed. Never mind. The system would simply redistribute its productive dollars to these people to keep them housed and fed. The system was maximizing its productivity and these uneducated people were an outcome of a production-maximizing system. Redistribution was considered a political concern, distinctly not an economic problem.

This might seem quite unfair to those who would like to have had a good job or a good education. After all, it was largely an accident of birthplace that determined whether one would have a respected place in society with a well-paid job, a valued education and the means to provide for a family. But economists believe one's contribution to society is to help maximize the overall income of the society. Fairness—while a good goal is the concern of a different field. Economists look for ways of maximizing income; politicians and sociologists look for ways of redistributing this maximized income. According to this set of theories, if everyone does their job well, then we all live in the best society possible.

One could also argue it is not fair that there is a system where some people, necessarily, are relegated to a position where they cannot contribute, do not have the dignity of a good job and cannot hope to support a family in a reasonable way. But a neo-classical economist would argue that maximizing the overall wealth of a society is an admirable goal for a society. It allows the society to live with the most wealth and best lifestyle. Providing all people with reasonable ways of living is not an economic problem, it is a social or political problem and therefore outside of the economic system to solve.

These are generally unsatisfying arguments and politicians, civic organizers, the media and ordinary citizens (and, to be fair, many diverse economists) can argue these points and never reach an agreement. But it does highlight a point of view—backed by neoclassical theory—that much of the world has come to believe we can neglect, essentially, the "north-east" corner of a country as a necessary consequence of economic growth. Stated another way, many have come to believe the counter-intuitive notion that we can neglect pockets of poverty and uneducated populations without any real consequences to the wealthy and educated.

If this economics ever worked—there was likely some logic to it in the industrial age—there is little logic left in the digital age of learning. Education is no longer an input only to industry; industry is no longer the single driver of social well-being. Moving goods across oceans in container ships, while still a major source of value for nations, is no longer the primary value moving around the world. The value of people's ideas and thoughts, innovation and the dynamics of learning is changing the way we interact, build our lives, restructure how we live every minute and how we use our time and link with our friends and change our values. Education is no longer primarily an input to industrial production; it is, rather, a resource in and of itself. In fact, schooling is no longer an end goal; the process of learning is likely more important than the final product of education. Your ability to re-form your ideas as you read this book is no doubt more important to your own growth than are the actual facts contained in the book. For the ideas you gain are a springboard to the next set of ideas you will build. The learning is more important than the facts.

So, back to the north-east corner of a country. What if we leave out one quarter of the citizens of a country? What if their ideas, their networks, their friends, their ways of communicating, their survival skills, their neighborhoods, their thinking and their logic are lying fallow? Each day they use their brains as much as we do. They figure out how to eat, how to survive, how to communicate, how to make deals, how to not drink polluted water, how to cure a disease without paying high doctor's fees, how to learn something without having to go to school, how to get somewhere without paying a taxi. In other words, they have networks, innovations and creativity that are untapped, and are not linked to the rest of society. It is a potential resource that is not being used by the other three-quarters of the country. Further, by not using this resource, food and housing for the poor needs to be supplemented, perhaps needlessly. The entire society is less stable because not everyone who can contribute and participate is doing so and the knowledge network that sustains the society is weakened. We also have one quarter of the total brain-power not being used; one quarter of our knowledge resources, our innovation power, our creativity and our diversity is untapped. Not only is one quarter of our resources lying fallow but, like a rowboat trying to get to the other side of a lake, we are dragging an anchor. We can't raise our test scores as a nation because that one quarter drags at us; we can't use all our national diverse thinking because some of our most out-of-the-box thinkers are not in the national pool. Our north-east corner does not only have to be supported by the other three-quarters, the missing one quarter is potentially more resource rich. We can't be a rich nation when other nations are using all their resources and we have to get to the other side of the lake with an anchor weighing us down. When other nations are using all their resources, some nations still hold on to the belief that it is economically viable to have pockets of unproductive people.

The security costs

Some controversy still exists as to the origins of the HIV virus. The most likely beginnings were that that the virus jumped from chimps to human—possibly when humans ate chimp meat—as chimps sometimes carry a virus similar to HIV. It was originally thought that the first traceable human case, was a flight attendant who was sexually active throughout the United States. His sexual encounters quickly spread the virus throughout the United States, and the virus quickly spread throughout the world. Other plagues have devastated populations in other previous eras such as the Black Death and periods of smallpox, but the spread of HIV shows us how vulnerable we all are to global disease in a world of global travel and global linkages. Long before modern medicine could even determine what the disease was or how it was spread, AIDS was killing people throughout the world.

Outbreaks of various strains of flu have put national health systems on similar alert as millions of people funnel through global travel centers daily. Flu is airborne and easily carried from Hong Kong to San Francisco to Melbourne or Lusaka in a day. The US-based CDC now has offices in 38 countries world-wide. This is not charity. This is a U.S. government agency with the charge to keep Americans safe and healthy. Keeping an eye on diseases abroad and carrying out research in the poorest countries is a means of ensuring that diseases in progress are diseases that can be halted early. If a country already has a good public health system, the CDC has a minimal presence.

The WHO works to eradicate diseases such as smallpox. It also works to get preventative health care—such as vaccines—and basic medical care to the world's poorest people. Simple medical procedures are researched for these populations, and protocols that may work in underfunded hospitals are researched and spread throughout the world. These global health organizations operate with bilateral donor and global funds, provided by the citizens of the wealthiest countries to mitigate the effects of disease among the poorest populations. In part, they do so because the poor cannot afford health care themselves. But it is an easy proposition to put to the taxpayers of these wealthy countries: global health of poor people is, in fact, global health of us all. If the meal of a Cameroonian rural dweller becomes disease spread by an airline worker that infects people throughout the United States and becomes a global virus that kills millions, then it is in the interests of the entire world to slow the spread of the diseases in their tracks. This means investing the in the health of the Cameroonian rural health resident and his food supply.

In 2011, millions of people in the Horn of Africa faced starvation. Although a severe drought was the most obvious immediate cause, there were underlying geo-political factors at work that exacerbated the situation: food aid to governments depressed food prices making it less profitable for local farmers to grow their own crops and fewer incentives were created to build irrigation systems. Political instability made transport costs rise, making what food there was difficult to transport, so people could not get food into their villages. Food prices rose beyond the ability of people to pay, with the result that thousands of people migrated—leaving their homes for refugee camps to find food and water. Various global and regional organizations and governments had to find a way to feed these people. For many, their lives have still not re-stabilized and their communities have not been rebuilt. The children lost education and development experiences during this time and many still suffer from the lack of adequate nutrition during the years when their brains and their bodies were growing. Years of productivity, creativity, political stability and civic life are lost in addition to millions of dollars. The human cost to the refugees is great; the global cost will be paid over generations.

No one really knows the costs of refugees. The UN High Commission for Refugees (UNHCR) coordinates a lot of the refugee work throughout the world, but many government and non-government organizations sponsor refugee camps around the world. Much of the cost is borne by host governments or even private citizens, who allow refugees access to their land or help in direct or indirect ways. The Norwegian government is helping one camp in Dadaab, Kenya and they estimated the direct and indirect annual costs of that camp at $100 million US. The camp has existed for 20 years and is taking in refugees from Somalia. It is also estimated that the UNHCR needs $30 million US annually simply to educate refugee children worldwide—much less to feed, clothe, house and provide medical care to the total refugee population worldwide.

A much cheaper solution would have been to prevent this refugee population from leaving their relatively stable lives where they could take care of themselves. We can all think of it as a large sink-hole of resources or the "north-east" corner, a large piece of humanity from whose creativity, brainpower, innovation, net-works, ideas and energies we cannot benefit; in addition, our own energies, productivity, stability and resources are being drained.

Amartya Sen comes to mind again here. His theory is that no society that has both the means to collectively build knowledge and also the ability to act on that knowledge will experience broad-scale famine (or the effects of many large-scale disasters). He reasoned that societies having the ability to collectively raise their knowledge of the circumstances at hand (through discussion, research, media, debate, networks), increase their ability to find means of dealing with the challenges. Since this knowledge became collectively understood, the society could then take action.[1] In the case of the Horn of Africa, awareness of an impeding drought could have spurred the society to start importing foodstuffs or worked collectively with agencies from abroad to get food into their villages before people were displaced. But the political disruptions around them— compounded by previous dysfunctional governments and the poorly educated citizens who had no means of understanding the dynamics of the political/ environmental/economic systems—meant that they had no means to take this action.

The lesson to learn from this situation is quite interesting: a small amount of education plus a dynamic learning system was truly the missing link here. If the population had a basic education plus a means to communicate, they would have done so with enough effectiveness such that they would have overcome a dysfunctional government and a corrupt political situation and managed to get the help they needed by taking the situation into their own hands. A dynamic learning system, such as active cell-phone communication and Twitter, YouTube or something equally simple, may well have done the job. Learning could be more powerful than politics. It was not really food that they needed or even rain; it was collective knowledge and a means of learning from each other plus a dynamic learning network.

In 2001, US President George W. Bush declared a "war on terrorism" in describing his determination to defeat Al Qaeda and other terrorists groups of global reach. Although his declared targets were Iraq and Afghanistan, for many, his speeches seem to encompass a distrust of the religion of Islam. He referred to the "enemy" as "these people" without reference to specific groups. The question was left open as to whether the declared "war on terrorism" was a war on nation states, on groups operating within specific nation states or on an ideology that extended somewhat more broadly across much of the Muslim world. This ambiguous message was interpreted by many young Muslims as a war on their core beliefs and lifestyles. During this "war," some who felt ideologically threatened volunteered to strap on bombs and detonate themselves in the name of core values to which they ascribed. Despite the dictates of the Koran against such acts, terrorist actions were heralded in the name of religion and the youths who volunteered were viewed—within narrow circles—as martyrs. How could such actions be viewed as heroic when their religion clearly forbade such actions?

The answer is not difficult to image. Throughout much of the world—say, in the "north-east corner" of some parts of some countries or in the poorest neighborhoods—are pockets of poverty; there are also people who feel otherwise marginalized. They are full of energy, creativity and intelligence and ready to begin making a difference in their worlds. For youth who are raised in healthy societies, with dynamic opportunities, this is the time when they try out ideas and possibilities and when they travel, try out a job or two or go to college and discover interesting courses, make new friends, go to rallies, explore new technologies, develop new hobbies or sports interests and delve into a new intellectual interest. But, if you are a youth in a poor neighborhood you may see little ahead of you. This may be especially true if the examples you have to follow—your uncles or your older sister— never had any of these opportunities.

If the world around you is particularly unfair or corrupt, your innovation, creativity and drive can take another turn. If you have been labeled unfairly, it will feel wrong. If your religion—the religion of your mother, your father, your grandfather, your ancestors, the people who taught you in school the people who looked after the poor who taught you honesty and fairness and kindness— is now being defiled by someone who does not even understand your society, then it is possible that your energies will begin to turn against this new threat. Put yourself in this situation: your energy is not going toward a positive interest such as work, college, a hobby or a sport. Rather, someone is declaring a war that comes very close to threatening something you hold dear, on which your values are founded. Then you get together with your fiends—what do you talk about? Soon, someone suggests that there is a group you can join that shares these values and is fighting to protect them.

You may not feel that you are being pulled into a political organization, but you are now very vulnerable toward political organizing. Maybe only one of 50 of you will actually turn into a violent terrorist, but perhaps one in ten will quietly support the actions of the other one and the rest will willingly pass messages or supply food or throw rocks or clear streets or collect money. Terrorism thrives when people are disenfranchised from their own society and when they have no way to make a positive contribution to their society. When their society is thriving and they have a positive role to play, terrorism cannot take root.

Now contrast George Bush's war on terrorism to the 2011 Arab Spring in Tunisia, Egypt and Libya. This is ending as I write the last chapter of this book, so, perhaps there is more to this Arab Spring than I can write here.[2] These are much the same people as those George Bush was worried about—youth, Muslims and Middle Eastern. But they were tired of their dictators; unlike those in the Horn of Africa, they had a basic education and they had, at hand, a simple, dynamic learning system—cell phones and the internet. They could do what Sen had theorized two decades before: they could build knowledge among themselves and then act on this knowledge. They could talk between themselves about their own society, its workings, its dysfunction and its corruption. They could raise awareness. Finally, sparked by a seemingly simple incident, they rise to action. Because they had a dynamic learning system (a social network from which they could inform each other and learn), they did not need to plan, per se; rather, a systemic force guided them. Their actions resulted in a democratic force that was more powerful, ultimately, than the totalitarian regimes they opposed.

Which forces were more powerful, ultimately, against terrorism in the Middle East? George Bush's "war on terrorism" or the "Arab Spring"? History books have yet to be written but one force tended to marginalize the youth, although it could be argued that it also found particular cells of Al Qaeda. The other was a force that provided that same youth with a democratic platform for a positive role to build their own societies. War or networks of learning? It might be argued that it takes a bit of both. But it would be difficult to argue that the forces of networks of youth who discuss, analyze, build their own understanding, raise awareness, redefine their own society and take action—that particular force is not the foundation upon which democracies emerge. It may take time and there may be many bumpy steps along the way, but giving a wider voice to people has generally resulted in more stable societies—a force for global stability in the long run.

This particular force is a good example of how the education of "the other" is a benefit to the world. The marginalization of the poorest people is not just a cost to them, but creates the pockets of unrest and instability for which we all pay a price. In the case of the Arab Spring, the youth rose up to protest about the unfairness of their own governments. Ensuring that all people have the ability to learn and have access to learning is a good way to increase global stability.

Momentum for change

The evidence is in: the old thinking is not just old, it is destructive. The old theories of development, economics, learning, communication and labor can be debated, but while they are, the youth of the world are connecting together in ways we could barely imagine a decade ago, a year ago, a week ago, or even when I wrote the first chapter of this book:

- Learning is a powerful, globally linked system that goes on continuously. People with common bonds, sometimes with cultural or linguistic ties, sometimes with professional or political interests in common, carry on dialogues and share ideas, raising consciousness, creating new knowledge, spawning new ideas and looking for ways of improving their lives and those around them.
- The knowledge and facts needed to support this learning is increasingly ubiquitous throughout the world. As I wrote this book, I frequently had to check a fact and quickly switched to the internet to find an obscure fact—I no longer needed to cite a source since the fact is now so easily available it can be treated as "common knowledge."
- Education viewed as formal schooling with teachers, classrooms and texts derived from an age when there were physical constraints to accessing knowledge sources. These constraints are being lifted rapidly. A more important question should now predominate, "How do we best learn?" Since some learning is often done best at an individualized pace and others

in a social environment, learning needs to be completely rethought by learning psychologists, not educational planners who think in physical terms.

- Knowledge workers can easily take their skills honed in a work environment and apply them to their civic, cultural, social and personal lives, so knowledge productivity goes beyond industry to affect the full range of human activity.
- This knowledge productivity can substantially increase the quality of people's lives without ever going to market, such as the example of teaching rural dwellers to rehydrate their babies. Thus, the quality of people's lives can be substantially improved through knowledge innovation that is rooted in civic, social, governmental, religious and other networks.
- As the cost of internet services become competitive in even the poorest parts of the world, people are finding creative ways of using communication to improve their lives, communicate, raise awareness and learn. Global networks are no longer the province of the rich.
- Curriculum need not be developed by curriculum specialists or professors. Knowledge is dynamic and evolves rapidly. Like open-source software, it is likely that open-source courseware—or some version of it, with some sort of accreditation—will replace stand-alone, static curriculum. Education will move from static to dynamic learning methods.
- Youth throughout the world are quickly adopting new technologies and finding ways to use them creatively for their own purposes. The rate of innovation, addition of networks of people, creativity and use are all exploding. No one is waiting for old systems to adopt or to sanction these new uses. This new world has arrived and its influence is growing by the day.

Let's return for a moment where Chapter 2 began—with the case of Rwanda. We asked how genocide could have occurred on such a scale without the wider world ever being aware. In fact, calls were being made to powerful people, but those people did not feel they had the means to take action. Action requires validation by the wider world in order to justify such action in a short time. Today's media, combined with the global linkages of cell phones, might now respond differently. Presumably, in today's media-linked world, Rwanda would be a different story.

Yet, starvation in the Horn of Africa is occurring in real time in 2011 and the world has chosen to ignore the geo-political which underpin it. In this case, global warming might be the apparent cause, but political instability in the region prevented people from taking the action needed that could have allowed them to stay in their villages. But, had they had a modest education and simple means of communication, they would have shared ideas, talked about a looming crisis, organized lines of communication and found ways to get supplies from foreign aid agencies. The organization that destabilizes the region can only do so because the population lacks basic education and the means to raise their own awareness and conversations.

Pima's mother can be forgiven as I speak with her in her small grass hut in rural Nepal. Little Pima will come home and tend to her little sister, prepare the fire for dinner and help cook dinner and study by the firelight for tomorrow's lessons. All will seem as if the world is relatively unchanged, aside from the fact that Pima is now spending her days in school rather than at home. None of the household members can know that the world is rapidly evolving, that the dynamics of learning are whirling around them and changing their physical environment, their health environment, their political stability, their life chances, Pima's ways of feeding herself in the future, of organizing their community and structuring their lives. They think their decision to educate Pima is a simple one, although not an easy one. Can they afford to lose her labor in order for the possibility of Pima to have a better life?

But this simple world view is the privilege of a simple life. It exists only because Pima's world is largely isolated from the rest of the world—at least for the moment. Her village has few links outside its borders. To get to the village one must walk across rice paddy barriers or have sufficient wealth to drive an expensive vehicle down a long rural road. There are no cell phones or landlines or internet connections; there is no CNN or BBC and no smartphones, although all that will be there in a matter of years—a few years.

But what of the rest of the world—those of us with smartphones and internet and educations and Al Jazeera and Google News? Those of us who pass news on at the speed of Facebook and blogs and email and usergroups? We live a different reality each day. We absolutely know that we live in an interconnected world and that the speed of information is also the speed of learning. We know that Pima's world is connected through climate, political and economic ties, migration and terrorism threats. Not only can we not tap her creative potential in a world of innovation and rapid civic re-creation, but the poor are a cost to us all. We have no excuse to see ourselves as isolated, as Pima's parents do.

There is no better example than the recent Arab Spring in Tunisia, Egypt and Libya. Despite rather low levels of income, these countries had relatively low costs of cell phones and internet for several years, and a literate youth for a number of years. The combination was enough to meet Sen's conditions of a population that was able to have meaningful conversations about their conditions and raise their own awareness, thereby creating new knowledge. This new knowledge consisted of an awareness of the possibilities of civic organization outside their own countries, of economic, political, social and civic structures that provided a better way of life. Raising their own awareness through informal conversations and using media to spur conversations and awareness, their knowledge-building increased. Then, when the right time occurred, they were able to take action. Contrast this to the countries of Somalia or Zimbabwe, which have much lower levels of education and internet coverage. They have no similar opportunities for raising awareness, engaging in conversations and building new knowledge. Even if the opportunity arises, they cannot take action. They do not have a learning base. In the case of the Northern African countries with relatively good internet linkages (and, hence the ability to use social networks), learning can move the countries forward largely on their own initiative. In the case of Somalia and Zimbabwe, where internet trunk lines had not yet reached, such shared knowledge and actions could not be organized virtually. In similar cases the international community faces long-term costs of instability, humanitarian crises and global problems.

Learning is no longer a privilege or something the rich can do for the poor. Nor can we afford to think that a teacher standing in front of a classroom is enough; it would not have been enough to stop the genocide in Rwanda or the massive migration in the Horn of Africa. It might be the case that a basic education in a classroom builds a foundation, but without the means to link to global conversations, without the means to build networks and raise awareness, then the means to build the knowledge to improve societies is absent.

As the most privileged of the world go about their daily lives, linked in to their online news sources, Facebook, radios, conversations, networks of informed friends, rich sources of information, computers, cell phones, tablets and other devices virtually plugged in during all their waking hours, it is easy to not rethink the paradigm that education was the classroom they were in until they were age 22 or 26. Learning is now their everyday luxury. It exists while they are having coffee with a friend and see the overhead TV with the newsflash; it is the conversation with friends about the news of the day; it is continuous at work as they build new ideas around their work. They wake up with it, are entertained by it, are accompanied by it while being transported and fall asleep with it. Learning has become ubiquitous and so pervasive that we no longer think of it as learning.

This learning world must become part of everyone's world—and rapidly so. It is a central component of helping solve the globally linked problems of the world. It is the means by which people can find networks, information and communications to inform themselves and begin dialogues that form the basis for building the foundation to tackle these problems. Societies that have the ability to discuss difficult issues tend to raise their own awareness and increase their knowledge putting them in a position to take action. Assisting in bringing access to global networks of knowledge, helping to build social networks and building the learning networks that help communities grow, are the most important things the world can do not only for development—and, ultimately for world stability. Very likely, with the cost of internet links falling rapidly, it will also be cheap.

Learning systems, like all large-scale systems, may well need some kind of regulatory framework around them to make them work in the public interest. For example, left alone, it is possible that powerful internet interests may begin to pay to make sure their "choices" appear first in search engines—or that small, new ideas are hard to find on the internet. It might also be the case that internet access might be expensive for rural dwellers. So, to ensure fair and equitable use, governments may need to set policies. If learning for all citizens is a priority, then governments may want to create incentives for learning software to be free or discounted and to make learning networks easily available. Public policy has a role to play in a global learning system.

The cost of not educating the poor is borne by the entire world. Not only is their creativity, innovation and ability lost to us all, but their poor education is a vulnerability we can ill afford in a globally linked world. But we must face up to our own mis-education. It is a comfortable world for the wealthy to see themselves as largely disengaged from the poor of this world—viewing the links to the poor as voluntary and self-regulated. But this is an illusion—albeit an illusion backed by years of outdated theories and the policies of world organizations. But the steps to rectify these misperceptions are not so difficult. Understanding how an integrated world works, understanding that learning is a powerful world system and that it is dynamic is a beginning. Understanding that everyone is part of a co-dependent, linked world is equally important. Once that is understood, we know we carry that understanding into our networks and are then part of a growing global momentum for change.

The world is a complex, global system and like all systems its weakest link is its point of vulnerability. The cost of not educating the poor is the cost of an unstable world. We need the poor's creativity, brainpower and innovation to join with us to help solve global problems such as global warming, pollution, disease, terrorism, political instability and famine. Moreover, we need to take advantage of the gains we can make in social progress from ideas. But, perhaps most of all, we need to capture this moment to regain our common humanity and realize that this is a profound cost to not educating the poor.

I have rarely been in a place where the people are not curious about my life, my world, my experience. If their culture does not find it impolite to do so, they pepper me with questions about what I've seen, where I've been, how I've lived. Students—no matter where I find them—ask me about far-away places and when I talk about another country, I notice that I have their rapt attention. Students talk about their dream of sometime going to the United States or Asia or Africa. Parents speak proudly and longingly of their children who are away in distant lands studying and show me the small gifts they sent from that land. Our televisions screens are filled with the images of distant cultures, and the latest award-winning movie gives us a glimpse of China or India or ancient Persia. We are intrigued, drawn in and curious about these places; we wish we could be transported and shown the lands and customs and cultures and languages.

All people want to learn more, explore the unexplored, try out new ideas and get to know someone who has had different life experiences. We all strive for a comfortable life, a stable life, a fixed notion of honesty, justice and civic participation. It is these very human qualities that bind us and continue to create the linkages. These human links are the foundation of the need for trade, financial linkages, technological advances, global disease control and the pressure on natural resources.

And so I turn back now to sitting in the Nepalese hut and listening carefully and intently to Pima's mother. Because of her and others like her throughout the world whom I have met, I have learned to live a simpler life—a life filled with solid friendships and world connections. It is a world, admittedly, highly dependent upon the computer in my lap and its silent, wireless link to her Nepalese world and beyond. As such, I've learned that fewer clothes, a modest car, minimal kitchen appliances and a small, reliable computer make my life richer. I have become a smarter mother through her because I understood that my son would compete in a different world—compete against the children in Nepal and Lebanon and Egypt that were learning two or three world languages, calculus at age 12 and were studying my people and my culture—and because I can see through her eyes and those I've visited in Eritrea, Micronesia, Jordan and Vietnam. I have become a richer, happier, more fulfilled person because she allowed me to come into her small hut, hold her baby and speak with her. We are connected at deeper levels than the obvious economic, educational and financial ties. We are connected as mothers, as neighbors and people with friends, hopes, dreams and shared humanity. It is that very human connection that is our most powerful tie.

Notes

1   This is the essence of his Nobel Prize-winning work on social welfare theory (Sen, 1995) which is discussed more thoroughly in Chapter 11b.
2   As I do the last edits of this book, I know now that the Arab Spring has had many repercussions that could not have been predicted and, likely there are many more to come. The rising awareness of a larger global world, its linkages and possibilities have freed many people to take action on their own behalf. It has also freed many negative forces to take action and organize. Both positive and negative social networks have evolved—freed from the constraints of oppressive and controlling national governments.

Reference

Sen, A. (1995). Rationality and social choice. *American Economic Review*, 85(1), 1–24.

Index

For Product Safety Concerns and Information please contact our
EU representative GPSR@taylorandfrancis.com, Taylor & Francis
Verlag GmbH, Kaufingerstraße 24, 80331 München, Germany